Public Corr

The Dark Side of So

Public Corruption
The Dark Side of Social Evolution

Robert Neild

Anthem Press
London

First published by Anthem Press 2002
Anthem Press is an imprint of
Wimbledon Publishing Company,
PO Box 9779, London SW19 7QA

British Library Cataloguing in Publication Data

Library of Congress Cataloguing in Publication Data

Typeset by Mudra Typesetters – Pondicherry, India.

Printed by Bell & Bain Ltd., Glasgow

For Virginia

Acknowledgements

I am indebted to a number of people who, as I rather slowly pieced this book together, read it in part or whole and offered me comments and encouragement. Without them I might have given up long ago. My particular thanks are due to Tony Weir, Garry Runciman and Sam Arnold–Forster, to whom I turned repeatedly. Others who generously spared time to look at what I was doing are Jean Blondel, Alan Doig, Alena Ledeneva, Anthony Sampson and William St Clair. I should also acknowledge my debt, which I explain in Chapter 1, to the late Gunnar Myrdal, and to the Master and Fellows of my college for providing me with facilities without which I could not have written this book.

Robert Neild

Trinity College
Cambridge

December 2001

Contents

I

Introduction

The typical reaction to the mention of corruption, at least of an Englishman of my generation, has been to ask why it is occurring and what can be done about it. We have implicitly assumed that the absence of corruption is normal in two senses: in the moral sense that people generally know that society should be regulated by established rules of the kind we take for granted; and in the statistical sense that most people obey those rules. The corrupt are a deviant minority, like naughty children in a well-ordered school: we must see why they are being naughty and do something about it.

Many years ago I was persuaded in a conversation with Gunnar Myrdal, the Swedish social scientist, that one should try turning this approach on its head.[1] If you look at history and across the world today you will see that it is uncorrupt government that is exceptional – and never totally attainable. For much of recorded history, societies have not been governed by rules of the kind we take for granted today. Rulers have been arbitrary and capricious. Where there have been rules, they have not normally been honestly enforced or closely observed. Most of history consists of the pursuit of power by whatever combination of physical force, tricks and deals seemed most effective to rulers and to their rivals. That has been the way of the world. Practices that we now call corrupt have been accepted as normal. The achievement of what I, for the moment, shall loosely call 'clean government' came about remarkably recently in a small group of countries: in the late eighteenth and nineteenth centuries in northwestern Europe – with ramifications in the colonies. Whether there was ever clean government in earlier times is a question I leave aside.

What I believe should be studied is what caused government to become relatively clean in this group of countries at this time. There are two questions to be considered. First, what were the political conditions that produced the pursuit of cleaner government? Second, what were the means by which it was achieved?

If we could begin to get answers to these questions, we might be in a better position to understand corruption in various parts of the world today and see which processes of political development and governmental reform may produce evolution towards cleaner government; and we might be better equipped to identify processes that destroy clean government. In short, to understand corruption and how to tackle it, try studying why and how it was ever suppressed.

It is a huge subject, which could absorb the minds of teams of historians and social scientists for a long time. Working on my own in retirement, I have had to be exploratory; I have had to rely for material on the work of others rather than dig into original sources. I am not a professional historian. The result is an essay – or a set of connected essays – in the literal sense of 'a first attempt in learning'. The conclusions I propose are tentative and limited. My object is to encourage others to address the problem. I should love to see others put me right and carry the subject further – or suggest how that might be done.

The order of the work is this. Having suggested some general hypotheses, in particular that military competition used to be important in inducing improvements in the efficiency of government, I look briefly at how standards of government evolved in France, Prussia/Germany and the United States in the eighteenth and nineteenth centuries; and more fully, at what happened in Britain in that period. I have chosen these four countries both because their history is accessible and because of the different incidence of military competition on them. I devote a chapter to the evolution in the same four countries of independent judiciaries, since that independence is a vital ingredient in the achievement of uncorrupt government, and it is convenient to compare in one chapter the experience of the four countries in this domain.

I then turn to the twentieth century and suggest that since the start of the Cold War military competition has changed radically and become damaging rather than helpful to uncorrupt government. Moreover, in the latter part of the century, the ability of traditional national institutions to uphold standards has been challenged by international and national developments, including a cult of personal greed and hostility to government. I again focus on what has happened in Britain. After a wave of scandals at the beginning of the twentieth century, standards appear to have risen, reaching a peak in the Second World War, only to decline again and give way to another wave of scandals at the end of the twentieth century. The nineteenth century apparatus for relatively uncorrupt government, which relied heavily on the sense of honour of elites, was then being eroded and, as regards the civil service, was emasculated in the name of efficiency. The response to the scandals has principally been to establish new bodies to monitor behaviour and report, but not as a rule to prosecute miscreants. The result is a shift towards a 'cops and robbers' approach to the prevention of corruption with the cops unarmed. That there has been a shift of this kind is, in part at least, an understandable consequence of the Thatcher–Blair policy of seeking to remodel the economy and society of Britain on American lines.

2

General

The Definition of Corruption

I shall concentrate on public corruption, meaning corruption by politicians and public officials of all kinds, including the judiciary. This is the area with respect to which the evidence is best and with which I am most familiar. But I shall also refer to private corruption since it is closely linked to public corruption: corrupt acts by public officials are usually deals with private citizens; and in societies where there is much public corruption there will usually be much private corruption; they tend to go together.

When we talk today of public corruption we mean bribery, nepotism, the sale of offices and jobbery in the appointment of public officials; we mean offences by politicians and public officials in such matters as the collection of taxation, the granting of contracts and the granting of cash benefits; and we mean fraud, bribery and other types of malpractice connected with elections, which benefit an individual or his party. In short, we mean the breaking of the rules, be they written laws or implicit codes of conduct, which we expect public officials and politicians to observe in the conduct of public affairs.[1]

As soon as one starts examining the history of public corruption one sees that the nature of the activities that are held to be corrupt has changed with time and has differed from one part of the world to another, in step with differences in the rules governing society. For example, it was normal practice for government ministers in England in the eighteenth century to lend out the public funds belonging to their departments and pocket the interest. Those practices were attacked; increasingly, they were called corrupt. As the attack succeeded, tighter rules of conduct were introduced and the meaning of corruption changed, becoming wider. To allow for this, I shall define public corruption, in this study, as follows:

> The breaking by public persons, for the sake of private financial or political gain, of the rules of conduct in public affairs prevailing in a society in the period under consideration.

The amount of corruption in any society will depend on the gap between:

(a) the number of decisions to be made by public persons (which, given the size of the society, will depend on the extent of government) and

(b) the extent to which those decisions are made dishonestly, i.e. influenced by the prospect of private gain.[2]

At first I was tempted to think there might be a simple relationship between the extent of government and the rate of corruption: that with more government and consequently more rules, there would tend to be a higher rate of corruption. But a moment's consideration of history shows that this is often not so. For example, the reduction in corruption and the great improvement in the quality of government in Britain in the latter part of the nineteenth century went hand in hand with an extension in the scope of government; they were both part of a general wave of reform. The introduction of new measures to improve education, public hygiene, factory conditions, the government of India and many other things, generated pressure for better administration and led to reform; and the utilitarian-cum-evangelical ethos of reform was conducive to the observance of rules. More generally, the improvements in government in northwestern Europe in the eighteenth and nineteenth centuries, which in the Introduction I described as the emergence of 'clean government', consisted of positive changes in both variables: new rules were introduced which forbade practices that previously were permitted, and the enforcement of rules was improved. Conversely, a policy of trying in a heavily governed country to reduce the scope of government, and hence the number of rules that have to be enforced, may be accompanied by denigration of the public service and by cuts in its pay and conditions of such severity that, in combination with an idealization of private gain, it may produce an increase rather than a decrease in the rate of corruption. Russia today is an example.

Of course, in those countries, principally in the Third World, that have limited capacity for government and yet attempt to enforce complex economic regulations, there is good reason to expect that corruption might be reduced by cutting back on regulation – provided it could be achieved without conducting a political attack on government and public persons that equally damaged the capacity for enforcement.

Clearly there is no general law as to the relationship between the extent of government and the rate of corruption. To understand what has happened we must look widely at the total evolution of those societies we wish to study; and we must recognize that there is likely to be complex causation in which many social and political variables interact and move at the same time: for example, the tide may flow towards better government, with honesty breeding honesty and then, perhaps after a long period, it may flow in the other direction with corruption breeding corruption. It is best to start from the view that anything can happen.

Some implications of the notion that the evolution of corruption depends on the relationship between changes in rules and changes in their observance are worth noting at this stage. An outburst of corruption does not necessarily mean that the standards of conduct of a society have become 'worse'. It may mean that new rules have been introduced, which demand higher standards of conduct than before and these are being resisted, in which case, the outcome, i.e. the new average standard of conduct, may be judged to be better than that which went before. In other words, new corruption round new rules may be an improvement on old corruption round old rules. For example, when in England at the end of the nineteenth century the introduction of electoral reforms stopped the sale of parliamentary seats and the bribery of electors, there was no law forbidding political parties from gathering money centrally and spending it on propaganda campaigns in the newly developed national press, nor on other means of rallying the electorate. In no time the rival political parties began to compete for money before elections; prime ministers, starting, surprisingly, with Gladstone, began to sell Honours, a practice for which Lloyd George became notorious and which subsequent prime ministers have not eschewed. Thus a new form of corruption replaced the old, but England's electoral system is generally judged to have been better after it was reformed than it had been before.

In other cases the introduction of new rules may induce more corruption than the rules are worth, causing a decline in the quality of government. This has often happened in Third World countries where governments have introduced complex economic restrictions, the manipulation of which has been profitable to public and private persons – and damaging to the economy.

In yet other cases, corruption may increase not because there has been any change in the rules of a society but because public and private moral standards have fallen following, perhaps, the accession to power of a bad ruler; or, conversely, corruption may decline following the accession of a good ruler.

It is self-evident that there will always be corruption. For there is always a temptation to break rules for the sake of economic or other gains – unless the rules are redundant, meaning that no one sees advantage in breaking them – and one can be sure that a fraction, large or small, of any population will yield to that temptation. It is true that those of us who grew up, as I did, in a society where there was little public corruption acquired the habit, wrongly, of thinking and speaking of our countries as not corrupt without qualification. Laziness of thought and expression is partly to blame. But there are other causes. One is that public corruption harms the community as a whole rather than individuals who might quickly protest at the damage they suffer. Hence it will not be noticed until it is exposed: like many diseases, it can exist invisibly. Another cause, which I suspect is important, is *esprit de corps*: we don't like to admit that there is anything wrong in the school, the college, the army, the civil service, the judiciary or the country to which we belong because to do so would be to blemish the reputation of that institution and therefore our own standing in the world. It might mean damaging the reputation of a colleague or colleagues, contrary to the spirit of loyalty that a good institution achieves and needs to achieve. Moreover, to admit that corruption exists may have the effect of causing those who are tempted to misbehave to yield to that temptation, saying, 'We all know others do it and get away with it, why shouldn't we?' Denial, whatever its cause, may serve in some degree as a means of enforcement, probably a dangerous one since it may cause us to avert our eyes for too long from evidence of corruption. In addition, denial may have a counterpart in a tendency to label as corrupt, without qualification, countries where corruption is acknowledged to be substantial. We must avoid black and white classification.

We must also recognize that the changing frontier between what in any country is regarded as corrupt and what is regarded as uncorrupt is likely at any time to look arbitrary and inconsistent. It will be the product of laws and conventions that have been, and are being, pushed this way and that as society evolves. Nor should we blindly condemn apparent inconsistencies. For example, it is not necessarily undesirable that, as is the case in Britain today, judicial appointments are made by patronage rather than by open competition or election, and contracts are not always awarded to the lowest bidder.

An Analytical Framework

I shall start from three broad propositions:

1. Changes in the quality of government, i.e. rules and their enforcement, will take place only if rulers introduce them.
2. Politicians whose prime aim is to gain office will not advocate reforms unless they believe that by so doing they will improve, or at least not damage, their prospects of acquiring power.
3. Once in power, rulers, regardless of how they got there – whether by inheritance, force or election – and regardless of what they promised in election campaigns, will not introduce reforms unless they believe that by so doing they will improve, or at least not damage, their chances of retaining or enhancing their power.

There have, of course, been exceptions to narrow power-seeking behaviour. Gladstone and Attlee come to mind. But they have been rare products of unusual social settings.

As soon as you consider these propositions and think about history, it is difficult to see how cleaner government ever came about. Indeed, you are confronted by a puzzle. For if, as is the case, government used to be 'dirty', meaning that those who sought power pursued it by killing their rivals and enlisting supporters by offering the prospect of jobs, wealth and a share in power; if, in other words, the pursuit of power was largely unconstrained and was based on what the sociologists call 'patron–client' relationships, how on earth did anyone gain power, or retain it, by renouncing the traditional 'dirty' methods and being clean? If anyone had tried being clean, would he not at once have been at a disadvantage, *vis-à-vis* his dirty rivals, and lost supporters, or been poisoned? Think how Shakespeare portrayed the pursuit of power in his plays. Yet somehow clean government did come about. How?

After reading a lot of modern history, looking for the causes of the improvements in government of the late eighteenth and nineteenth centuries, I see a tangle of politico-social forces operating in different ways within each country; and, standing out from these, one powerful force, military competition, which is external to each country and has operated upon each with a strength determined by its strategic location.

Social Forces

The principal social forces that stand out are the Enlightenment, religion and the pursuit of efficiency.

So much has been written about the Enlightenment that I shall simply take it as a stylized fact that in the eighteenth and the first half of the nineteenth century, European rulers were faced by a tide of intellectual criticism, by the terrifying example of the French Revolution, and then by powerful popular demands for reform sweeping across Europe and accompanied by widespread uprisings. These threats to established rule and the ideas underlying them were a potent force making for improvements in the quality of government.

As regards religion, there can be no doubt that the variations in corruption between the countries we shall examine, and the changes over time within those countries, have been associated with variations in personal-cum-public moral standards. Nor is there any question that, for most of the period at least, these standards were influenced by religion. But it is very difficult to assess the importance of religion relative to other factors. One is tempted to grab at the common observation that the Protestant countries of northwestern Europe – Scandinavia, the Netherlands, Germany and Britain – seem to have achieved cleaner government than the Roman Catholic countries of the south – Italy, Spain and Portugal. Several differences in the two types of Christianity can be adduced to explain this north–south divide.

In the first place, it can be argued that the Puritan conscience is more demanding of good behaviour in public matters than the Catholic conscience. The Catholic can confess his misdeeds to a priest, do penance and shed his sins, whereas the Protestant is stuck with his: he must judge for himself the extent of his sins and live with them. The Catholic is concerned about the judgement of God mediated by his priest; the Protestant is concerned about the judgement of God, which he can infer only from his conscience and from the judgement of his fellow men.

A second argument is that Protestants came to extol industry, thrift and discipline, worldly virtues that, particularly when combined with the utilitarian calculus of the common good, led to respect for public service, rather than the service of God.

A third is that the Catholic is subject to dual claims on his political loyalty. The Church of Rome has been a highly political, territorial entity, a religious empire dominating kings, receiving money from all over the world. The Reformation was, *inter alia*, a revolt against that religious imperialism. But in the post-Reformation world Catholics still have looked to the Pope, an authority outside their nation state, for guidance on moral, sometimes highly politicized, matters, for example, anticommunism in the Cold War and contraception. Protestants have looked for moral guidance to their local Protestant church, which is often not subordinate to any outside authority, let alone to an autocratic authority abroad.

These are plausible reasons why Protestants should be more conscientious in their public conduct than Catholics, but as soon as one asks oneself how far they explain the apparent north–south divide in Europe, one sees other possible contributory causes. To start with there is geography. Before urbanization, much of Scandinavia had such a small dispersed rural population (because of the lack of fertile topsoil) and such a harsh climate, that in order to survive it was necessary to behave in a cooperative manner, for example, offering hospitality to travellers, keeping your section of the local road clear of snow, or helping neighbours if they were in trouble. Around the Mediterranean, on the other hand, a relatively benign climate, fertile soil and dense population has meant that relatively selfish behaviour has been consistent with survival: a hungry person at the wayside has needed help less urgently in Sicily than in Sweden; and in Sicily, unlike Sweden, the dense population has meant that passers-by could plausibly say to themselves, 'Someone else will take care of him, I needn't.' Geography may have helped to induce a sense of public duty more strongly in the north than in the south of Europe.

And then there is national unity. Consider Sicily, admittedly an extreme case. It is a strategic island at the crossroads between Africa and Europe and between Christianity and Islam. It was invaded by the Greeks, the Romans, the Phoenicians, the Normans, the Bourbons and many others, and for much of its history it was under foreign rule. Eventually it was formally integrated into Italy, a nation of which it has been an island appendage, remote from Rome and from the economically dominant north. Little wonder if the view exists amongst Sicilians that government officials are intruders to be evaded and swindled, not obeyed. The same explanation may have validity in Greece and other countries that have long been ruled and dominated by foreigners or by remote autocrats of their own nationality.

One can only suppose that differences in all three factors – religion, climate and national unity – and others, have contributed to the apparent north–south divide in Europe, and that their relative importance and the way in which they have operated will have varied from country to country.

As for the pursuit of efficiency, it is clear that one motive for reforming government has been to stop theft, waste, incompetence and inefficiency. Reform of this kind was often triggered by scandalous failures of the system for supplying armies in war, for example, the British Army in the Crimea. This is not surprising, since public expenditure until modern times consisted almost entirely of military expenditure and the servicing of debt incurred through war.

In a less visible manner, reform came about piecemeal as new tasks were taken on by governments and new kinds of staff and new methods were seen to be needed; and it came about when new notions of social justice, as well as arguments of efficiency, led to the introduction of new recruitment practices. The principal example is the introduction of open competitive recruitment to the civil service and armed forces in place of patronage – which is not to say that patronage was invariably inefficient or corrupt.[3]

Efficiency is not, of course, the same thing as honesty. An uncorrupt system may be inefficient, for example through excessive form-filling and niggling; a corrupt one may be efficient at misappropriating public resources. Moreover, the achievement of efficiency within the apparatus of government does not mean that the government will achieve its desired politico-economic ends – let alone ends that the international community would approve today. The efficient application of a misguided economic policy may produce politico-economic failure; an efficient government apparatus may be used for torture or genocide. But the point remains that the pursuit of greater efficiency has often reduced corruption; and, conversely, the hounding out of corruption has often increased efficiency.

Mechanisms of Reform

We should also note two mechanisms by which reform was achieved. Firstly, the creation of career élites has been an important means of achieving high standards in public service. The establishment of a career public service, selected by competition and given security and high status, was the common means of reforming the civil and military services in Europe; and on the Continent the same method was applied to the judiciary. Of course, these elites did not come into being by an act of creation in a vacuum. They are institutions, comprising persons of high competence, that have come into being because they have helped rulers to exercise and maintain their power; they displaced, or evolved out of, precursors that were generally less professional and less disciplined; they have been able to reproduce themselves from one generation to another, exercising power and enjoying their status.

Secondly, transparency i.e. the exposure of what is going on in government, is helpful if the media and public is critical of corruption and able to call effectively for reform; it is unhelpful if it causes the behaviour of a rotten ruler or rulers to be imitated by the people of the country so that corruption and cynicism spreads.

The introduction of democracy is commonly said nowadays to be a way of suppressing corruption, but the history we shall examine does not bear that out. In France and Germany autocrats cleaned up government; and in the United States Jacksonian populist democracy led to increased corruption. One needs to keep an open mind towards the relationship between democracy and clean government.

Runciman's Approach

Since these various factors do not fit coherently together, I have sought a theoretical framework within which to try to bring them into some order. The most interesting I have found is that proposed by Garry Runciman.[4] Greatly simplified and stripped of its refined theoretical structure and terminology, it states that the evolution of society is similar to Darwinian genetics. People pursue power of three kinds, economic (emphasised by Marx to the exclusion of the other two), coercive (the use or threat of force) and persuasive (religious or political propositions propagated through the pulpit, political meetings, books, pamphlets and the modern media). New mutations and recombinations of these three kinds of power occur randomly as technical progress and human knowledge advance. Since these developments are random, we cannot predict the evolution of society any more than a biologist can predict the evolution of living species – except perhaps in the short run when a new mutation or recombination has shown itself and has begun to make progress. But in retrospect we, like biologists, can see when a mutation or recombination has been successful, and with luck we may be able explain why, i.e. we may be able to explain how it found a niche. At this very general level I find Runciman's approach most attractive. But, as an amateur exploring a huge field, I find myself unable to use the refined sociological concepts he builds on this basis.

But I have derived from Runciman two ideas. The first is that when we look at changes in the level of corruption it is useful to think of them as parts of a process of evolution and to try to think how they were related to the pursuit of power. The second concerns a different evolutionary process, operating through relations between nations. It is that military competition between nations has favoured the expansion of the less corrupt *vis-à-vis* the more corrupt: those nations that have developed efficient, relatively uncorrupt government have been able to mobilize their resources for war and military domination more effectively than the more corrupt and less efficient; as between nations of similar economic potential they have therefore had the capacity to expand at the expense of their neighbours. Prussia's expansion and its leadership of the unification of Germany is a strong example. The military threat posed by such nations may also promote efficient government abroad by causing their neighbours to try to reform government for the sake of military security. On the other hand, military expenditure in war and peace is singularly vulnerable to corruption; though where a corrupt nation is defeated but survives, the response can be reform – by peaceful or revolutionary means. In short, war has been a significant, albeit brutal, test of government efficiency and has thereby been a selective force favouring the more efficient, which as a rule are the less corrupt.[5] This process was important in the eighteenth and nineteenth centuries when it was a part of the building of nation states.[6] Thus, Martin van Creveld argues cogently that the need to wage war was a prime cause of the rise of the nation state and the development of its apparatus of bureaucracy, taxation and even welfare services.[7] But now the process has gone into reverse: since the middle of the twentieth century military competition has had a predominantly corruptive effect on the quality of government, and at the same time the nation state has been in decline. This apparent change, which I shall explore in Chapter 9, is of the greatest importance. It is relevant to the problems of many countries where corruption is rife today.

Military Competition

Adam Smith, whilst advocating that markets should normally rule economic activity, saw 'three duties of great importance' that the ruler must attend to, of which the first was 'the duty of protecting the society from the violence and invasion of other independent societies'.[8] He described how military technique and organization had advanced since the earliest times to become the art of specialists – an example of the division of labour – and to become more costly, but he did not consider the effect of military competition on the quality of government.

To see how military competition worked in the eighteenth century and nineteenth centuries, it is useful to look right back to the feudal system. That system meant, in theory at least, that the king or prince was the ultimate owner of all the land in his kingdom or principality. He could expect some rent from his land and he could expect his vassals to come and fight for him. If they were barons with extensive lands, he could expect them to bring with them knights who for limited periods were expected to fight without payment, but for a long war were meant to receive pay.[9] Thus the economics of the feudal compact in its ideal form were that the ruler, in exchange for conceding the use of land, obtained some free military service (a form of rent in kind) and some rent. On the expenditure side he had to run a court and government of sufficient scale to maintain the command and respect of his people and maintain some measure of law and order. If he became engaged in war he incurred extra expenditure with no easy means of paying for it, other than making his armies live off the land, i.e. looting, which was more viable if you were gaining territory than if you were losing it. This system was obviously precarious. It suffered erosion over the centuries for many reasons.

Firstly, the loyalty of the nobles was not guaranteed. Collectively, their association with the ruler was essentially voluntary. They had an interest in having a ruler who would defend and run the country in a manner that allowed them to enjoy their power and wealth. If that compact was betrayed they might break away or challenge the ruler by backing a rival. He had no army other than the nobles with which to impose discipline on the nobles. If they combined, he was impotent. Think of what happened at Runnymede in 1215. Since the ruler's power was circumscribed, his claim to the ultimate title of all the land was always somewhat precarious.

Secondly, to buy the loyalty of nobles and advisers the rulers often gave them land, thereby reducing the royal rental income and creating a need for taxation.

Thirdly, military expenditure became more costly as professional armies became more effective than traditional armies, as weaponry advanced and, on the Continent, as neighbouring nations adopted standing armies. This practice, once begun by one nation, had to be followed by its neighbours on land if they were not to be caught defenceless. It did not have to be followed by neighbours protected by a sea, for example, Britain and North America. Military practice advanced in fits and starts. Two key developments were the arrival of gunpowder in Europe in the fourteenth century and the huge increase in the size of armies and in the numbers deployed in the field of battle in the seventeenth century.[10] Not only was the cost of armies driven up, but years of war became almost as frequent as years of peace. Out of the hundred years ending in 1815, Britain was at war for 46 years and France for 45.

To pay for their professional armies, rulers needed money; and the same was true of their navies, though they were made to depend partly on private enterprise in the form of prize money and privateering. Sometimes kings were strong enough to improve their rental income by taking back royal lands. Usually they had to turn to taxation, supplemented by borrowing. But borrowing was not a permanent substitute for tax revenue, and it was dangerous: if it was excessive in relation to the revenue, the result could be a spiral of rising debt requiring rising interest payments which in turn required more borrowing, until there was a financial crisis when the Treasury was empty, the lenders would not lend and the state was left with no alternative but to default, temporarily at least, on part or all of its debt. When war broke out borrowing was almost inevitable since war would usually cause a surge in military expenditure that governments were unable to match immediately, or perhaps ever, by increased taxation or from accumulated reserves. The problem was to avoid borrowing too much (or borrowing on terms that were too extortionate) in relation to the flow of tax revenue that could be achieved.[11]

Where then did tax come from? In the pre-industrial world, agriculture was the predominant economic activity. Those who owned land earned rent, a windfall income, which, according to all schools of economic thought ought to be taxed – and according to one school of thought fashionable in France in the eighteenth century (the Physiocrats) was the only thing that ought to be taxed. But the nobles, who held much land, no longer paid rent in kind in the form of knight service, which was obsolete, or other feudal dues or charges of any substance. The ruler needed their support. Many of them had provincial loyalties and pride. To impose taxes on them presented obvious political problems. It was tempting to grant them partial or complete exemption in order to buy their loyalty. But that meant that the burden of land tax became concentrated on the peasants, and they were poor and were hard to tax without using punitive methods. There remained indirect taxes (including those levied through state monopolies of the sale of such products as salt and tobacco). The scope for these increased as internal and international trade displaced the consumption of one's own produce, but again they were unpopular, not always easy to collect and in wartime liable to interruption by naval blockade. There were also taxes on property other than land, often assessed by reference to objects that signified wealth – carriages, clocks, manservants, windows.

The Problem of Taxation

But the problem was not just to decide what and whom it would be judicious to tax. At least as important were the problems of how to (a) collect tax; (b) ensure that all or at least a large part of what was collected reached the state coffers; and (c) ensure that it was spent properly and not diverted into the pockets of corrupt officials and corrupt contractors.

As regards collection, the principal alternatives were:

(a) Collection by government officials, appointed from the centre or locally, often backed up by military or police forces. This required a good bureaucracy and good forces of law and order.
(b) Telling local communities that they had to appoint a tax collector and deliver so much, and backing up that demand by use or threat of force.
(c) Tax farming, meaning that the task of collecting a tax in an area was farmed out to a private individual on condition that he delivered a specified sum each year; anything he collected in excess of that sum he could keep. It is an ugly but arguably efficient way of organizing tax collection in countries at an early stage of development. Britain, France and Germany all used it; it was used in the Mogul and Ottoman empires; in Sicily, where it had been a traditional method of tax collection since the time of the Bourbons,

it was reintroduced in 1952[12]; it is still used in the Third World. Its attractions have been that it has offered the prospect, not always fulfilled, of reliable predetermined revenue and the prospect of diverting some of the odium of tax collection from the government to the tax farmers.

On the expenditure side, one of the crucial issues was whether the money that was collected was properly accounted for and brought into a single kitty (a treasury or exchequer) where its spending could be centrally related to income and controlled rather than being left in many different funds in the provinces and the centre where it could be used and misused by a multitude of sticky-fingered officials, tax farmers and courtiers.

To sum up, as professional armies displaced amateur armies and as military techniques advanced, rulers had to raise increasing amounts of revenue for military pay, munitions and supplies. This required an administration sufficiently clean to be capable of both gathering and spending revenue efficiently. If a ruler were not as good at gathering taxes and mobilizing resources as his neighbour, he would be vulnerable (assuming all other things were equal) to attack by him. In this way the competitive pursuit of military power generated pressure to extend and improve government for the sake of revenue. But that was not all. More expensive armies and navies also brought with them more scope for corruption on the expenditure side: there have always been rich pickings to be had from military procurement. An essential element, therefore, in the competitive development of military power was improved administration on both the revenue and expenditure sides taken together, when faced by the need to mobilize resources.[13] The reactions of countries to the need to mobilize resources would take time to unfold and might go in any direction. The corrupting effects of increased military expenditure might debauch a nation with an initially weak administration, or it might react positively and introduce reforms. A nation with an initially good administration might extend and strengthen that administration to meet the needs of military competition – or it might fail to meet the challenge and suffer defeat and, perhaps, internal upheaval.

Of course, the efficiency of governments in gathering revenue and spending it was not the sole determinant of military strength. The whole pace of development, economic, social and political, was important; and the pursuit of military power and the development of new weapons and new modes of fighting influenced each of these elements in development in all sorts of ways.[14] Furthermore, military power depended on the quality of military leaders and their forces, and on all the intangible factors that contribute at any time to the fighting spirit of a nation. All that matters to our enquiry is that efficiency in gathering and spending revenue was a necessary condition for the achievement and exercise of military strength. It follows that, *other things being equal*, countries with relatively uncorrupt government in this respect would tend to prevail in war and diplomacy over those with relatively corrupt government.

Recapitulation

In a complex way that we shall never fully understand, competition for power evolved in northwestern Europe in the late eighteenth and the nineteenth century in such a manner that public corruption was suppressed to an extraordinary degree and new standards of government were introduced. In this period, scientific knowledge expanded and political ideas changed at an extraordinary pace. There were strong popular demands for better government; and military competition, shaped by changing technology, took a form that favoured those nations that were best able, by means of improving their standards of government, to mobilize their resources for war. In these ways a combination of domestic and international forces combined to foster less corrupt government.

I shall explore these notions not in the belief that I can reach unassailable conclusions but in the hope that I can stimulate others to investigate them further.

3

Prussia/Germany

Prussia, which was to bludgeon and weld Germany together, is the case where the military motive and the military approach to organization can be seen at their most potent; where popular demands for reform were met cynically but effectively; and the result was an efficient, hierarchical, bureaucratic monarchy. By the middle of the eighteenth century the bureaucracy was remarkably uncorrupt by the standards of the times, but any strong ruler who could master that machine could do with it more or less what he liked, fair or foul.

That Prussia, formed by the Hohenzollerns out of bits of the Holy Roman Empire, sought military strength is understandable. The Hohenzollerns had suffered terribly in the Thirty Years' War (1618–48), losing half their inhabitants and much territory. When Louis XIV pursued grandeur and military strength, building palaces and creating a large standing army, it was understandable that the Hohenzollerns should react by doing likewise. They expanded their territory by marriage, purchase and conquest, and they copied Louis XIV in seeking to build a strong national monarchy and a strong standing army. But to acquire the necessary power and economic resources they had to dominate the landowners, guilds and other local interests that had enjoyed feudal powers in a highly articulated form under the Holy Roman Empire; they had to break those traditions and establish the primacy of duty to the national ruler and to public law. Several things helped them in this endeavour. The Reformation meant that they ruled a Protestant state in which religious division was not acute and was not associated, as it was in France and England, with conflict with a partisan monarch; it meant that the people had a strong sense of duty; and it also meant that the monarchy enjoyed large rents from lands it had confiscated from the Church. Furthermore, Prussia was a frontier state where the

Germans faced the Slavs, periodically fought them to keep them at bay and colonized them. In the colonized areas the Junkers were colonial settlers with no obligations to their Slav workers; they stayed on their estates managing them; they were very different from the leisured land-owners of France or England, who spent much of their time at Versailles or London. The pursuit of profit and efficiency came as naturally to them as it has done to other colonizing farmers.[1]

The organization of Prussia as a hierarchical military state had proceeded far by the reign of Frederick the Great (1740–86). After the Thirty Years' War, Frederick William the Great Elector (1640–88) had built up the army, centralized power and started using military administrators to help run the country. He established military commissars (*Kriegskommissare*) to enforce central authority in the country. At first they organized support for the army but they soon became involved in economic and social administration.[2]

The next important reformer was King Frederick William I who ruled as king (Prussia having by now become a kingdom) from 1713 to 1740. While avoiding war, he obsessively pursued personal power and order, and he built up the army with a passion for complex, formal drill and parades; he established a General Directory to supervise military, fiscal and legal activities throughout his dispersed lands, but he kept a strong personal grip on the bureaucracy he was creating to implement his will; he wrote at the end of the decrees establishing the General Directory, 'We remain King and Lord and do as We please.' Under him, the army became the pre-eminent force in society. He enmeshed the aristocracy into the officer corps, so increasing the prestige of the former and the loyalty of the latter. Officers dominated the court, served in local government and held important ministerial positions. He enmeshed the peasants into the army by making each area (*canton*) responsible for providing the standing army with a certain number of able-bodied peasants. This system produced an army superior in quality to the mercenaries and misfits obtained by other armies; it knitted the army into the social structure; and it 'gave Prussia's characteristic blend of state power and aristocratic privilege a military dimension. Just as the aristocratic officer affirmed his loyalty by his service to the king, who exercised absolute rule over his army, so the trooper reaffirmed his obedience to his master, who was both his military and social superior.'[3] The king seems, however, to have tested the loyalty of his nobles to the limits by persistently confiscating slices of their land for the Crown, a policy that improved the royal finances but led to so dangerous a discontent that Frederick the Great, on his accession to the throne, at once put an end to it.[4]

Frederick the Great (1740–86), that 'enlightened' despot, found that his military conquests, the extension of the state's civil activities – he expanded the state's role in education and the economy – and the demands of frequent wars required not just strong government but wider government. To strengthen the existing means of power, he raised the status of the nobility, making aristocratic rank a prerequisite for advancement in the officer corps, and he confirmed the power of the nobles over the peasants. To widen government he created a bureaucracy of state servants exercising new powers alongside those of the army and the nobility. He delegated the task of executing his policies to this new apparatus – though the new bureaucrats did not always do – or succeed in doing – what they were told. An official commented that Frederick's directives were in danger of remaining a 'platonic republic, so good on paper, but impossible to put into practice'.[5]

Betty Behrens tells us quite a lot about the quality of government in Prussia under Frederick the Great. He totally forbade the sale of offices, which had been practised in a small way by Frederick William I; he did not ennoble bureaucrats or sell titles; the bureaucrats generally remained members of the estate of the burghers (Bürgerstand). But bureaucrats were made a privileged sub-category of the Bürgerstand called the Beamtenstand (the estate of the bureaucracy). Like the nobility, its members were not subject to town courts, only to higher courts; they were exempt from libel and slander laws; they, unlike other bourgeois, might marry into the nobility; and they and their sons were exempt from military service.[6] The barrier between the bourgeois bureaucrats and the nobility was thus preserved in form but eased in substance. It was all very orderly, pragmatic and peaceful compared with what happened in France.

Until the 1770s, the Prussian civil service made its initial selection of recruits without formal examinations. Those who were chosen had to serve as unpaid apprentices for several years, after which they were examined to see if they should be taken on for regular paid service. In 1770 a standing civil service commission was established and the civil service followed the judiciary in adopting competitive examinations for the selection at the first stage; they continued to examine the trainees at the end of their apprenticeship. University degrees were made a requirement for recruits at the beginning of the nineteenth century.[7] The long apprenticeship deterred the sons of parents without means, but the ambitious sons of landowners and high officials took to studying law (widely defined in the continental tradition) at the universities in the second half of the eighteenth century, since that was the best way to improve their chances of success in the two-stage procedure for entry to the upper bureaucracy and the judiciary. It is striking that in Protestant Prussia education, training and application were emphasized as early as this, and that service of the state was a career that was much sought after. Hard work, sober living, thrift, honesty and careful accounting became official gospel in the Prussian state service and in the social elite in the eighteenth century to an extent they never did in France.[8]

But perhaps the most striking contrast between Prussia and France lies in the condition of the official finances. Frederick the Great, who cared passionately for sound finance, perhaps because he knew what had happened in France, refused to get into debt to pay for his wars. Rather, he managed, in spite of being often at war, to run budget surpluses sufficient to build up during his reign a war reserve of bullion, which at his death was equal to three years' revenue and was reckoned to be sufficient to pay for a four-year war. He was helped by the fact that at the beginning of his reign 50 per cent of government revenue was rent from the royal estates, which had no doubt been boosted by his father's policy of confiscating land from the nobles; and he was helped by the subsidies from England which in the Seven Years' War equalled 20 per cent of his war expenditure.[9] He increased indirect taxes rather than direct on the grounds that they were felt less, an approach that ran counter to the Physiocrat doctrines fashionable in France; he tried to make existing direct tax tolerably fair by ensuring that the land surveys on which it was based were kept up to date and by refusing to enlarge the tax exemptions of the privileged; and he established grain stores so as to ward off famine. But he was not soft in his methods of tax collection. To collect indirect tax he introduced French tax farmers who became so unpopular that they were quickly dismissed by his nephew when he came to the throne.[10]

The state accounting system was fragmented: money came into and was held in many different funds with the result that financial planning was hard to conduct efficiently. Nevertheless there seems to have been relatively little dishonesty. In 1807 a reformer, Freiherr von Altenstein, judged the system, despite its deficiencies, to be more honest than that of any other contemporary government.[11] What that means by comparison, for example, with standards in Germany or Britain today, it is hard to say. There were financial scandals, but the very fact that a number were reported and the culprits punished is evidence that standards of some sort were being enforced, not neglected. Moreover the machinery for collecting the direct tax was elaborately designed to stop fraud. Not only were many persons made to sign the local accounts, but the king had his own extensive system of spies, normally advocates by profession, who constituted a secret police whose principal task was to watch for financial malpractice by officials.

The Prussian Achievement

The remarkable achievement of Prussia in the eighteenth century was that it matched France militarily although its population was only about one fifth of that of France. (The French population in 1789 has been estimated at 26 million, the Prussian a few years earlier at 5.5 million). Prussia's system of government was so effective that it was able to maintain an army of no less than four per cent of its population without incurring any debt; and at the same time the economy grew healthily.[12] France, constrained by its rotten financial system, could maintain an army equal to only about one per cent of its population, and even then the French public finances were in chronic state of disarray that was ended only by revolution and the assumption of power by Napoleon.[13] One must not forget the social flavour of this efficient authoritarian nation. Describing the militarization of society by his tyrannical father, Frederick the Great said that Berlin became:

> ...the Sparta of the North. Its entire government was militarized. The capital became the stronghold of Mars. All the industries which serve the needs of armies prospered... Frederick William strove less to create new industries than to abolish useless expenditures. Formerly, mourning had been ruinously expensive; and funerals had been accompanied by extremely costly festivities. These abuses were abolished. Horses and carriages were no longer allowed to be draped in black, nor were black liveries to be given to servants. Thenceforth people died cheaply. The military character of the government affected both customs and fashions. Society took a military turn. No one used more than three ells of cloth for a coat. The age of gallantry passed away. Ladies fled the society of men and the latter compensated themselves with carousals, tobacco and buffoonery.[14]

The Prussian Reaction to the French Revolution

With the French Revolution we enter a new era as regards the problems of how to command power and govern in Europe. The dominant problem now was how to ride or crush the discontentment and political demands of the masses and at the same time maintain military strength *vis-à-vis* neighbours.

In 1806 Napoleon, after roundly defeating Prussia at Jena and Auerstedt, made her pay a huge indemnity, surrender a large part of her territories and submit to an extremely harsh occupation of the territory that remained to her. The effect was to discredit the liberating message that Napoleon had proclaimed as he invaded his neighbours and to 'rouse nationalism among the young Germans, who, fired by secret societies, were sick of being overrun by the French, as the German states had been since the wars of Louis XIV.'[15]

Prussia's defeat partly stemmed from the extravagance of Frederick the Great's feeble nephew, Frederick William II, who succeeded him and ruled from 1786 to 1797. In those eleven years he managed to empty Frederick the Great's war reserve of bullion and run up debt of almost that amount again. His son and successor, Frederick William III (1797–1840), a man no more decisive than his father but of restrained habits, could not repair the financial damage that had been largely responsible for the vacillating foreign policy and military unpreparedness that led to the disastrous defeats at Jena and Auerstedt of 1806.[16] Since the days of Frederick the Great, the Prussian Army 'had become a creaky affair led by antique generals'.[17]

Before 1806, ideas of reform, inspired partly by the French Revolution and partly by the works of Adam Smith, were discussed, but it was only in the recovery from military defeat that reform got under way, implemented principally by Stein and Hardenberg. To these two strong men, one an aristocratic bureaucrat, one an officer, the weak and indecisive king was ready to delegate his power more or less completely, something that was to happen again when William I, who ruled from 1861 to 1888, relinquished power to Bismarck.

As an urgent task the army was reformed. The French example had convinced the Prussians that men who were treated like human beings and trained to use their reason were more effective than brutalized over-disciplined cannon fodder; and the government also needed to circumvent the limit of 42,000 set by the French on the size of the army. To meet these needs the structure and tactics of the army were reformed. A system was introduced whereby a large number of recruits were called up and trained for short periods, thereby creating a large trained reserve to back up the limited number of men in uniform at any time.

On the civil side, the approach articulated by Hardenberg and adopted in Prussia was that the right response to the French Revolution was a revolution brought about through the 'wisdom of the government' not by popular violence; what was needed was 'democratic principles in a monarchical government'. By 'democratic' was meant economic freedom and social emancipation – the opening of careers to all men of talent, religious toleration and civil liberty for Jews, freedom of opinion and the provision of education by the state. But the state was to retain virtually unlimited powers in the conduct of public affairs.[18] A decree in October 1807 abolished serfdom, which had been the status of about half the peasants, and also the legal distinctions between the members of the three estates (the nobles, the burghers and the peasants). 'Henceforth no occupations, trades or professions, including particularly the ownership of land, were closed to anyone. Nobles might engage in trade; bourgeois or successful peasants, if they could afford to do so, might buy what had hitherto been noble lands. Careers, in other words, were thrown open, in law, to talent in accordance with the principles of Adam Smith; and, also in accordance with those principles, the monopolies of the guilds were abolished and, in the course of time, the government monopolies. The provincial tariffs were replaced by a single tariff enforceable at the state frontiers – the famous tariff of 1818.'[19]

The reforms of Stein and Hardenberg and their successors changed an absolute monarchy into a bureaucratic monarchy. While the king remained an absolute ruler, not subject to laws interpreted by the judiciary nor displaced as law-maker by a democratically elected Parliament, he was now reliant on a bureaucracy that was so extensively involved in managing the affairs of the nation and that enjoyed such high status that he could not readily command its actions; he was as much ruled by the bureaucracy as he was ruler of it.

Behind the strengthening of the bureaucracy lay the view, enunciated by Stein after the debacle of defeat and occupation by Napoleon, that arbitrary and irresponsible rule by royal cronies drawn into a personal cabinet by the king should be replaced by orderly and responsible government by ministers chosen from the bureaucracy to run five departments into which government should be divided according to function. With the implementation of this system, ministers drawn from the bureaucracy acquired a monopoly over both the formulation and the execution of policy.[20] A further element in the strength of the bureaucracy was the principle of collegiate responsibility in decision-making, which meant, we are told, that 'all members of an agency' (whatever that means) took part in the discussion of every major question within the field of responsibility of that agency and shared responsibility for it. An American academic has this to say of the collegiate system:

> The collegiate principle was the symbol of the corporate tradition of the bureaucracy. Though it was less efficient than monocratic organization, early nineteenth-century officials were strongly attached to it... Collegiate responsibility protected their profession against corruption and the threat of arbitrary intrusions from higher authorities...
>
> ...although personal initiative was encouraged, it was the will of the group that was decisive...[21]

The author, while critical of the collegiate system, recognizes that it kept corruption down.

The introduction of the new system, with five bureaucrat-ministers operating under the king, was taken a step further in 1817 when the ministers were formally incorporated into a Council of State without whose consent the king theoretically could not, and in practice did not, issue any laws. But the apparent emasculation of the king in favour of the bureaucrat-ministers was in some degree illusory since the king retained the right to appoint and dismiss the ministers and to intrigue behind their backs, with the result that '...he was still in a position to determine the broad lines of policy'.[22] Nor was there any move towards popular representation. With the defeat of Napoleon the need to move in that direction was not felt to be compelling.

The nation's finances were in disorder after the war. Rearmament, war and indemnities had caused a large national debt. To meet the problem the king was persuaded to consolidate the debt, to schedule its amortization and to reform the tax system, all of which he did by edict on the advice of his ministers and bankers. As a sop to his subjects, he promised to consult the estates before he incurred any new debt. The importance of revenue from royal domains, monopolies and loans had now declined significantly: in 1821, 70 per cent of the Prussian state's income came from taxes, including tolls and tariffs. In the same year, nearly half the budget went on military expenditure, but in the next 25 years civil expenditure took an increasing share of the budget as money was put into state education, public health, the building of roads and railways, and other forms of economic development. In education Prussia was far ahead of Britain. By the middle of the nineteenth century over 80 per cent of children received some kind of formal training.[23]

The power of the bureaucracy came to be clearly recognized. Hegel, in his *Philosophy of Law*, published in 1821, extolled the merits of rule by neutral bureaucrats who, believing that they represent the divine ideal of the state, stand above 'civil society', meaning the realm of sectional interests and market forces, which, in his view, may become chaotic and self-destructive if not tamed by reasoned action for the general good by bureaucrats.[24] And Weber, writing a century later, said:

> The absolute monarch...is powerless in the face of the superior knowledge of the bureaucratic expert... Under the rule of expert knowledge, the influence of the monarch can attain steadiness only through continuous communication with bureaucratic chiefs which is methodically planned and directed by the central head of the bureaucracy.[25]

By the third decade of the nineteenth century, the pattern of Prussian modern government, which was later to be extended to the united Germany, seems to have been largely set. The revolutionary disturbances of 1830 and 1848 produced firm reactions tempered by few lasting concessions of a constitutional kind. In 1830 the fall of the Bourbons induced no significant formal change in the government of Prussia, though at the time criticism of the officiousness of bureaucratic rule was increasing. More important were the revolutionary uprisings across Europe in 1848. In Germany and Austria the uprisings were, in the end, put down by a combination of force and concessions. In Frankfurt delegates from the various states laboriously negotiated an all-German parliamentary constitution that would have turned the various German states into a constitutional monarchy headed by the king of Prussia, Frederick William IV, but he refused the crown regarding it as 'not really a crown at all, but actually a dog collar, with which they want to leash me to the revolution of 1848.'[26] Meanwhile the future of Prussia was resolved in Berlin, where in May 1848 a constituent assembly, similar to that of Frankfurt but more sharply divided between left and right, had been established. It spent months debating what kind of constitution should be introduced in Prussia and what balance there should be between monarch and parliament. The king, after order had been forcefully restored in Berlin, took the wind out of the sails of the reformers in December 1848 by suspending the assembly and introducing by decree a new constitution with two chambers: an upper house chosen by a restricted suffrage, the lower by almost universal male suffrage; the sovereignty of the monarch was clearly spelt out, as were ample emergency powers for the executive. Elections were quickly held and the parliament met for the first time at the end of February 1849, but when, after only two months, the lower chamber challenged the king, he and his ministers, who had been biding their time, dissolved the lower chamber and suspended the upper.[27] The tide of revolution was spent. In place of the democratic parliament the king introduced a constitution with a 'Three Class' suffrage system that was weighted according to wealth (as measured by tax obligations) in a manner that could be expected to ensure that the king and his ministers did not again face a hostile majority. The system, which remained in force until the monarchy was abolished in 1918, divided the electorate into three groups, each of which voted for electors who, in turn, met to choose one third of the members of the new *Landtag*. Nearly all men were eligible to vote, but the voting was extremely heavily weighted by wealth: the richest 5 per cent of the electorate chose as many members as the poorest 83 per cent (one third each); in between were 12 per cent of the population who chose the remaining third. When the electors chosen by this method were brought together to choose who should be members of the *Landtag*, they voted not in secret but in public, with one class voting at a time, starting with the poorest. As Sheehan, on whom I have relied heavily, observes:

> This suffrage system is of interest not only because it regulated Prussian elections until the end of the monarchy, but also because it so accurately reflects the combination of forces at work in the Prussian reaction: a bureaucratic preference for legal equality, an implicit faith in the conservative influence of property, and a desire to preserve the power of traditional deference communities.[28]

Reforms to the Judiciary and Bureaucracy

When order was restored in 1849 a series of laws and edicts was issued with the purpose of calming the populace by meeting their demands for reform and yet retaining or reinforcing the authority of the state.

Major changes were made to the legal system. Feudal forms of justice were abolished: nearly a thousand patrimonial courts were replaced by state courts; the hierarchy of courts was rationalized by the introduction of new appeal courts and a supreme court; a State Prosecutor's Office (*Staatsanwalt*) was established; and qualifications for legal officials were raised and standardized. This rationalization of the system produced an expanded, highly-trained professional judiciary and a legal profession of enhanced status, but it also reduced the autonomy of the judicial process. The number of positions directly appointed by the Ministry of Justice was substantially increased, with the result that the Minister of Justice, who was a political appointee, had greater say than before in the naming and promotion of judges; while the creation of the State Prosecutor's Office meant that the cases brought before the courts were dependent on the will of the administration.[29]

The administrative bureaucracy, some of whose younger members had supported the revolutionary movement, was brought to heel by a revised disciplinary code. Officials were made liable to dismissal if they violated 'the duty of loyalty' or showed themselves guilty of 'hostile partisanship against the government'. For most officials these rules were applied through disciplinary procedures that served to ensure that they were not dismissed arbitrarily. But this protection was denied to a top layer of 'political officials' which included directors of central ministries, under-secretaries, presidents and vice-presidents of district governments, state prosecutors, state police chiefs, diplomats and more. They were liable to suspension at the discretion of their superiors with no right of appeal guaranteed.

Reform extended to other fields. Local government, which had been essentially feudal, was reformed; new factory laws were passed. Through all these reforms a dominant pattern can be seen. Previous governments had ruled the individual through traditional institutions with feudal roots. Now, in response to pressures for political, social and economic change, the government was to rule more directly than before from the centre, using as its instrument a hierarchy of civil servants in the administrative and judicial services, who were more highly professional and subject to tighter formal discipline than before. A further factor strengthening the confidence of the government was the increasing effectiveness of the security forces, including the secret police.

Through all these upheavals the individual integrity of the Prussian bureaucrat appears not to have been corrupted. 'On the contrary, the Prussian bureaucracy remained remarkably free of petty scandal; its reputation for honest, efficient government was hardly challenged...'[30] But the bureaucracy was made to bend to the will of its masters. The most willful of these in the nineteenth century was Bismarck. In his ruthless pursuit and use of power, he is alleged to have bullied and bought newspapers, introduced censorship, corrupted the appointment of judges and civil servants, made financial gains for himself using inside information, undertaken unauthorized military expenditure, used secret funds for political ends, used the police to spy on his political opponents and manipulated the press and the votes of his bureaucrats in an attempt to get his son elected.[31] Yet Bismarck, by domestic modernization, diplomacy and war, was immensely effective in building up and expanding the powerful German nation. By introducing improvements in education, training, social security and promoting economic expansion, he and his predecessors appeased the popular demands for reform – though they also met them with harshness – and by the same means built up the economic and military strength of the nation till it outstripped its neighbours and could defeat them. Prussia (with Austria) invaded Schleswig-Holstein in 1864; she defeated Austria and expanded southwards in 1866; and she defeated France and took Alsace-Lorraine in 1871, in which year the king was proclaimed German emperor. The efficient society he ruled was authoritarian in the extreme.

Conclusion

By way of an interpretation of Prussia's achievement we might say that here was a society whose rulers, because of its geography and history, needed ready military strength if they were to survive or expand. Remarkable was the way in which coercive and economic power were used in combination to create a government that could generate extraordinary military strength with strong financial foundations. The use of those two forms of power was at least aided, and perhaps conditional on, the change in persuasive power resulting from the Reformation and from the Enlightenment. But these new intellectual tides found expression in an unusual way in Prussia: reason was applied to the analysis and shaping of society with unusual freedom and vigour but only so long as it did not undermine obedience or in any other way threaten the efficiency of the absolute ruler's pursuit of his objectives. Liberty was both encouraged and circumscribed, a point typified in Frederick the Great's phrase 'argue as much as you want and over whatever you want, but obey,' a remark akin to Henry Ford's statement about his Model T motor car, 'You can have any colour you like so long as it is black.'

4

France

France is a case of a country with land frontiers where military competition, combined with a defective financial system, helped to cause a deterioration in the quality of government that ended in revolution; and where reform was then made effective and enduring by a military autocrat, who was driven by military competition and who harnessed the legacies of the revolution.

In the reign of Louis XIV (1645–1715) the French public finances slid into what proved to be a politically irreversible mess. The essence of the problem was that the king spent money on wars regardless of the fact that the tax system was inelastic as well as inequitable, and there was no formal capital market on which he could borrow on a sound basis. The essential prerequisites for the financing of a war – an ability to borrow on reasonable terms backed by the prospect of tax revenue sufficient to give lenders confidence in the ability of the government to service their borrowings – were lacking. More and more of the revenue was lost in servicing debt and raising money by desperate means. The devices used were unusually varied; the ways they were administered were unusually rotten. The result was that in relation to its population, which was the largest in Europe, France managed to raise remarkably little revenue.

The Flawed Fiscal System

The only significant direct tax until the middle of the eighteenth century was the *taille*. Originally this was a charge on non-combatant serfs, but between the fourteenth and sixteenth centuries, when royal rents became an inadequate source of income, it was developed into a crude property tax. It remained essentially a tax on the peasants until it was abolished during the French Revolution. The nobility and the Church were exempt from the *taille* – though where nobles let their land to tenant farmers or *métayers*, a practice which spread in the second half of the eighteenth century, the *taille*, which was levied on the tenant, will have tended to lower the rent their landlords received. Towns were exempt on the grounds that there were no means of assessing business activities.[1] As to assessment and collection, the government, with little knowledge of what was reasonable, would decide what sum to exact from the population; that sum was divided up between provinces in each of which the *intendant*, a kind of provincial governor, served as collector. He, after struggling with Paris to get his quota reduced, would continue the process of dividing up the quota and passing on the task of collection to subordinate authorities until there was a given sum to be collected from each parish by a collector chosen from among the parishioners. Theoretically, the collector was elected by the parish, but the office exposed the incumbent to so many dangers that in the reign of Louis XIV 'there was no one, even the most miserable who would not sell his shirt to escape this servitude.' The more powerful among the villagers pushed the job onto the most defenceless who, in the nature of the case, were impoverished, ignorant and illiterate peasants. Unable to write, they would have to employ a literate person to prepare a register; and he would use the opportunity to protect himself, his friends and relations at the expense of the other *taillables* and the collector himself. The collector, poor wretch, if he failed to deliver his quota would be thrown into prison; and if he did deliver enough to satisfy the government, he was as likely as not to be beaten up or have his property destroyed by angry parishioners.[2]

The indirect tax system was no better. It covered a wide range of commodities many of which were government monopolies. These included salt, on which the tax – the notorious *gabelle* – bore heavily on the poor and yet yielded most revenue. The indirect taxes were administered by tax farmers whose privately employed police used such violent and arbitrary proceedings in pursuit of smugglers and other tax evaders that the indirect taxes caused as much discontent as the *taille*, or more. These taxes had been exploited to their limits by the beginning of the seventeenth century.

A principal means of filling the gap between spending and tax revenue was venality, which French kings had begun to use as a means of fund-raising in the thirteenth century. By the beginning of the sixteenth century, the way in which offices of the crown were sold, held and transferred from one holder to another was well established; and during that century the system was used increasingly to pay for wars. It was not regarded as corrupt; it brought benefits to both the office holder and the king.[3] From the king's point of view, the sale of offices, besides bringing in money, had the politically advantageous effect of turning into clients those with money who bought offices: having invested in a job the value of which depended on the authority of the king, they were unlikely to defy him. From the point of view of the buyer, the absence of a reliable capital market meant that a venal job, which he could always sell to a private buyer, was the best asset other than land in which to invest – even though it carried the risk that the government would default on its commitment to pay the salary – and it was also the best road to social advancement, including the acquisition of a hereditary title. The financial and social privileges that could be gained by the purchase of an office were numerous. One of the most sought after was exemption from the *taille* since it put you on a par socially with the nobility as well as being a valuable financial perk. It has been said that the exemption of the Church and nobles from the *taille* was of little consequence compared with the enormous mass of privileged commoners. But the essential point is that the rich, whether nobles or commoners, avoided tax, and were offered better opportunities to do so when the state was desperate for money with the result that the burden was passed on to the poor.

The state sold venal offices not just for the life of one incumbent, but with hereditary rights, with the consequence that for the sake of ready money revenue was committed in perpetuity to paying the salary of the venal office. In addition, more and more unnecessary offices were created in order that they might be sold for the sake of immediate money. Short of default it was impossible to abolish these offices unless there was enough money in the royal kitty to pay compensation, which naturally there almost never was.

The laws of demand and supply came into play in both economic and social terms. If the king sold too many offices, the price he could get for them would fall and the existing holders would be upset by the fall in value of their assets and also by the feeling that their status was being degraded as new upstarts were admitted to the privileges they enjoyed. By the end of the reign of Louis XIV, this had happened to the point where venality as a source of money was exhausted and was never revived on the same scale.

The economic trouble with venality is that it is just a form of borrowing. To obtain a lump sum for an office in exchange for the promise of a future salary is no different from borrowing a sum in exchange for the promise of future interest payments: for the sake of ready money, future income is mortgaged. The same is true of the other devices that were resorted to. Where those who bought offices were granted exemption from the *taille* or from other charges and fees, future income was lost. Where, as happened on a large scale, trades were turned into royal monopolies so that only traders who had paid for a licence were allowed to sell a commodity or service in a particular place – for example, in 1691 the oyster-sellers of Paris, Normandy and the royal court were made to buy a licence – a burden akin to a tax was imposed on the people.

Similar things happened with tax farming. The future income from the tax farmers was increasingly promised to financiers in exchange for ready money. The tax farmers – who had combined to form a cartel, the General Farm – and the financiers became one community. The same persons gathered tax, using subcontractors, with one hand and lent with the other. They worked their way into the court, marrying their rich daughters to courtiers, thus acquiring status and gaining contact with the men of influence and power around the king. It would be hard to contrive a system with stronger incentives to corruption or greater opportunities for it. Julian Dent has described it with much financial and social detail.[4]

As the Crown's demand for money became more desperate, the formal financial system within which the state's finances were meant to be conducted, was circumvented until it became a fiction. Resort was had to 'extraordinary means of finance' (*affaires extraordinaires*), this being the umbrella under which tricks were developed for disguised borrowing. The Crown could not borrow directly (which is one reason why there was no proper capital market) partly because the Crown, being the supreme maker and judge of the law, could not be obliged to honour its obligations by due process of law.[5] Various devices were used.

There were *Rentes*, which were loans raised by using the *Hotel de Ville* as intermediary and guarantor. But by the 1630s the payment of interest had become so irregular and defaults by the Crown in times of financial stress had occurred so often that the acceptability of *Rentes* had been undermined, leaving them a vehicle for manipulation by the financier-tax farmers. They 'had become useless save as vehicle of corruption'.[6] To replace *Rentes* a new means was found of giving the financiers the steep interest they demanded without the Crown being seen to pay it. The financiers made loans at high interest to a top financial official, usually the *Surintendant des Finances*, against his personal word, whom they trusted because he was sufficiently high up in the corrupt hierarchy to be in a position to pay what he promised from the funds he handled for the king.

The most notorious of these officials was Fouquet who in his financial operations as a servant of the king acquired such a vast personal fortune and spent it so conspicuously that he was sacked and put on trial by Louis XIV when he, no longer a child, took power into his own hands following the death of Mazarin. Fouquet's most notable extravagance was the building of *Vaux le Vicomte*, a palace and formal park of great grandeur, which was a precursor of Versailles. He seems to have been remarkably brazen. His emblem was a squirrel and his motto *Quo non ascendam*. (How high shall I not climb.) But it was perhaps bad luck that he fell foul of a formidable young king intent on taking power into his own hands and kicking aside those who had been using and abusing it on his behalf. It was not extraordinary for those in the top positions of power to build magnificently. Sully and Richelieu built several châteaux apiece and each also built a whole town. Compared with what they did, Fouquet's château at *Vaux le Vicomte* does not seem far out of the ordinary.[7]

Attempts at Reform

Colbert, who soon replaced Fouquet, his former master, did a great deal to reform the financial and economic administration of France, and he helped to improve the centralized bureaucracy that had been established by Mazarin and his predecessors. Entrusted with ever more offices by the king, he became in effect 'the dictator of the whole economic life of France'.[8] But his achievements were lop-sided as regards the income and expenditure side of the state's affairs. On the expenditure side, he seems to have been able to send orders from the centre and see grand policies executed, for example the creation of shipyards and an effective navy, the creation of great public buildings and of state enterprises such as the *Gobelins* and the construction of roads and canals – at one time 12,000 men were at work on the great *Canal du Midi*. On the income side of the royal accounts he achieved very considerable improvements. He set up a *Conseil de Finance* to manage the finances and a *Chambre de Justice* to judge and punish the conduct of officials and financiers. Many titles to offices were scrutinized and many were cancelled with minimal compensation to the holders who had bought them; the holders of *Traités* and *Rentes* were treated similarly. The proceedings were essentially those of a bankruptcy. Colbert got away with it because the titles to the offices and loans were so dodgy that their holders would not argue for fear of punishment.[9] And he displayed the circumspection so necessary to the acquisition and retention of a position of power at the court of such a wilful king. To avoid trouble for himself and for other influential people around the court and financial world (his own past actions would presumably not have borne close scrutiny), Colbert edited the record of the trial of Fouquet, his predecessor, as before the trial he had edited Fouquet's papers so as to deprive Fouquet of evidence with which he could defend himself.[10] Ugly, but understandable.

Colbert managed to improve the yield of the indirect taxes by holding what amounted to auctions for tax farms, giving contracts to the highest bidder, rather than behaving like his predecessor and arranging corrupt deals for his own gain. (A civil service to collect these taxes was lacking.) But he achieved little as regards direct tax. He was fully conscious of the defects of the existing regime. In his own words:

> In almost all the parishes, the chief inhabitants and the rich easily found means to avoid the *taille* and shift it to the shoulders of the poorer inhabitants; while the latter were forced to acquiesce in the shifting, because the rich were their employers, and their only resource for help in all their necessities.[11]

He knew the evils of the methods of collection: the seizure of the goods, chattels and livestock of defaulters, and the imprisonment of defaulters and collectors. For the practical purpose of gaining more revenue Colbert sought to spread the *taille* more generally, reform it and reduce it. His general aim was to reduce tax rates and improve the yield by better administration and by plugging the gaping holes in the tax base, but there was a limit to what he could do without challenging the privileges of the Church, the nobles and the ignoble rich in a manner that the king would not sanction. Once the king had embarked on the Third Dutch War (which was partly the consequence of Colbert's policy of challenging Dutch commercial strength in the name of mercantilism) Colbert could raise the money that was needed for the war only by resorting to the old tricks. He was compelled to undo his own reforms – to raise tax rates, sell offices and borrow in defective ways. His influence declined until his death in 1683.

Louis XIV's pursuit of ever more megalomaniac wars on top of his lavish expenditure on his court and palaces and his failure to reform the tax system, reduced France's public finances to disarray by the end of his reign. The economy was in a terrible state: schemes for empire and navy were shattered, agriculture was impoverished and the population fell by more than 2 million as a result of famine and disease.[12]

The underlying political problem was that France was a mosaic state whose pieces were regions with strong autonomous traditions over which, more influential than any one region, lay the Church. The country had been united by strong monarchs. During Louis XIV's minority, the nobility together with the bourgeoisie – by this time towns were important – took part in the *Fronde*, a series of uprisings partly in protest against taxes imposed on them by Richelieu and Mazarin. This caused Louis XIV and his successors to be circumspect in their treatment of the nobility and other beneficiaries of privilege. (It was the last time the nobles took arms against the king of France.) After Louis XIV had gathered the reins into his own hands on the death of Mazarin, he established himself as an absolute monarch, taking unprecedented power unto himself. Intentionally and unintentionally, he and his successors let the system of exemptions and privileges produce increasing inequality of burdens between town and country, and amongst the provinces and social groups, to the point where these groups directed much of their anger at one another rather than at the monarchy.[13]

Like other strong kings before him, Louis XIV never summoned the Estates General, the traditional channel through which the elites were represented.[14] Instead he gathered the high nobles, who might have caused trouble in the provinces, around him and made them dependent on him for their financial and social privileges, as well as preoccupied with the rituals and jealousies of court life. He reduced their power in the provinces and built up direct rule from the centre under ministries, dividing the country into *généralités* (the precursors of Napoleon's *départements*) using as his principal agent in each *généralité* a royal *intendant* whom he appointed personally and whose office was not venal. These *intendants*, who were not drawn from the hereditary nobility, were paid salaries from the centre so that they could be kept under control and replaced at any time. They were the eyes and ears of the king. 'Through their correspondence the whole life of France passed in review like a great and unending panorama before the king's council, sitting in its various divisions day after day.'[15] Louis XIV's absolutism was distinguished from earlier types of royal power because, in Professor Mousnier's words, the king was held to share his power with no one; he exercised power through a standing army, and through royal officials in the capital and the provinces, who are commonly described as constituting a bureaucracy.[16] But the bureaucracy was weakened by venality. Since the officials below the *intendants* had usually bought or inherited their offices, they were of uneven quality and could be dismissed only if money could be found to buy them out. Indeed it is at first sight surprising that Colbert managed to get so many grand plans executed using this defective apparatus. The explanation would seem to lie in the fact that in his heyday when he was introducing his main plans Colbert, as we have seen, was also attacking and abolishing venal offices in the interests of efficiency; that must have helped him to get things done; but it did not last: venality returned.

The monstrous defects of the tax system and the system of borrowing did not go unrecognized. A succession of persons analysed the problem clearly and proposed reforms. The best known is the great Burgundian general and military architect, maréchal Vauban who, having spent most of his life away from the court travelling to the frontiers of France to build fortifications and conduct sieges, knew the condition of the people and the miseries inflicted on them by the tax system. He proposed that the existing jungle of taxes and exemptions should be swept away and a single tax introduced, the royal dime (*dîxme royale*), levied at 10 per cent on the estimated product of every piece of land and at a lower rate on commerce and industry. But the courtiers and financiers, fearing their ruin, poisoned the king's mind against the scheme. Vauban, in a last effort to sell his scheme to the king and his ministers, revised his proposal and had it printed as a book for private circulation. But an order was made that the book should be seized, and a week later, in March 1707, Vauban, already a sick man, was dead.[17]

The development of a relatively effective administrative system for the expenditure of public money on the development of the economy and navy on the one hand, and the debauchery of the system for gathering taxation (and for borrowing) on the other, can be seen to be a product of the lop-sided basis of the monarch's political power. The exercise of his absolute power did not meet great political obstacles when it came to expenditure, but with respect to taxation it was undermined by the need to keep sweet those with the greatest taxable capacity – the Church, the nobility and the newly-moneyed elite.

Louis XIV's successors did no better. Immediately after the king's death, John Law, the colourful Scottish financier, caused temporary relief followed by collapse with his unconstrained schemes for issuing paper.[18] Wars continued to cause financial crises. Venality, though revived, was never again a prime source of money. A new direct tax on land – the *dixième*, succeeded by the *vingtième* – from which the nobles were not exempt, assumed some importance in the middle of the eighteenth century, but there was much avoidance by the rich – both privileged commoners and nobles. Louis XVI inched his way towards reform, but he could not do away with all the privileges and patronage that held the system together. He turned to Necker, a Swiss Protestant banker, to save the financial situation. Necker, having managed to trim some bits of expenditure and produce an apparently balanced budget, for a while reassured the financiers and induced them to lend again. But confidence in him collapsed and he was ousted amid accusations that he had cooked the books – though how far he had really done so is a matter of contention today.[19] Nobody had the political power and resolution radically to reform the tax system or heed the limits of the revenue it produced.

The Revolution and Reform

In the earlier years of revolutionary government, the ways of the *Ancien Régime* were rejected: the nobles lost their privileges, the Church lands were confiscated, tax farmers and the indirect taxes they collected – including the notorious salt tax – were abolished. But the new leaders scarcely knew what to put in place of the old financial disorder. A new, comprehensive tax on land and other property was devised by a committee which largely adopted the Physiocratic notion that tax should be levied on land and which, furthermore, naively believed that if the old rotten tax system were replaced by a just one the people, inspired by the new spirit of democracy, would pay willingly.[20] In the event, the collection system, new and complex in design, failed to produce adequate revenue. As the revolutionary governments became more desperate, collection became crude and savage until, in the words of an historian of the French financial system, 'the countryside was ravaged by hordes of tax collectors who made it look as if it had been invaded and pillaged by an invading army.'[21] As regards appointments, venality was out, and since no agreement could be reached on a method of avoiding patronage, the selection of civil servants was left to the free choice of ministers.[22]

That Napoleon decisively reshaped the government of France is beyond dispute, but there is debate about how far he was an innovator and how far he was building on the steps towards efficient centralized government that were initiated under the *Ancien Régime* and continued under the revolutionary regimes that preceded him. Certainly reforms of enduring importance were introduced before he came to power. For example, the *École Polytechnique*, that fount of the technocratic tradition of modern France, was established in 1794 during the last days of the Convention. Moreover, Napoleon pragmatically reinstated selected institutions of the *Ancien Régime*, for example, a number of faculties of law, all of which had been closed by the revolutionaries.

The Napoleonic legacy is well known – centralized power; formalized rule by detailed laws and decrees; an imperial structure of government operated through prefects (the successors of the *intendants*) acting as guardians of law and order in their departments and implementing orders received from Paris; a large public service with all school teachers, the staff of universities and research institutes, judges and postmen on the payroll of the central government; and a professional civil service with a technocratic-cum-legal tradition, with education and training the key to entry. In short, a highly professional system of government.

One of the weakest parts of the Napoleonic legacy was the tax system. He kept the direct tax structure he inherited from the revolutionary government but since it provided no exemptions to any class of property owner it was unpopular with them all; it was not feasible to raise more revenue from it. Therefore Napoleon, who took the view that the only quality of a good tax system was its yield, pragmatically reintroduced indirect taxes, applying them to drink, tobacco and similar things, though never again to salt, and introduced a new rigour into the assessment and collection of taxes.[23] At the same time he reformed the financial administration and passionately stopped waste. Even so, such was the cost of his military adventures that he managed to avoid deficits, an aim to which he was dedicated, only by living off the territories he conquered and extracting money from them, a path followed by two other notable conquerors of Europe, Gustavus Adolphus in the seventeenth century and Hitler in the twentieth.[24] It is a precarious path. When you suffer defeat and have to retreat, you suffer financial implosion. But it has the advantage of relieving the dependence of an army on its supply train and so increasing the speed with which it can move forward.

The failure to establish a better direct tax system must have had many causes. One is that it is always hard to tax peasants who own their land and who consume a part of their produce and commonly do not keep accounts, the more so if they have acquired the habit of resisting brutal tax collectors. Another cause, perhaps of more importance as regards the upper and middle classes than the peasants, is that some of their members felt loyalty to the Crown and the Church, others to democracy and free thinking: there were two factions with rival political-cum-religious loyalties. As the country chopped and changed between republican and royalist government in the nineteenth century, one faction or the other would always be out of sympathy with the government of the day, reluctant to pay tax to it and probably feeling that their religious – or anti-religious – feelings gave moral sanction to the steps they took to avoid or evade tax. Such a pattern of behaviour is likely to become ingrained and not to be altogether abandoned when your own faction is in power.

Besides professionalism, Napoleon imparted another characteristic to the French public services: he personalized them, in this respect behaving as monarchs had done under the *Ancien Régime*. The top civil servants were selected by him for their personal loyalty to him; and judges, though state servants for life, were promoted by him, as of course were the generals. Even today one's French academic colleagues (who are all on the public payroll) seem to feel, in a muted way that I as an Englishman find hard to fathom, that they are answerable to their government. In short, dependence on the government of the day became a feature of the French system. After 1830, for example, 95 per cent of the prefects of France were replaced; and later in the nineteenth century, under the Third Republic, there was a great deal of lobbying by elected representatives for public jobs for their constituents and for themselves. In order to buy the support of deputies, who had little or no loyalty to political parties, governments gave them jobs on the public payroll.[25] The use of patronage to buy political support was far from dead. Furthermore, the constitution of 1958 was so framed that the president could interfere with the judiciary (Chapter 8).

Conclusion

What can one say about the forces behind reform in France? Military competition was plainly important, first as a negative force contributing, in combination with all the defects of the tax structure, to the deterioration in government and the slide into revolution. Later it became a positive force, providing a motive for reform and a pretext for Napoleon to appeal to patriotism and to the spirit of the revolution as he reorganized – and mobilized – the nation. France, it must be remembered, was at war almost continuously from 1792, when war broke out with Austria, until 1815, when Napoleon was finally defeated. As regards social forces, the popular demands for reform that helped to produce the revolution were an expression of a desire for more just and efficient government, a desire which was eventually met by Napoleon, who pursued efficiency and economy with zeal. Religion can scarcely be invoked as a factor that contributed to an improvement in standards of public conduct: the revolution was antireligious.

Though France inherited from Napoleon a professional public service and a clearly articulated and efficient system of centralized government, it did not clean up its politics. France's political history in the nineteenth century and beyond was so turbulent, so often punctuated by changes in regime between various forms of republic and monarchy, that central government never settled into a mould in which constraints on the means used to gain and maintain power became well established. Corruption amongst politicians, far from being severely stamped upon, has tended to be regarded as inevitable at the national as well as the local level. But, as we shall see later, that tradition is now being challenged.[26]

5

The United States

The United States is the extreme opposite of Prussia/Germany and France. Once it had been brought into being by revolt against colonial rule, military competition and social pressures for reform of government were absent or weak.

As regards military competition, North America, situated thousands of miles across the sea from Europe, and with weak or negligible neighbours to the north and south, was so far from external military threats that, when the time came for constitution-making, there was no necessity for strong central government to organize and finance standing military forces. A significant standing army was not introduced until the Cold War.

As regards popular demands for reform, the European inhabitants of North America, having fled from religious intolerance, overbearing government and poverty in order to start afresh in a new country, carried with them an antipathy for strong central rule, indeed for government in general. They had left behind forms of government against which their European cousins were to revolt; they had cast off colonial rule; they were in no degree influenced by such forms of government as had been evolved by the native 'Indians', against whom they – or rather we, for to start with our British ancestors were the dominant rulers – directed their superior armament and organization to generate a process of genocide that had been started accidentally as infectious diseases were carried to the New World.[1] The earliest recorded case of biological warfare, other than the placing of human and animal corpses in wells, occurred in 1763 when Sir Jeffry Amherst, British Commander-in-Chief in North America, wrote to a subordinate 'Could it not be contrived to send the Small Pox among those disaffected tribes of Indians [in the Ohio-Pennsylvania area]. We must on this occasion use every stratagem in our power to reduce them.' His proposal was acted upon. A few months later smallpox was prevalent among the tribes in the Ohio area.[2]

Collectively, the European inhabitants of North America were free, to an extraordinary degree, to choose how to rule themselves. Individually they also enjoyed a great degree of freedom because there was apparently limitless land to be appropriated at low cost. With land almost free, any adventurous man could acquire property, and property meant freedom from direct economic dependence on other men. The early America can perhaps be described as a huge 'desert island democracy'.

Narrative History

The constitution was designed to limit the authority of the state by means of the separation of powers: the executive was made weak by design. There was no provision for political parties since society was not perceived to be divided by issues. The Founding Fathers 'held to a sort of "amateur" theory of politics according to which men were called from their private affairs to take care of political business and returned to their previous occupations.'[3] In the event, there was an early division between Federalists representing the propertied and mercantile interest, who were headed by Alexander Hamilton and were in favour of relatively strong central government and mercantilist protection, and were also hostile to the French Revolution, seeing it as a challenge to order. On the other hand were the Jeffersonian Democrats, representing the agrarian interest who were opposed to Federal power, were in favour of popular government, and were sympathetic to the French Revolution, seeing it as a struggle for the cause of liberty.

Hostility to elites and to central power, combined with faith in democracy and the belief that anyone could do anything, meant that there was no initial provision for an independent, professional civil service. The judiciary was insulated from short-run political influence at the level of the Supreme Court, but it was vulnerable to political influence at the state and local levels, where judges were appointed by the local legislatures or by direct election, though practice differed from one state to another according to the constitution each adopted.

The Spoils System

There were soon problems over patronage. When Jefferson became president in 1801 he inherited from President John Adams public servants who were almost entirely Federalist. Offices were already regarded as rewards for service and Jefferson's followers were eager to have them. Jefferson, succumbing to pressure to use his absolute power to hire and fire, replaced significant numbers of inherited officials. But it was under Andrew Jackson, who became president in 1829, that the use of patronage for political ends became extreme. Having been elected in a dirty election campaign in which he accused John Quincy Adams, the previous president, of corruption, he pressed no charges against Adams when he came to power. However, in the name of cleaning an Augean stable, he removed every civil servant suspected of supporting Adams, thus audaciously bringing the 'spoils system' from the states where it had always existed, into the federal government. His justification, not in itself ridiculous, was stated in his first annual message:

> ...the duties of all public offices are...so plain and simple that men of intelligence may readily qualify themselves for their performance; and I cannot but believe that more is lost by the long continuance of men in office than is generally to be gained by their experience... No one man has any more intrinsic right to official station than another.[4]

The result was that:

> Aged and respectable Jeffersonians were replaced by young, often disreputable, and sometimes corrupt Jackson men. The spoils system did not noticeably increase the power of the President, for even Jackson had to please congressmen, and the Senate negatived many of his nominations; but it greatly increased the power of party and of the professional element within parties, by offering tangible rewards for faithful service.[5]

Several other developments were important around this time. One was the introduction of universal suffrage (for men), which the new western states were writing into their constitutions and the older states now adopted in place of property qualifications. With the electorate widened, the competitive harvesting of votes by fair means or foul was a more challenging exercise than before for the party machines. Secondly, immigration brought in many people seeking to make their way and ready to vote for anyone who looked as if he might help them: the annual inflow grew from an average of 10,000 in the 1820s to 50,000 in the 1830s. Thirdly, tremendous temptations for business to bribe politicians were introduced when the federal government offered grants of land to companies as an incentive to build railroads that would open up the west. It has been said that in the nineteenth century 'the US railroads virtually stole 190 million acres of land by bribing Congressmen'.[6]

But it was after the Civil War (1861–65) that behaviour deteriorated so far that corruption was seen to be really scandalous. There seem to have been many reasons for this. Firstly, the Civil War saw much self-ishness, indifference and defeatism on both sides and left a legacy, most extreme in the south, of lawlessness. (A civil war seems more certain than an international war to cause disorder and unscrupulous behaviour; there is no single enemy against which to unite; and government and administration are sure to be fractured with damaging consequences for law and order.) Secondly, industry and big business grew fast, based on unrestrained capitalism protected from foreign competition; and, in the period up to the First World War, the poor of Europe poured into the United States to work in the new industries and live in burgeoning cities. The sleepy agrarian society was being displaced by a raw urban society where there were few social constraints on behaviour.

Precisely because it was a period of increasing corruption, the years from the end of the Civil War to the start of the First World War saw the development of reform movements, formed in reaction to what was going on. As they went into battle, the reformers, understandably, met fierce resistance from all those with an interest in the existing state of affairs. A long struggle followed, in which the tide went to and fro. The result was limited progress for the reformers.

Civil Service Reform

One of the main issues was civil service reform, meaning the replacement of the spoils system by selection by merit.

> Every President since Polk (1845–49) had complained of the demands that patronage made on his time, energy and judgement, and Lincoln had expressed fears that the spoils system was 'going

to ruin the republican government'. Scandal had followed scandal in the civil service; yet the spoils system had been extended even to cleaning women in the public offices.[7]

In 1864 there had been an ineffective move, backed by East Coast intellectuals, to introduce a Civil Service Reform Bill. By 1871, the year when Gladstone finally managed to introduce exams for entry to the top of the British civil service, dissatisfaction with the spoils systems had become widespread in the United States. A civil service commission was established which submitted a list of reforms. President Grant (1869–77) promised to give them a fair trial but soon 'scuttled the commission and jettisoned the reforms'. He packed the civil service with party henchmen and, in the words of a contemporary observer, there was 'an utter surrender of the civil service to the coarsest use by the coarsest men'. In 1875 the civil service commission itself was discontinued.[8]

Grant's administration was so tainted by scandals that there was something of a revolt in which discontented old time politicians now joined liberals and reformers. Civil service reform was the issue on which they could unite, and it was tackled, rather ambivalently, by Grant's successor, President Hayes (1877–81). He appointed a civil service reformer to the Department of the Interior and seemed to have good intentions, but these he quickly breached, scandalously, by rewarding officials who had engineered his election by ruling in his favour when investigating disputed election results.

In the early 1880s civil service reform at last made some progress under President Arthur. He was a nonentity of a vice-president who succeeded to the presidency when, soon after being elected, President Garfield was shot by a disappointed office seeker and killed. Unexpectedly, Arthur became something of a reformer and is remembered for the Pendleton Civil Service Reform Bill that became law in 1883. It introduced entry to the civil service by merit in open competitions. The new system applied to only about 12 per cent of posts, but the president was empowered to extend it at his discretion. Although the step forward was modest, Pendleton, a Democratic senator from Ohio, so displeased his party by curtailing the spoils system even thus modestly that they denied him re-nomination.

President Cleveland, a reformer, extended competitive entry to more posts, but under President Harrison (1889–93) a Republican 'who lacked the ability to control the spoilsmen of his party' the actions of the government swung in the other direction. In particular, the Postmaster

General made a clean sweep of Democratic postmasters, removing 30,000 of them in a year, more than double the rate at which Cleveland had dismissed them.[9]

Between the turn of the century and the Second World War, Theodore Roosevelt, Woodrow Wilson and F D Roosevelt extended the merit lists, and most states passed civil service reform laws of their own. Yet Professors Morison and Commager, on whose admirable history of the United States I have drawn heavily, concluded in 1942:

> Yet it would be idle to pretend that civil service reform has ful-filled the expectations of its advocates. The emoluments are not sufficiently high, or talent at such a premium as to attract university graduates and other able men from business and the professions. There has been, however, a great improvement in morale and efficiency; and it was fortunate indeed that the merit principle was adopted before the twentieth century when administrative expansion greatly increased the need for honest men and expert service.[10]

Although the United States followed Britain in adopting civil service reform, it did not give civil servants the high status accorded to them in Britain and many other European countries. It did not create an elite. The Congress, expressing its devotion to democracy, a devotion perhaps tainted by a hankering after patronage,

> refused to adopt those provisions of the British model that, by setting age and other restrictions on entry opportunities, and by strengthening tenure and other inducements to stay in the service, encouraged the development of a permanent body of civil servants with little or no turnover... American civil servants remained a loose and flexible group, whose turnover and mobility remained almost as high as in the private workforce. Also, lacking any special social status, American civil servants did not develop anything like the *esprit de corps* through which European bureaucracies policed their own ranks. This held true especially for the lower echelons of American public service, where patronage prevailed much longer.[11]

Civil service reform was important not just for the substance of what it achieved but also for its symbolism, for the focus it provided for intellectual reformers who were better suited to campaigning for an abstract cause than to exposing and hounding particular villains. But to focus on civil service reform is to direct one's eyes at a reassuring part of the picture, rather than at the dirt of what was going on in politics. It is as if one were looking at a painting by Pieter Bruegel and had focused on an upper corner where priests are guiding virtuous people away from a village binge and had not lowered one's eyes to the scenes of lust and debauchery in the rest of the canvas. Let us turn now to three things – the nature of the political machine in the United States, city politics and the links between government and business.

In considering what went on, it is important to remember that the United States, having derived its laws and moral code from England via the founding fathers and the constitution makers, inherited the same notion of corruption as we have. Later immigrants coming from different parts of Europe and from other parts of the world may often have arrived imbued with un-English moral codes and un-English habits with respect to observance of the law, but once they entered the melting pot they were expected to revere the constitution and to observe a system of law derived from England. The United States is not a society that evolved separately from Europe with a different moral code and different set of laws; it is not a society where actions we regard as corrupt are legitimate and morally normal. Rather, it is a society that has experienced an unusual struggle between the codes to which it aspires and the conduct of its politicians and its citizens; it is a society with plenty of ambivalence in its attitudes to good conduct. The battle cry 'corruption' has often been heard as accusations of misbehaviour have been made, justifiably, against politicians. But, as Bryce observed at the end of the last century, there is in the United States 'a disposition to be lax in enforcing laws disliked by any large part of the population, to tolerate breaches of public order, and to be indulgent to offenders generally.'[12]

The Political Machine

The characteristic of the American 'political machine' emphasized by historians is that it exists to pursue power for itself. In American politics, issues have generally come second. In what I have called their 'desert island democracy' there have not been groups or classes – other than Native Americans and Africans – welded together by different values and the pursuit of different collective aims. The people have been politically apathetic, content to pursue their own interests with the minimum of government interference: that was the meaning to them of the freedom they had found in the United States. But in pursuing their interests, as individuals or in business enterprises, they would take any help they were offered by the politicians – and any help they could extract from them. In exchange, the politicians wanted their votes; and once they had power, and the command over economic resources that power gave them, the politicians' aims were to reward themselves and, of necessity, to reward their supporters sufficiently to ensure that their party won again. The party machines have engaged in 'winning, keeping and using political power'.[13] They have been 'far less under the control of one or two conspicuous leaders than are European parties.'[14] Power has lain with the bosses across the nation.

City Politics

The cities are where corrupt machine politics have been most conspicuous and shameless, and of all the machines Tammany Hall was the most infamous. From the latter part of the nineteenth century to the 1930s Tammany was the most powerful faction in the Democratic party in New York City which, despite a few setbacks inflicted by reformers, ran the city. The most notorious of its bosses was William Marcy Tweed. He and the few cronies with whom he shared power came to be known as the Ring. Their antics, which were minutely described by Lord Bryce, beggar belief. Having succeeded, by means of bribery and electoral frauds of unprecedented magnitude, in gaining a majority in the State legislature, they caused it to change the city's charter in 1870 in such a manner that control of the city's finances was concentrated in the hands of the mayor and a few officers whom the mayor was now given the power to appoint. The results were predictable. In the calm words of Bryce:

> In the reign of the Ring there is little to record beyond the use made by some of them of the opportunities for plunder which this control of municipal funds conferred. Plunder of the city treasury, especially in the form of jobbing contracts, was no new thing in New York, but it had never reached such colossal dimensions.[15]

He gives as examples the purchase, by members of the Ring and their friends, of land where street widening was due to take place, for the purpose of profiting from compensation payments and contracts the value of which was rigged; the payment to three companies in which the Ring was interested of no less than $3 million in two years for stationery and printing; and the payment of a total estimated between $8 million and $13 million for a courthouse that was initially estimated to cost $250,000.[16] The escalation in expenditure on the courthouse (and on city contracts in general) was achieved by requiring contractors to add to their bills large sums that were then appropriated by Tweed and his associates. A particularly extravagant case which gained publicity was that of a plasterer named Gray, dubbed by the *New York Times* the 'Prince of Plasterers', who was paid $2,870,464.61 for nine months' work.[17]

Tweed's behaviour was so extreme that, caught out when the press obtained copies of municipal accounts, he was eventually indicted for felony. After being in and out of the courts and running off abroad twice, he died in gaol in 1878. Some reforms were introduced but, to the despair of reformers, Tammany was soon back in power.

A fascinating account of the attitudes of a Tammany politician is to be found in the discourses on politics of George Washington Plunkitt who, having started as a butcher's boy became, by political means, a millionaire. His words of wisdom were delivered from the bootblack stand at the county courthouse in New York City. A journalist took down what he said and, having put it into shape and probably embellished it a bit, published the edited transcript in 1905.[18] Plunkitt at that time was a well-known figure in New York politics. Most famous is his distinction between honest and dishonest graft:

> There's all the difference in the world between the two. Yes, many of our men have grown rich in politics. I have myself. I've made a big fortune out of the game, and I'm getting richer every day, but I've not gone in for dishonest graft – blackmailin' gamblers, saloon-keepers, disorderly people, etc. – and neither has any of the men who have made big fortunes in politics.
>
> There's an honest graft, and I'm an example of how it works... Supposin' it's a new bridge they're going to build. I get tipped off and I buy as much property as I can that has to be taken for the approaches. I sell at my own price later on and drop some more money in the bank. Wouldn't you? It's just like lookin' ahead in Wall Street or in the coffee or cotton market.

The merit of sticking to honest graft, he explains, is that when a reform administration comes in and looks for evidence of wrong-doing:

> The books are always all right. The money in the city treasury is all right. Everything is all right. All they can show is that the Tammany heads of departments looked after their friends, within the law, and gave them what opportunities they could to make honest graft.[19]

He detested civil service reform, condemning it on the grounds that it would destroy patriotism. 'How', he asks, 'are you goin' to interest our young men in their country if you have no offices to give them when they work for their party?'[20]

Tammany was not unique. Chicago was notorious and so was Philadelphia where the Gas Ring, a Republican machine managed from the city's gas department, took control of the city, including the police department, and the control of the electoral register and achieved massive swindles.[21] Similar things went on in every great city.

Three principal causes have been suggested for the corruption of American city politics. First, the political system devised for an agrarian society, on the assumption that people would generally behave cooperatively and virtuously, was unsuited to the conditions of the new industrial and commercial cities thronged by immigrants, mostly not Puritans, from the poorest parts of Europe, in particular Ireland and Italy, desperately seeking to make their way. Secondly, Tammany and similar city machines succeeded because they met a real social need. They helped immigrants to get papers and find jobs, and they might help them when they were in trouble. It is a point that appealed to Denis Brogan:

> The real role of Tammany was to "organise" the newly enfranchised voters… It gave some kind of coherence to a society in perpetual flux, in which even the natives were bewildered by the new problems of urban life in cities growing like the prophet's gourd. And it did this at a price. To the poor it gave favours; if it controlled the police, it could moderate its zeal; it could give and withhold minor favours like peddlers' licences; it could give jobs; it could arrange naturalisation; it could act as a kind of charity organisation society, helping with coal and food in domestic crises; and, with its parades and excursions, it provided circuses as well as bread.[22]

Thirdly, Tammany (and the other city machines) and big business supported each other in various ways. They had a common interest in not making trouble for each other, and they did deals when they needed each other's help. Thus we are told that Tammany was in partnership with Gould and Fiske of the Erie railroad scandal, who were then reaping great harvests on Wall Street, and that when accusations started to be made against Tammany it 'adroitly invited a committee of prominent and wealthy citizens, headed by John Jacob Astor, to examine the controller's accounts,' a committee which, after a brief inspection, certified that 'the affairs of the city under the charge of the controller are administered in a correct and faithful manner.'[23] And in 1929 it was observed that 'It was the alliance of the "Underworld" and the "Upperworld" that explained the deep roots of graft and crime in Chicago'.[24]

A further suggestion, made in 1904 by H J Ford, is that political corruption is common in the United States because the constitutional checks and balances that separate the executive and legislative branches of government at the Federal and state levels cause such acute paralysis that government cannot be carried on without corruption:

> The boss, the machine, the political party, the bagmen, all these operate...to concert the action of legally independent branches of government through the exchange of favours.[25]

A European is likely to note another constitutional point, namely that the central government seems to have no power to intervene in scandals at the state level, let alone the city level. That the centre might have more power, as it usually has in Europe, is a point to which Americans seem to give little or no attention, so strong is their respect for their constitution and for states' rights.

Reform

At the end of the nineteenth century, there was a wave of protest against corruption by writers and journalists who exposed the scandalous things that went on in the cities and in big business and who earned from Theodore Roosevelt the epithet 'muckrakers', derived from Bunyan's *Pilgrim's Progress*. The classic work of the muckrakers was *Shame of the Cities* in which Lincoln Steffens, the greatest of them, gathered together articles he had written about major American cities. In all of them he had found conditions that were similar and rotten. Privilege, he concluded, controlled politics; neither morals nor law had anything to do with it. He followed it with *The Struggle for Self Government*, which he dedicated ironically to the Tsar of Russia whom he addressed in an introduction, explaining, 'we Americans have what we call "representative democracy"; but we have Tsars, too. It is true we do not call them by that title; we call them bosses.'[26]

Other books exposed the doings of business, for example, how Standard Oil had crushed competitors, seized natural resources and purchased legislative favours. Protest was not confined to journalism. Novelists, historians, economists, sociologists and philosophers also played their part. Two whose analyses of American society provided enduring ideas for the reformers were Henry George (*Poverty and Progress*) and Thorsten Veblen (*Theory of the Leisure Class* and *Theory of Business Enterprise*).

In 1942, Morison and Commager judged that the muckrakers, meaning those who produced the entire literature of exposure and protest, 'aroused public opinion to the point where it was willing to support men like Roosevelt and Wilson in their reform programs, and they planted the seeds of progressivism which the politicians were to harvest.'[27]

That reform came late in the United States, compared with those European countries we have looked at, is pretty clear. Nothing much seems to have been achieved before the beginning of the twentieth century. Power to change the state of affairs at the state and municipal levels has belonged to politicians and voters of the individual states, each with its own constitution. Steffens entitled one of his articles 'Chicago's Appeal to Illinois – showing how, since the Corruption of a State and its Cities is all one System, Municipal Reform must include State Reform'.[28] The cry of the reformers was that the people should throw out the corrupt bosses and so achieve true self-government. In Heidenheimer's volume of readings on political corruption, published in 1970[29], it is claimed that there had been an improvement in the standards and honesty of public servants in the cities in the last 20 years but not in the states. That conditions have still not changed totally can be illustrated by a story of Las Vegas in 1993.

An Englishman, having just arrived in Vegas for the first time, took a cab. After the usual pleasantries with the driver about such things as where are you from and the heat, the visitor, after a lull, asked the driver, a large friendly black man, if he owned his own cab. 'Naa,' said the cab driver, 'We don't own our cabs.'

'Oh' said the visitor, 'don't any of you drivers own your own cabs?'
'Naa', said the driver.
'Who owns them then?' said the visitor.

'Why, they do.' replied the driver.

'Who is they?' said the visitor, puzzled.

'Why, *theey*' said the driver, lengthening the word.

'Oh, I get it', said the visitor, 'You mean the mob, or whatever you call it?'

'I didn't say that, did I' replied the driver, chuckling.

Sensing that his passenger, now silent, might be worried by what he had heard, the driver, when stopped at some traffic lights, heaved himself half round and said, 'You don't need to worry, you know. This is the safest place in the USA. You can walk around this city with your money bulging out of your pocket. Nobody will take it; nobody will touch you.'

'Oh,' said the Englishman, 'that's surprising.'

'It isn't surprising when you think about it,' said the driver. 'They don't want trouble, do they? They don't want people scared away from their hotels and the gambling.'

'How do they do it?' asked the visitor.

'Well,' said the driver, 'in the past few years there have been 30 cases (or some such figure) of homicide by the cops. Every one of those cases has been judged justifiable homicide. And then', he added slowly in a philosophical drawl, 'the desert is very big around here.'

'You mean they dump people out in the desert?'

'Well,' said the driver, 'they get lost, go missing...they find bones sometimes.'

This story, which I know to be true, is a reminder that, since reform cannot constitutionally be imposed from the centre by the federal government, government at the state level (which can be dominated by the politicians of a major city) is a game without a referee. But it also illustrates a more interesting point. It is surprising at first sight that the reputedly lawless men who rule Vegas should impose a strict regime of law and order as regards the protection of property and persons – except when it comes to dealing with those who disobey their rule. It seems paradoxical until you realize that in this case you must stop thinking of the mob as people who lack property and therefore prey upon the property of others; here is a case where they have become property owners on such a scale, and with sufficiently legitimate titles to their property, for them to develop an interest in the existence of an orderly political regime within which to preserve and expand their wealth and power. The current mayor, formerly a lawyer well-known for defending mafia figures, said when he took office in June 1999 that he wanted to make Las Vegas a better place by revitalizing the downtown area through taxing developers and attracting clean industry like that of the Silicon Valley. It has been suggested that the Russian mafia may be reaching the point in the expansion of its wealth where it will be interested in the restoration of law and order of some sort.

Conclusion

In the United States the absence of serious military competition from neighbouring states meant that there was no compelling external force in the nineteenth century to induce the reform of government. The nation could survive in spite of burgeoning corruption and avoid the burden of maintaining standing military forces.

Its experience illustrates three points. Firstly, democracy does not necessarily produce clean government, a point it would not be necessary to emphasize if, since the end of the Cold War, it had not been so naively asserted that democracy is a cure for corruption. One can see many reasons why the United States experienced so much corruption after it began its extraordinary period of industrial expansion in the nineteenth century: the lack of common moral standards once successive waves of new immigrants flooded in; the absence of elites governing the country; the absence of any lasting cause or causes to bind the people into political parties held together by forces other than pork-belly politics; in addition to the absence of sufficient military competition from neighbours to force a permanent strengthening of government.

Secondly, much corruption in public life is compatible with great economic success – a point that should not to be interpreted as meaning, without qualification, that more corruption means more economic success. Russia today is a warning against that nonsense.

Thirdly, in a democracy where elites are absent or are weak, the improvement of standards depends particularly heavily on the existence of a free press and independent-minded legislators ready to investigate scandals: political muckraking is a necessary and honourable activity.

6

Britain in the Eighteenth and Nineteenth Centuries

Britain occupies an interesting intermediate position between Germany and France on the one hand and the United States on the other, as regards military competition and social pressures for reform in the eighteenth and nineteenth centuries. Helped by the protection of the Channel – which, though much narrower than the Atlantic, is still a formidable military barrier – Britain after 1688 never suffered invasion. Nor, thanks to the taming of the monarchy in the Civil War, and to the Glorious Revolution, did it experience revolution. It escaped those two violent triggers to reform which on the Continent produced spasms of change. All the same, Britain became heavily engaged in war at sea, on the Continent and overseas; and, following the French Revolution, pressures for reform were strongly felt in Britain, even if in less violent form than on the Continent. The reaction to them, mediated through the British democratic process in which power was contested between Parliament and the Crown and between rival groups in Parliament, consisted principally of reforms of the electoral system and of relatively slow, piecemeal reforms to increase the efficiency of government and reduce corruption.

The Background

England in 1688 was a country that had broken the domination of the Church as an independent power exercising authority in politics, possessing large lands or claiming tax exemption, as it did in France; the government was no longer run by a medieval household of the king staffed by men selected from the Church and household; it was run by ministers who selected and promoted men to serve them – a patronage system which continued until civil service exams were introduced in the late nineteenth century. Revenue went through a central Exchequer. In these respects government had been modernized in Tudor times.[1]

But after two centuries or more of low military expenditure compared with her continental neighbours, England now entered an era of expensive external wars. Immediately after 1688 she fought in the Nine Years' War (1688–97) and after a short interval of peace she mobilized massively in the War of Spanish Succession (1701–13). At the peak in 1710 it is estimated that military expenditure took 10 to 15 per cent of national income; it accounted for 80 per cent of government expenditure (there was little civil expenditure in those days) and paid for 300,000 men under arms, including men in foreign armies paid for by British subsidies.[2] But in peacetime military expenditure was quickly cut back. After the experience of the Civil War, the country was prejudiced against a strong professional army and, since its potential enemies were across the seas, it had no need of one.[3]

The army was not a tool of the monarch, as it was in France and Prussia. The power of the monarch was contained by Parliament, which had powers over taxation; by the power in the country, as well as in Parliament, of the land owning elite; and, later, by the power of the financial elite. Central government depended on compromises between all these elements.

The Fiscal System

How then did the government pay for war? The answer has been well provided by John Brewer on whose admirable study I have drawn heavily.[4] At the time of the restoration of the monarchy (1660) the state finances were in poor shape. There was little rental income since most royal lands had been squandered by earlier monarchs or had been confiscated and sold during the Civil War. The main sources of revenue were three types of indirect tax – customs duties on imported goods; excise duties on home-produced goods and a hearth tax, all of which were collected by tax farmers; and direct tax, essentially on land, the collection of which was the responsibility of the local landowners. As in France, money was borrowed at short term from the tax farmers. But England, having been relatively little involved in war on the Continent and having, in particular, escaped the Thirty Years' War, was not at this time heavily burdened with debt; nor had it resorted on a large scale to the sale of offices, which, as we have noted, was an alternative form of borrowing.

After the Restoration, steps were taken to escape from the tax farmer-financiers. The customs tax farm was abolished in 1671, the excise tax farm in 1683; the hearth tax was abolished in 1684; and the Bank of England was created in 1694, providing a new and much better means of borrowing. But the collection of taxes was still extraordinarily uneven and remained so during the eighteenth century. The land tax was in the hands of the landowners who served as local tax commissioners employing local agents of their choosing, a system which softened the impact of the tax though it did not altogether prevent it raising useful amounts of revenue in time of war, particularly during the Nine Years' War. The landowners who dominated Parliament seem to have seen the need for tax in time of war and also the advantages of the land tax, which, since it had to be approved annually by Parliament, gave them the power to check the monarch. But their liking for it was not unbounded. During the eighteenth century they ensured that it remained based on an assessment of land values drawn up in 1692, with the consequence that the yield did not increase as it should have done.

The Customs service was run directly by the Treasury, which meant by the politicians, with the result that it was corrupt in a different way. The service was full of political appointees – of men put there for their votes and to exert local political influence, and men given sinecures. There was much smuggling and much corruption of officers by smugglers. On the other hand, the Excise, as a result of reforms in 1677 and 1683, became a model of a new kind of bureaucracy. A board of commissioners ran it, and its officers, initially appointed by patronage, were subsequently moved around the country by the commissioners so as to keep detaching them from local political influences and local rogues. They were paid salaries and were little reliant on fees; they were promoted by merit after review; there was a drill book on how to assess and collect excise taxes; and the country officers were subject to unheralded inspections. The commissioners were backed by strong legislation under which they were the ultimate judges in excise tax cases. There was no appeal to the ordinary courts, a point that did not go uncriticized by champions of liberty.

Excise duties, because they were collected relatively efficiently, were extended in the eighteenth century from beer and spirits to such everyday articles as salt, soap and candles, and also to luxuries such as gold and silver wire and carriages; and the rates of duty were raised. The result was that in the 100 years between 1690 and 1790 the share of the Excise in total revenue went up from 25 to 45 per cent. The share of direct tax went down from 40 per cent to about 20 per cent – though it went up and down with war and peace as the gentry who commanded Parliament showed their greater willingness to be taxed in war than in peace. The share of the Customs, the revenue from which was reduced by wartime interruptions of trade as well as by corruption and smuggling, wobbled about, but it did not rise even though the rates of duty were raised. With the tax farmers out of business, government borrowing, which was resorted to heavily in the eighteenth century, now took the form of borrowing at short term on bills managed by the Bank of England, and borrowing at long term by funded debt, i.e. loans to the service of which revenue from specified indirect taxes was pledged. To raise more long term loans it was necessary to raise more indirect tax; and conversely tax cutting had to be cautious or it would endanger service of the public debt.

While the government finances were in these ways improved and made relatively sound, what we would now call corruption was rife in the eighteenth century.[5] Public offices were private property to be bought and sold; patronage, including the granting of sinecures, was regarded as normal, indeed necessary to stability and efficient government; smuggling was an accepted game; the rigging of elections and bribing of voters were accepted features of life; so was the temporary use by ministers for their own profit of public funds held by their departments – a practice which merged invisibly into more questionable ways of enrichment.[6] Politicians enriched themselves through office without inhibition. For example, Robert Walpole, who became remarkably rich, building himself a grand country house and filling it with a remarkable collection of pictures, was uninhibited about how he acquired his fortune. When accused in 1830 of corruption, he answered in a bold, almost 'brazenfaced' speech in the House of Commons. 'Of course,' he said, he had 'got a great estate, a very great estate, and having held some of the most lucrative offices for nearly 20 years what could anyone expect, unless it was a crime to get estates by great office; if so' – and here he turned the tables on his accuser – 'how much greater a crime it must be to get an estate out of lesser offices.'[7]

These things came to be seriously attacked only towards the end of the century at the time of the American and French Wars. The unpopular and disastrous American War left the country with high tax, a huge debt and a tide of criticism that was principally directed at two things, corruption, of which the City was most critical; and the power of the king, who was felt to have been overbearing. The attack was led by

Burke and was two-pronged. He pursued 'Economical Reform', meaning a reduction via the purse strings in the powers of the monarch to exercise patronage, offer sinecures and in similar ways exercise political power; and secondly he attacked 'corruption', meaning not the ending of what we would call corruption today but the checking of what he, passionately, but not always with consistency, deemed excessive. Thus, while objecting to patronage by the king, Burke, when he gained office, sought jobs for his brother and others near him as a matter of course.[8] As regards corruption, he went passionately for Warren Hastings, and started proceedings for impeachment against him that ran on for seven years. His motives were complex, but one observation is in order. It must have been politically advantageous to accuse those who ran India, rather than those who ran England, of corruption. (Clive had been accused and acquitted earlier.) For then the victims of the accusation of corrupt dealings – whether donors or recipients of bribes or favours, or victims of extortion or violence – were Indian and did not count in English society, even though they were rulers of great territories; they were native rulers who did not know better, who perhaps should be set an example by the rulers of the Raj; their standing would not be ruined by the accusations made against them, for they had no standing in England. Or to put the point another way, it is hard to conceive that had Burke accused Warren Hastings of corrupt dealings with people at the top of English politics and society the trial would have been allowed to run on for seven years: the potential damage to individual reputations and to society would have been so great that the matter would surely have been settled quickly, and quite possibly quietly. Altogether the proceedings against Warren Hastings look rather bogus if they are judged as an attempt to remedy British corruption. But they served to keep the word corruption in the air. Hastings was acquitted; he was taken care of by his employers, the East India Company, and was made a privy councillor.

Fiscal Reform

Recommendations as to how the government finances and administration might be improved were made by the 'Commissioners for Examining the Public Accounts, 1780–87', who were appointed by Lord North with the aim of meeting, or at least defusing, the crisis over the public debt and the accusations of incompetence and corruption made by the Whigs after the American War.[9] In pursuit of what they called the 'principle of public economy' the commissioners recommended that the costs of collecting and managing the revenue should be reduced, that the running of government offices should be simplified and regularized, and that salaries should be made general and uniform. They drew on the bureaucratic model of the Excise. In pressing their opinions the commissioners appealed to the notion of 'public trust', which implied that all positions in Government, including Parliament and the bureaucracy, were public trusts to be discharged for the benefit of the public, not to satisfy rights inherited or acquired by their incumbents. The work of the commissioners has been hailed at different times as the inspiration for most of the administrative reforms of the next half century and as the source of a new bureaucratic ideology of public service.[10] The leading member of the commission, who wrote most of its reports and took over the chair when its first occupant, General Sir Guy Carleton, retired, was a Master in Chancery, Thomas Anguish. Poor man, he lived up to his name. After the commission had delivered its last report, he died, according to the diagnosis of the time, 'of indigestion, occasioned by eating a quantity of cold oysters for supper, whilst he had the gout in his stomach.'[11]

William Pitt the Younger, in a quiet, piecemeal fashion, introduced the main reforms of the turn of the century. He set an example of being an honest, public-spirited man, and a believer in sound finance. He abolished a number of sinecures, paying compensation to the incumbents; he introduced salaries extensively in place of fees in government departments; he put through an Act for the provision of retirement benefits (in place of life sinecures); and he brought patronage under the immediate control of the Treasury, a move that was interpreted by Whig critics as a dangerous increase in the influence of the prime minister and hence the Crown. An article in the *Edinburgh Review* in 1810 trumpeted that this centralization of patronage in the hands of the Treasury

> ...has given that great and overwhelming department such additional influence in every branch of the state, that its hand has been thrust in all the Boards from the highest to the lowest; and patronage, formerly vested in the members of those Boards, is now wholly in the minister's possession; so that he now, in every part of the country, gives away clerkships and smaller employments without number – which used formerly to be in the gift of the chiefs of particular departments. What is the consequence? We now see no

such thing as an *opposition man* in any office – no such thing as an opposition member having the power to provide for a single friend or dependent – no such thing as a county or parish, in which every other man you meet is not bound to the minister, and to all ministers, by some place of convenience, state, comfort or profit.'[12]

The prime minister exercised his patronage through a secretary at the Treasury. Later, the post, labelled 'patronage secretary to the Treasury', was to be occupied by the chief whip.

The centralization of patronage may have eased the introduction of civil service reform when it was politically desired but, as we shall see, the ending of patronage was resisted for a long time. The extent of patronage after Pitt's time in office was illuminated in the 1820s when John Wade, a journalist, published a remarkable list of suspect offices and payments in *The Black Book, or Corruption Unmasked! Being an Account of Persons, Places and Sinecures*. The book sold 50,000 copies and was reproduced in 1831, 1832 and 1835.

Pitt left his mark on the public finances. He strengthened control of public expenditure. He attacked smuggling by drastically cutting the duty on tea, which was so high that it encouraged smuggling rather than yielding revenue. He applied the same approach to wines and spirits. He strengthened the enforcement of the Customs duties. And in 1799 he took the step, which was brave even in time of war, of introducing a true income tax in place of the previous jungle of taxes related to wealth, which had included taxes assessed by reference to carriages, clocks, man-servants, windows and other symbols of wealth.[13]

In the event, Pitt's war income tax, which relied on declarations by individuals or firms of their income, brought in disappointingly little revenue. Nevertheless it paved the way, politically, for Addington who was prime minister from 1801 to 1804, to introduce in 1803 a new version of the income tax that incorporated the more effective device of deduction at source whereby the collectors went straight to the source of income instead of going to the recipient of income[14]. For example, in the case of holders of the Funds, the source of income was the Bank of England, which paid the interest. If tax, which was at a flat rate, was deducted from the interest before it was paid, the government was sure of 100 per cent collection of tax on that type of income and the recipient had no means of evasion. That is the simplest case, in theory at least. In practice, political opposition led by Pitt delayed deduction at source with respect to the Funds, but when it was finally introduced in 1806, it produced a marked increase in the revenue.[15]

A more interesting case is the application of the system to land, to which deduction at source had been applied in a more rudimentary way under the old land tax. By Addington's time most agricultural land in England had been enclosed. That is to say, tenant farmers had been established on large farms to which they applied new methods of agriculture from the profits of which they were able to pay good rents to their landlords. (It is the pattern of income that is reflected in the substantial farm houses, which landlords built for their tenants, and the grand country houses which they built for themselves, houses we all admire as we tour England today.) Tax on rents was collected directly from tenants, who suffered no loss by paying 5 per cent of their rent to the tax collectors rather than to their landlords. The landlords, who as a class were still involved in tax collection as local commissioners of tax, were trapped. They could not readily evade the tax; and while war against Napoleon continued, they could not politically oppose it without restraint – though they saw to it that the income tax was abolished as soon as the war was over. The government trapped the tenant farmers as regards their profits from farming by the device of assessing those profits at three-quarters of the rent they paid their landlords.

The collection of the tax from traders and manufacturers was less easy, since the source of income and the recipient were usually one and the same person, and their accounts must often have been rudimentary. Nevertheless, enforcement seems to have become relatively efficient as regards traders and manufacturers. One can see a possible explanation. Once the landowners and rentiers were caught by deduction of tax from their incomes at source, they may have resented the idea that traders and manufacturers should escape. Previously, the landowners, rentiers, traders and manufacturers must all have been doing their best to avoid the assessed taxes, bricking up windows and concealing taxable objects, with the result that there was an implicit alliance, or at least a common interest, in tax avoidance and evasion amongst the classes. The new war tax may have broken that alliance: the landowners and rentiers, caught unequivocally by the tax, must have felt sore when they heard evidence or rumour of their social inferiors in trade and manufacturing avoiding it; and if that is right, they are likely to have used their influence in Parliament and in the country to support the enforcement of tax collection from the traders and manufacturers.

Tax enforcement was strengthened by Parliament in 1805, 1806 and 1808 when more powerful central tax collecting machinery, run by civil servants, and including itinerant inspectors, was superimposed on the traditional local machinery run by the local elites. This was done in a very English manner. 'Nothing was abolished, and, in theory, and to some extent in practice, the balance between national administrative needs and local representation and influence was maintained.' Yet a new conception of administration was brought about. Indeed it has been argued that, 'The process which resulted in the development of the Victorian civil service and the technique of modern administration began in the war years, and not least in the organization for assessing the War Income Tax.'[16]

Compared with France and Germany at that time – and with many countries of the world today – England at the time of the Napoleonic wars must have been a relatively easy place in which to make an income tax work. Enclosure and the development of a capital market lent visibility to major flows of income. Moreover, the class structure and the play of political power had evolved in such a way that the landed class, which had most interest in defending the country against Napoleon and the tides of revolution, owned the rents and had responsibility both for agreeing in Parliament to the imposition of the new tax and for supervising its collection in the country.

England after the Napoleonic Wars

Once the Napoleonic wars were over, England, benefitting from its secure insular position and from a long period of peace, cut back its armed forces and did not quickly increase the civil activities of government. Military expenditure, having been £72 million in 1815, was reduced to £18 million by 1818 and stood at only £15 million in 1850. Civil expenditure by the central government, excluding debt charges, was £6 million in 1815 and only £7 million in 1850 and was far outweighed by debt service, the legacy of wars, to the reduction of which much political attention was paid. Since the price level fell between these dates, real expenditure was not quite as severely restrained as these figures indicate. It was only in the last two or three decades of the nineteenth century that civil expenditure other than debt service rose substantially. By 1895 it stood at £20 million, with the increase going mostly towards education; and there was a similar increase in spending by local government, again mostly on education.[17]

In contrast to France or Germany, where the government became engaged in fostering and financing economic development, England was a country where an agricultural revolution and then an industrial revolution took place spontaneously without government participation. The doctrine of laissez-faire took hold: government involvement in the economy was minimal. Popular pressure for reform, though provoked by economic hardship, was expressed most powerfully in demands for reform of the electoral system, demands which were met by a series of electoral reform Acts during the century; and in demands for the reform of the Corn Laws. When the activities of government were extended, it was to curb the excesses of runaway capitalism, not to foster capitalism: it was to limit the employment of children, or to ensure safety in factories, or it was to provide basic education for the benefit of the masses, scarcely at all technical training for the benefit of industry: apprenticeship within firms and trades was relied on for that. The role that bureaucrats played in central government has been likened to that of referees or nannies; a great deal was left to local government that operated on an essentially feudal basis until late in the century.

Compared with the Continent, the pressure of military competition was slight (until the end the century) as also, again compared with the Continent, was the apparent pressure of popular demands for reform – though here the difference with the Continent may principally have been that the violence of demands for reform in Britain was directed at electoral reform, and was met slowly and moderated by democratic processes. Yet, by the end of the century, there had been great improvements in the cleanliness of government, particularly with the displacement of patronage in the civil service by entry through competitive exams, so tailored that they selected a remarkably high-minded elite.

The reasons why this came about have been much debated. There is wide agreement that non-conformist religion and irreligious utilitarianism, both of which were peculiarly powerful in Britain, generated powerful notions of duty amongst the people at many levels. It has been argued that reform was part of the process whereby the bourgeoisie and bourgeois values, including bureaucratic rationality, displaced the aristocracy and their values. On the other hand it has been argued that there was not much of a bourgeois revolution in Britain. Rather, 'Pitt and his successors were faced with what they considered a serious challenge to elite political authority, and were themselves convinced that state structures needed to be made more efficient, and administrators more attentive to an emerging ideology of public service shaped in part by Evangelical morality'; through reforms and the cultivation of an image of disinterested management, they succeeded in preserving the authority of the British political elite.[18]

The Reform of the Civil Service

Remarkably, reform of the civil service in Britain was led by reforms first introduced in India by the East India Company. Indeed the company gave to the English language the term 'civil service' which it used to distinguish its non-military from its military officers. By the middle of the nineteenth century, the ICS (Indian civil service) was ahead of the home civil service as regards training and recruitment and also in bureaucratic methods;[19] and it was with respect to the ICS that the nineteenth century image of a British civil servant became prominent, with its morally-charged emphasis on serving the public interest, never one's own, and always telling the truth. It is an ideal that had a seminal influence on the standards of integrity of British public life.

In 1853 the East India Company agreed, under pressure from the government, to abolish patronage and introduce entry by competitive exam; in the same year the Northcote–Trevelyan report recommended the same change for the home civil service; and in 1854 Macaulay headed a committee that recommended what the content of the ICS entry exam and subsequent training should be.[20] This multiple assault on patronage was the work of the leading reformers of the day. The persons principally involved were Macaulay, who had led the campaign for the abolition of Indian patronage; his brother-in-law, Trevelyan, a passionate reformer who had served long in India and was now a senior civil servant at the Treasury; Gladstone who as prime minister had appointed the committee on the home civil service; and Jowett of Balliol (father, with Arnold of Rugby, of the Victorian approach to education based on the classics, Christianity and sports) who had urged Gladstone to appoint the committee on the home civil service and who served on Macaulay's committee on the Indian civil service.[21] This close-linked group of formidable, like-minded men set out their views with remarkable certainty and brevity.

Macaulay's report argued that the entry exam should be designed to select those men who had excelled in the kind of education offered by Oxford and Cambridge (the only English universities until 1825), since that was where the best men would be found; specialized training in Indian languages and other skills useful in their work should follow. The report did not have to argue against patronage since its abolition in the ICS had already been accepted. The report on the home civil service advocated much the same kind of exam but first it made the case for the abolition of patronage. This it did in a diatribe, written by Trevelyan, which gives one a measure of the zeal of these men:

> It would be natural to expect that so important a profession would attract into its ranks the ablest and the most ambitious of the youth of the country; that the keenest emulation would prevail among those who had entered it; and that such as were endowed with superior qualifications would rapidly rise to distinction and public eminence. Such, however, is by no means the case. Admission to the civil service is indeed eagerly sought after, but it is for the unambitious, and the indolent and incapable, that it is chiefly desired. Those whose abilities do not warrant an expectation that they will succeed in the open professions, where they must encounter the competition of their contemporaries, and those whom indolence of temperament, or physical infirmities unfit for active exertions, are placed in the Civil Service, where they may obtain an honourable livelihood with little labour, and with no risk...
>
> ...the comparative lightness of the work, and the certainty of provision in case of retirement owing to bodily incapacity, furnish strong inducements to the parents and friends of sickly youths to endeavour to obtain for them employment in the service of the Government;
>
> ...The result naturally is, that the public service suffers both in internal efficiency and in public estimation.[22]

Criticism of the reformers was not lacking. Lord Salisbury was scathing about competitive exams: they were a method of bestowing appointments 'not upon persons who are qualified for them, but upon those who had shown their fitness for something else'; Anthony Trollope, who satirized Trevelyan as Sir Gregory Hardlines in *The Three Clerks*, thought the criticisms of the existing system made by Northcote and Trevelyan were quite excessive and that patronage, of which he was a beneficiary, can produce good results, a point made again recently by J M Bourne.[23] It is remarkable that although the

Northcote–Trevelyan report criticized patronage so vehemently for producing inefficiency, it said nothing about patronage possibly being a disreputable means by which prime ministers could buy political support. Perhaps Trevelyan, the dominant partner in the production of the report, felt as a civil servant appointed by the prime minister that to criticize prime ministers would be inappropriate and might prejudice the adoption of his recommendations.

In fact, Trevelyan was himself a product of patronage, and a very remarkable one at that. A member of a land-owning family, educated at Charterhouse and East India College, he was a talented oriental linguist and a staunch liberal, keen on improving Indian education and the lot of the Indians. Having entered the Company's service in 1826 and risen to be secretary to the board of revenue in Calcutta (where he married Macaulay's sister), he returned in 1840 to England to be assistant secretary at the Treasury. There he remained 19 years, during which time he administered famine relief (or lack of it) in Ireland and produced the Northcote–Trevelyan report. In 1859 he returned to India as Governor of Madras but disgraced himself by making public a difference of opinion over financial policy with his superiors in Calcutta. But he soon triumphed and was himself appointed to Calcutta as finance minister in 1862. There he stayed until he retired in 1865.[24] He has been described as 'a civil servant so zealous that he seemed more like a politician than an administrator'.[25] The opposite might perhaps be said of Northcote, who comes across as an unassertive person.[26]

The Northcote–Trevelyan report has come to be seen less as a revolutionary manifesto than as a rallying cry which helped forward and shaped a process of reform which was already erratically in motion, sometimes thrust forward, sometimes stalled by the workings of democracy. Thus before 1853, when the Crimean War was a spur to action, there had been a good deal of piecemeal reform in the administration of the army and in other government departments, much of it motivated by the desire for greater efficiency.[27] Amongst other things, the choice of persons appointed (by patronage) came to be guided to a greater degree than before by efficiency and less by nepotism as the government assumed more responsibility, albeit limited compared with the governments of France or Germany, for education and other new functions.[28] It has also been argued that the political pressure that led to the Northcote–Trevelyan report stemmed more from the concern for greater efficiency and economy than, as has sometimes been suggested, from the desire to find jobs for the educated sons of the new middle class who were now emerging from Oxford and Cambridge – a proposition which does not contradict the notion that the outcome was more jobs for boys in that category.[29]

The recommendations of the Northcote–Trevelyan report took time to be implemented. Entry by merit to the lower and middle ranks of the civil service was introduced quite quickly, but entry by competitive examination to the higher civil service was not pushed through the Cabinet until 1870. Britain lagged far behind Germany, which had adopted that procedure 100 years earlier, and France, which had followed not much later. There was a similar lag in the adoption of competitive entry for officers in the army. The abolition of the purchase of commissions (including promotion), a practice that had been defended by the Duke of Wellington (on the grounds that patronage and favouritism would produce worse officers), and had been attacked by Trevelyan in an eloquent tract in the 1860s, was finally abolished, with compensation to holders of purchased commissions, in 1871.[30]

A principal reason for the delay in the reform of entry to the higher civil service was the reluctance of governments to lose the political power they still gained from patronage at this level. It was still the practice that the government chief whip (officially the 'Patronage Secretary to the Treasury') induced members of the party, in Parliament and elsewhere, to support the government by offering them the gift of offices in the civil service.[31] It was against this background that Gladstone, late in 1869 when he was again prime minister and was finally rallying the support of ministers for the introduction of open competition for the higher civil service, wrote to the Chancellor of the Exchequer 'There is another person whose position is more delicate, I mean Glyn [the government chief whip] as the change would affect more or less the basis of his office, his *quid pro quo*,' a view from which Glyn certainly did not dissent.[32] When informed that ministers had decided on competitive entry, he wrote to Gladstone saying that he accepted the decision but ventured to explain that 'Your patronage at the Treasury which has been left to me as "Secretary" is *entirely* swept away... I lose, without notice, and at once, the great advantage of the daily correspondence and communication with members of the party which the ordinary dispensing of the Treasury Patronage gave me, to say nothing of the power it placed in my hands.'[33]

Professor Matthew, the editor of Gladstone's diaries, remarks in his biography of Gladstone that the dismantling of the patronage system in the previous 50 years had meant that 'the party in power had little of the "pork-barrel" left to offer its supporters save honours... Patronage in the civil service had been almost the last *"quid pro quo"* left of the old system of familial government; there remained after 1870 only the odd Lord-Lieutenancy, the Church, the colonies, and the Justices of the Peace.'[34]

An explanation offered as to why civil service reform was implemented in 1870 is that 'the great extension of the franchise in 1867...threatened the transfer of effective patronage from the magnates to publicans and radical agitators who were beginning to create something like the American machine. The spoils were removed before these upstarts became the victors.'[35] According to this view, the ruling elite preferred to abolish patronage rather than let it fall into the hands of upstarts.

Conclusion

The cleaning up and shaping of modern government took place later in Britain than in France and Germany, and through a markedly different process. Because of the Channel, military competition was less important; and with the monarchy already largely emasculated, the political structure was more elastic. A democracy of the privileged responded to fear of revolution by conceding electoral reforms that permitted utilitarian, liberal and puritanical ideas and values to flow into politics and into the conduct of government, in particular the government of India. By the end of the nineteenth century the public services – the civil and military services and the judiciary – had been substantially reformed, and the tone of the new civil service was unusually high-minded.[36] But politics and commerce were another matter. The turn of the century was a period notable for scandals in those realms of society, as we shall see in Chapter 10.

7

Britain's Indian Connection

The Background

In the first half of the eighteenth century, the East India Company, which had been trading in India under privileges obtained from the Mogul emperors, found Mogul rule to be weakening. The Company became increasingly assertive and so did local rulers.[1] The French stirred those rulers against the Company and engaged in war against the company's army. After Clive defeated the French, famously in English eyes, and dealt ruthlessly with various local rulers, the Company in the middle of the eighteenth century found itself militarily and politically dominant in large parts of India. Having set out to trade under a royal charter granted by Queen Elizabeth, the Company now found itself governing a large part of the sub-continent.

In the next 100 years the Company was subjected, step-by-step, to the curtailment of its trading privileges and to supervision by the British government until, after the Indian mutiny of 1857–58, it was dissolved and the British government finally took over. This transition involved an extreme change in notions of corruption as regards patronage and the pursuit of personal gain. Standards first deteriorated disastrously but then, initially in reaction to that deterioration, they were raised until they were ahead of those in the home civil service. Remarkably, the Indian civil service became in some degree a model for the home civil service.

The standards that prevailed in India before the collapse, and their relationship to eighteenth century standards at home, were admirably described by Lucy Sutherland:

To make a comfortable fortune in the public service and to establish those dependent on him in situations of profit was the major and (to contemporaries) the legitimate ambition of the ordinary politician. Such a man's obligations to his patron, his loyalty to his friends, and his duty to himself made up the main tenets of his political creed. But the results of this attitude...were not as disintegrating as might have been expected. This was chiefly because the ambitions of such men were kept within the bounds of moderation by the dominance of a wealthy aristocracy whose main sources of riches remained outside the sphere of politics and by the traditions of a governing class, which (though sympathetic to such views if pursued in moderation) in the last resort felt some responsibility for, and interest in, the maintenance of the king's government and in the prosperity and prestige of the country...

...within the [East India] Company, as within the State, a certain conventional balance between public and private interests (though an even more precarious one) had grown up... A man should if he survived (as many of course did not) make a considerable fortune in the Company's service, but only if he had worked his twelve or fifteen years through the ranks and given the Company the benefit of his industry and acquired experience. While making his fortune through the recognized channels of perquisite, private trade, and money-lending, he need not reject presents from wealthy and important Indians, but he ought to do so if in return he had to sacrifice his employers' pecuniary interests, and he must not permit his private concerns to monopolize his attention to the detriment of his public duties. If these conditions were fulfilled his colleagues and he considered that he had served the Company loyally.[2]

The deterioration in the conduct of the Company's servants followed the mid-eighteenth century military victories and the collapse of the Mogul empire. The opportunities for enrichment were so tempting that the company's servants cast aside restraint. In the opinion of Sulivan, one of the great statesmen of the Company, the Company's servants, having gained a sudden affluence, became 'quite unmanageable'.[3]

What followed was well summarized by Furnivall:

In the early days the Company had been content with trading privileges but, with the dissolution of the Mogul empire, it began to trade in kingdoms, seeking profit in tribute rather than in commerce. Most of the profit, however, went to its servants in bribes and booty, and their corruption and misrule were disastrous to the Company and to its subjects. Within a few years it was threatened with bankruptcy and had to seek aid from Parliament. Meanwhile its servants were using their huge gains to corrupt home politics, and party jealousy impelled the British government to use the financial difficulties of the Company as a lever for insisting on its responsibility for good administration. At the same time the Company, in the interests of the shareholders, was aiming at reforms.[4]

But that was not all there was to it. At the end of the eighteenth century and thereafter the Company's ways were increasingly challenged by the new ideals that were to become fused into English liberalism. Humanitarian sentiment grew and was played upon brilliantly by Burke in his denunciations of the abuses of power in India. Adam Smith's doctrine of free trade told against the Company's trade monopoly; the evangelical movement aroused concern for the condition of the Indians and pressure for missionaries to be allowed into India; and utilitarianism provided a rational basis for calculating what policy would contribute best to the welfare of the Indians.

Moreover, the energies of reformers of all these schools, humanitarians, evangelicals and utilitarians, were diverted to India. At home the reformers were frustrated by the power of the aristocracy. But the aristocracy was not much concerned about reform in India. Their wealth and power derived from ownership of land in Britain and command of Parliament; they despised the nabobs who came back from India with ill-gained fortunes; they cared little about Indian patronage: it was only the financially-straitened members of their class who joined the middle class in seeking places for their sons in India.

The leading British liberals engaged themselves in the formulation of policy towards India: James and John Stuart Mill worked for the Company at its headquarters in London, India House; Macaulay at different times worked for the Company and for the government-appointed Board of Control that supervised the Company in its later days; and Bentham's ideas had a seminal influence on policy. Moreover the ambition of the Company's men who rose to the top in India was often driven by reformist ideals. India was thus an experimental ground, an outlet for the expression, and often for the implementation, of the ideals and prescriptions of the reformers. As Eric Stokes put it:

The whole transformation of the English mind and society, as it expressed itself in liberalism, was brought to bear on the Indian connexion. And it was brought to bear – it is this which makes Indian history important to the most insular of English historians – by its most distinguished representatives, James and John Stuart Mill, Bentham and Macaulay.[5]

The Task of British Government in India

As it became ruler, the Company faced the same task of government as was faced by the governments of the other countries we have considered: to extract revenue, principally from the land, with which to support an army and other agencies of government. The first purpose of that army and those agencies was to maintain internal law and order – in this case amongst a subject people – so that revenue could be collected. Beyond this closed circuit in which revenue was absorbed in gathering revenue and providing a measure of law and order for the people, the further British objectives for which the army and other government services were maintained changed over the years. They included keeping India passive and open for British trade; keeping the princes of areas not under direct British rule in their place; keeping frontiersmen in the northwest at bay; keeping Russia out of Afghanistan; and supporting an Indian army that could be called upon to fight for Britain outside India.

The Company experimented, principally in the north, with building up large estates under zamindars who were given responsibility for collecting the land revenue from the peasants, keeping part for themselves. But this system, which appealed to those with liberal convictions who favoured indirect rule as a means of achieving minimum government similar to that which they knew at home, was not a success, essentially because the zamindars often behaved like French tax farmers, not like the ideal English landlord.[6] The Company therefore turned mostly to the ryotvari system whereby the person who cultivated each patch of land was identified and revenue was collected directly from him. Building on the relics of the machinery for collecting revenue and maintaining order that had existed before the breakdown of Mogul rule, the Company evolved a regime that relied on (a) gaining the support of the headmen of villages, landowners and other influential persons by enrolling them formally or informally into the work of revenue collection and the job of keeping the peace;

(b) establishing a police force and an army led by Britons but manned predominantly by Indians; and (c) being ready to use force firmly if British authority was challenged. By relying on Indians, treating them relatively favourably and thus enrolling them as beneficiaries of British rule, the Company was able to run India with remarkably few British men. Each young British man who went out to India in the civil service of the Company was quickly given responsibility for huge numbers of people. The key position to which he would be promoted after learning the job under an older hand was that of 'collector'. Besides being responsible for revenue collection, he would be magistrate and have command of the police in his district. Like English landlords who, besides gathering their rents, commonly held authority as magistrates, the collectors were powerful in the areas for which they were responsible, though their actions were constrained by the existence of revenue boards and law courts to which cases might be carried. That they were called collector is significant. Collecting revenue (which involved establishing in a reasonably just manner who held and cultivated each piece of land) was the first priority in establishing government and it remained the very foundation of government.

It was in recruitment to the Indian civil service that patronage was first ended and the British ideal of public service came conspicuously into being. In both these respects reform of the British home civil service followed considerably later. Moreover, whereas the reform of the home civil service was a rather invisible affair which, as we have seen, was finally settled in Cabinet when Gladstone put pressure on his colleagues, the reform of the ICS (Indian Civil Service) was the result of open battles between reformers and the owners of patronage, partly conducted in Parliament, of which there are good records.

The Struggle to End Patronage

In the mid-eighteenth century recruitment to the Company's service was by patronage of the directors with no constraint on whom they chose. Boys for whom places had been solicited or purchased from directors of the Company (or intermediaries) went out to India to make their fortunes and serve the Company when they were extraordinarily young and totally lacking in qualifications.[7] There was no minimum age for recruits. They were taken on either as 'cadets' in the Company's military service or as 'writers' in its civil service.

William Hickey in his memoirs, racily described how the system worked. The year is 1768. After disgracing himself in London through a life of dissipation, Hickey, aged 19, is told by his father, 'William, I lament that you should once again have deceived and disappointed me... As I find you cannot settle yourself to any thing in your native land, we must try another line and another country for you, and may the Almighty in his unbounded goodness vouchsafe to turn your heart... Since I saw you last I have procured for you the situation of a cadet in the East India Company's service, and God grant you may do better in future than you have done hitherto. And now leave me, I feel too weak and exhausted to say more.'[8] Poor man, his wife had just died, an event that seems not to have touched his son. Hickey describes what followed:

> ...my father took me to visit Sir George Colebrooke, the director who had nominated me a cadet. The Baronet received us with great politeness, telling my father it afforded him pleasure to have it in his power to comply with his request... From Sir George Colebrooke's, we went to Mr Laurence Sullivan's, then a man of great influence and a leading Director. He likewise was very kind, and promised to give me letters that would be of essential service to me... From Mr Sullivan's we went to the India house, where I was introduced to Mr Coggan, one of the Company's principal officers, who being then very busy desired I would call the following morning and he would put me in the way of doing what was required.[9]
>
> ...Towards the end of the month by desire of Mr Coggan, I attended before a Committee of Directors to undergo the usual examination as a cadet. Being called into the Committee room after a waiting of near two hours in the lobby, at which my pride was greatly offended, I saw three old Dons sitting close to the fire, having by them a large table, with pens, ink, paper, and a number of books lying upon it. Having surveyed me, as I conceived, rather contemptuously, one of them in such a snivelling strange tone that I could scarcely understand him, said:
>
> "Well, young gentleman, what is your age?"
>
> Having answered "Nineteen," he continued:
>
> "Have you ever served, I mean in the army? Though I presume from your age and appearance that you cannot."
>
> I replied, "I had not."
>
> "Can you go through the manual exercise?"

"No, sir."

"Then you must take care and learn it."

I bowed.

"You know the terms on upon which you enter our service?"

"Yes, Sir."

"Are you satisfied with them?"

"Yes, Sir."

A clerk who was writing at the table then told me I might withdraw, whereupon I made my *congé* and retired. From the Committee room I went to Mr Coggan's office, who after making me sit down for near an hour, presented me with my appointment as a cadet.[10]

An extreme example of the youth of the recruits is John Malcolm, a Scottish son of the manse who became one of the leading rulers of India and a distinguished self-educated scholar, author of histories of India and Persia. In 1781 he was accepted as a cadet and sailed for India at the age of twelve. At his interview a director asked him 'Why, my little man, what would you do if you were to meet Hyder Ali?' He replied, 'I would out my sword, and cut off his head.' 'You will do,' said the director, 'Let him pass.'[11] (Hyder Ali of Mysore, like his son Tippoo Sahib, was notorious for his military attacks on the Company.)

One hundred years later all that had been changed. Patronage had been replaced by competitive exams designed to select the best young graduates from the universities; the pursuit of private gain had been replaced by dedication to public service; the new civil servants who, typically, had been given a Victorian classical education at fee-paying schools and the older universities, far from pursuing trade, turned their backs on any of their compatriots who were in business, sometimes referring to them contemptuously as 'box wallahs', a term for native peddlers who travelled with boxes of goods.[12]

The achievement of that transformation was not quick or simple. The process of 'turning a group of merchant buccaneers into a set of disciplined administrators' involved a complex set of institutions and interests.[13] The directors of the East India Company were politically influential. As individuals, they had links with the banking and shipping worlds; many of them were Members of Parliament, as were some proprietors of the company on whose votes the directors depended for their election to the Court of Directors. Their job was to run India and to run the 'Grandest Society of Merchants in the Universe'.[14] Their actions could bring war or peace and could influence the capital market so strongly that the terms on which the government could borrow were affected. Through these and other common concerns the company and the government were bound together. India House was a centre of power with which governments had to come to terms.

In the middle of the eighteenth century Clive began introducing salaries and trying to restrain the behaviour of the company's servants, but the directors in London disapproved of the salary system he introduced. Cornwallis, backed by the younger Pitt, introduced more successful reforms towards the end of the century: decent salaries were established; corruption in India by the company's servants was attacked; and the company's trading activities were separated from its administrative functions. But patronage was not tackled. Rather, the idea that the government might take over the company was opposed on the ground that it would cause an unhealthy increase in the patronage, and hence the political power, of the government, which meant the Crown until its power was curtailed. To bring the company under greater government control without taking it over, Pitt's India Act of 1784 created a government-appointed Board of Control to superintend the actions of India House.

An important step was taken in 1800, when Richard Wellesley, the Duke of Wellington's older brother who had been made governor-general in Bengal by Pitt, became fed up with the inadequacy of the young men who were sent out to him as civil servants and set up a training college in Bengal, the College of Fort William. When the Court of the Company in London received a message from him saying what he had done, the directors felt he had exceeded his authority and decided that the school in Bengal should be cut back and should confine its activities to teaching local languages and local law; they would set up a training school in England.[15] That was the origin of East India College, which was opened at Hertford Castle in 1806 and soon afterwards moved to Haileybury. The curriculum included education relevant to the job to be done in India. In particular, the college created the first chair in economics in Britain and chose Malthus to occupy it, which he did from the time the college opened until his death in 1834. He and his successor, Richard Jones, taught the young men the theory of rent, a subject directly relevant to their future task of supervising the collection of land revenue.[16] But the students, who had the right of appeal to their patrons, the directors, over the heads of the college authorities, were so unruly that one wonders how much they learnt.

'There were riots in 1808, 1809, 1810, 1815, 1822 and 1837. Drunkenness, assaults on the long-suffering inhabitants of Ware and Hertford and damage to college property were common occurrences.'[17]

Patronage continued. Each director had the power to appoint one youth per year to the school; the chairman and deputy chairman of the Court two. There was a committee at Haileybury to vet the candidates, but it included six directors and appears to have done little to moderate patronage.

After 1800 attempts at reform were made at 20-year intervals when the company's charter came before Parliament for renewal. That happened three times – in 1813, 1833 and 1853 – before reform was complete. In 1813 a policy of free trade was applied to the company. It lost its monopoly of trade with India but continued to run the country subject to government supervision. Lord Grenville made an eloquent plea for selection of the company's civil servants by open competition. Speaking of Indian patronage, which had increased as the responsibilities of the company had been expanded, he asked:

> Is it self-evident that because we fear to give this vast influence to a party, we must therefore vest it in an exclusive corporation?... Patronage is by far the most considerable source of that great political influence which the company does now actually exercise in this country; and its abuse, for who will deny that abuse there is, would in no way be so well controlled as by the competition of a free trade... The most obvious course would be to choose the young men who are destined for the civil service by free competition and public examination from our great schools and universities.[18]

Although he was speaking only a few years after a scandal in 1809 over the sale via intermediaries of cadetships and writerships with the company, he received little support. The new 1813 charter stipulated that the nominated candidates for writerships should spend four terms at Haileybury, but the directors retained the right to nominate whom they chose, provided he was between the ages of 15 and 23.[19]

In 1833 a radical reform of the company might have been expected. The Whigs had been victorious in 1832; the political climate had changed; Macaulay, a liberal reformer, was secretary of the Board of Control. When the Company's charter came up for renewal, two main questions were debated, first, whether the company's exclusive right to trade with

China (its one remaining monopoly) should be ended, which it was; and second, whether the company should go on running India. Parliament and the country were preoccupied with the Reform Bill and were content to leave things largely as they were. The company's assets in India were nationalized, with compensation, but it was allowed to carry on running India, under government supervision. William Cobbett, who had previously been a critic of company rule, conveyed the mood. 'My impression', he wrote, 'is that the country [India] is governed well by the Company. I am sure they [the Government] will not govern it better.'[20] As regards patronage, Macaulay, the leading advocate of open competition, was opposed by the Directors who fought against the loss of their patronage and settled for a compromise: the directors would retain their exclusive right to nominate candidates but for every vacancy they would nominate four candidates; the best would then be selected by examination. In the House of Commons Macaulay used his ponderous eloquence to advocate the scheme:

> India is entitled to the service of the best talents which England can spare. That the average of intelligence and virtue is very high in this country, is matter for honest exultation. But it is no reason for employing average men where you can obtain superior men. Consider too, Sir, how rapidly the public mind of India is advancing, how much attention is already paid by the higher classes of the natives to those intellectual pursuits on the cultivation of which the superiority of the European race to the rest of mankind principally depends. Surely, under such circumstances, from motives of selfish policy, if from no higher motive, we ought to fill the Magistracies of our Eastern Empire with the men who may do honour to their country – with men who may represent the best part of the English nation. This, Sir, is our object; and we believe that by the plan which is now proposed this object will be attained.[21]

He went on to argue the case for recruiting the men who did best at university regardless of the relevance of the subjects they had studied to the tasks they would face in their careers. This is, I believe, the first appearance of the argument for the 'all-rounder' that he deployed again 20 years later (in less colourful terms) in the House of Commons and again in his famous report on the Indian Civil Service of 1854. For a century or more it was to shape the character of not only the Indian civil service but also the British home civil service; it was still a subject of controversy when it was criticized in the Fulton Committee's Report on the Civil Service of 1968. His words in 1833 were these:

> It is said, I know, that examinations in Latin, in Greek and in mathematics are no tests of what men will prove to be in life. I am perfectly aware that they are not infallible tests; but they are tests I confidently maintain. Look at every walk of life – at this House – at the other House – at the Bar – at the Bench – at the Church – and see whether it be not true, that those who attain the highest distinction in the world are generally men who were distinguished in their academic career...
>
> Whether the English system of education be good or bad is not now the question. Perhaps I may think that too much time is given to the ancient languages and to the abstract sciences. But what then? Whatever be the languages, whatever be the sciences, which it is, in any age or country, the fashion to teach, those who become most proficient in those languages and those sciences will generally be the flower of the youth – the most acute – the most industrious – the most ambitious of honourable distinctions. If the Ptolemaic system were taught at Cambridge, instead of the Newtonian, the senior wrangler would in general be a superior person to the wooden spoon. If, instead of learning Greek, we learned the Cherokee, the man who understood the Cherokee best, who made the most correct and melodious Cherokee verses – who comprehended most accurately the effect of the Cherokee particles – would generally be a superior man to him who was destitute of these accomplishments.[22]

The proposal that all candidates, though nominated by the Directors, should be sifted by competitive examination met with dissenting voices, including that of Mr Charles Grant, the president of the Board of Control (of which Macaulay was secretary). He advocated the retention of direct patronage for at least some posts, on the grounds that it would permit the appointment of young men to districts where their fathers had served and were held in respect by the people; and, he argued, it would be 'a natural and legitimate manner of rewarding those who had discharged important functions in the country'.[23] This dynastic argument failed to convince the Whig parliament; Macaulay's proposal was passed into law.[24] But the directors fought back and prevented the law being put into effect. A clause in the new charter made the directors subject to the supervision of the government's Board of Control in all their activities apart from patronage, for which specific exemption was written in.[25] The directors failed to implement the scheme, raising difficulties; and in 1837, by which time Macaulay had gone to India, there to produce his penal code, they persuaded the government to pass an act suspending the scheme. But the adverse effect on the quality of writers sent to India may not have been acute. East India College, to which the lower age limit for entry was now raised to 17, established a system of frequent exams and prizes. If a young man was found to be 'too idle and stupid' it was a convention that the director whose turn it was to nominate to the cavalry, a branch for which no test of intellect was demanded, would postpone his choice and nominate the dunce from Haileybury. About one-fifth of Haileybury students are said to have been weeded out.[26]

In 1853 the political climate was different. Popular demands for political and economic reform had become more potent and effective; Victorian values were taking hold. The matter for debate was whether the charter of the Company should be renewed at all; and at the heart of the debate was patronage. Since the Company no longer had any commercial function, the main consequence of its abolition would be the end of the directors' patronage: India would still be governed by people appointed from London, but they would be paid and appointed by the government, not by a private company under government supervision. There was little more to it than that.

The government proposed that the Company's charter be renewed but that the patronage of the directors should cease; entry to the civil service of the Company should be by competitive examination; the Board of Control should make regulations setting out the conditions for entry to both the civil and military services; and the Board of Control should lay before Parliament all regulations it made under the Act within 14 days of making them. The Bill was debated at length and led to several late night sittings of Parliament. Disraeli made an ineffectual speech criticizing the Bill; an attempt to partially retain patronage was defeated; Macaulay, now returned from India, repeated his arguments for entry by competitive examination; and the chairman of the Company, Sir Charles Wood, acknowledged defeat, saying that the Company would obey the new charter even though they had objections to many parts of it.[27]

After the Bill had been passed, the Company appointed a committee under the chairmanship of Macaulay to propose what the nature of examination for the Company's civil servants should be, in particular what the subjects should be. Belief in the new educational regime of the public schools and the older universities was now in the ascendant. Benjamin Jowett, the Master of Balliol College, Oxford, who, along with Thomas Arnold of Rugby, was a father of that regime, was a member of Macaulay's committee; and all the members shared that belief so closely that they let Macaulay draft the report and adopted it without amendment. In the report Macaulay again displayed his exuberant confidence in the education system through which he had passed – he had been a Fellow of Trinity College, Cambridge – and the merits of the system of entrance examination he was proposing:

It is with much diffidence that we venture to predict the effect of the new system; but we think that we can hardly be mistaken in believing that the introduction of that system will be an event scarcely less important to this country than to India. The educated youth of the United Kingdom are henceforth to be invited to engage in a competition in which about forty prizes will, on an average, be gained every year. Every one of these prizes is nothing less than an honourable social position and a comfortable independence for life. It is difficult to estimate the effect which the prospect of prizes so numerous and so attractive will produce. We are, however, familiar with some facts which may assist our conjectures. At Trinity College, the largest and wealthiest of the colleges of Cambridge, about four fellowships are given annually by competition. These fellowships can be held only on condition of celibacy, and the income derived from them is a very modest one for a single man. It is notorious that the examinations for Trinity fellowships have, directly and indirectly, done much to give a direction to the studies of Cambridge and of all the numerous schools which are the feeders of Cambridge. What, then, is likely to be the effect of a competition for prizes which will be ten times as numerous as the Trinity fellowships, and of which each will be more valuable than a Trinity fellowship? We are inclined to think that the examinations for situations in the civil service of the East India Company will produce an effect which will be felt in every seat of learning throughout the realm, at Oxford and Cambridge, at the University of London and the University of Durham, at Edinburgh and Dublin, at Cork and at Belfast.[28]

The proposals made in Macaulay's report were adopted without delay. When, within a few years, the government took over the rule of India from the Company following the mutiny of 1857–58, it retained the new method of examination; and the reformed Indian civil service came to possess a remarkably high reputation for efficiency and incorruptibility in the modern Western sense of the word although, as we shall see, it did not attract Macaulay's academic stars from Oxford and Cambridge. Macaulay had recommended that once they had been selected the new recruits should be on probation and under training for one or two years, at the end of which they should be examined in Indian history, jurisprudence, financial and commercial science and an Oriental language.[29] He saw the need for relevant training after recruitment.

Patronage Debated

The debate of 1853 produced longer and more detailed criticism of patronage and more outspoken defences of it than had been heard in Parliament in 1813 or 1833. In the House of Lords, the Earl of Ellenborough, a former Governor-General of India who had served several times as a Tory minister and several times as President of the Board of Control, compared the glories of being a director of the Company with those of being a government minister:

> The holder of a government office is there for public and not for personal purposes; the Director desires to hold his seat solely for personal objects, since he has no real power at all – the actual government is really carried on by the Board of Control. But the moment a gentleman becomes a member of the Court of Directors he becomes a great man. The day before he is a Director, he is nobody; the day he is made a Director, he becomes a man of great social influence; he hears knocks at his door by parties applying to him for the good things known to be at his disposal; and he is a member of one of the bodies which is supposed to exercise an influence over the affairs of India. His social position is very much improved; he holds his office for life; he possesses the semblance of great power and great authority.[30]

In the House of Commons, Lord Stanley said he believed the patronage of the Company had been better distributed than might have been anticipated – that is to say the men were better than the system; but since the Directors received patronage in lieu of adequate pay the necessary inference was that the patronage was not entirely for the public benefit.[31] Macaulay passionately denounced a proposal to let the Governor-General choose personally who should serve under him in India:

> My firm conviction is that the day on which the civil service of India ceases to be a close service, will be the beginning of an age of jobbery – the most monstrous, the most extensive, and the most perilous system of abuse in the distribution of patronage that we have ever witnessed... I believe most firmly that instead of purity resulting from that arrangement, India would soon be tainted; and that, before long, when a son or brother of some active member of this House went out to Calcutta, carrying with him a strong letter of recommendation from the Prime Minister to the Governor General, that letter would really be a bill of exchange drawn on the revenues of India for value received in Parliamentary support in this House. That would be no new traffic, but only an old traffic revived.[32]

When it was asked if the salaries of the Directors were to be increased to compensate them for the loss of patronage they were going to suffer, Sir Charles Wood, the President of the Board of Control, responded in the most lofty manner: 'He had never connected the patronage with the salaries, and had all along repudiated the idea that the directors received any personal benefit from the patronage'. He went on to protest indignantly that John Bright earlier in the debate had told the House that he had recently come across a case of a job with the company being offered for sale; he demanded that Bright produce evidence. Bright was able immediately to call upon another member of the House of Commons, Mr Wilkinson, who told the House how in the previous year his brother had been offered a cadetship with the company for his son for £300 or £400, but finding that, unlike the purchase of a commission in the British Army at that time, the transaction was illegal, he had withdrawn from it.[33]

Altogether it is hard to know how clean or dirty was the use of patronage in the later days of the East India Company. How far were young men chosen who were inferior to those that might have been recruited by open competition? How far did the directors put personal gain, whether of a pecuniary or nepotistic kind, before the interests of the company? The answer must surely be that both these things happened in some degree but we cannot know in what degree. In the last days of patronage, an anonymous critic of the company writing in *The Times* offered an acerbic view:

> Nobody accuses the directors of selling their patronage for money; they very carefully avoid doing that; but they daily and notoriously exchange it for almost every commodity which can be purchased for £1,000 notes. Nay, it becomes from its very nature a more dangerous instrument of social corruption than money can be, because they can bribe with it parties whose worldly position places them beyond the influence of money bribery.[34]

In the 1930s an historian, writing a more bland view, suggested:

> ...on the whole the Directors, who were usually persons of wealth and independence, distributed their patronage honestly and well, although, when so great an amount of patronage and so large a number of persons were involved, it was inevitable that irregularities should occur.[35]

The Ideal of Public Service

The essence of the ideal of what a civil servant should be, which burgeoned in the Indian civil services (ICS) and later permeated the home civil service, was the notion of public service, the idea that you should be an English gentleman, should serve the public interest, never your private interest, and should always tell the truth. It began to take shape in the latter part of the eighteenth century; in the nineteenth century it gained extraordinary power in the minds of those who served in India, and that vision continued into the twentieth century. In *Competition Wallah*, his record of a journey through India in 1863, George Otto Trevelyan, (son of Sir Charles Trevelyan of the Northcote–Trevelyan report), described the men he met, many of whom must have joined the ICS before competitive selection was introduced:

> It is impossible for [the Indian civil servant] to have any misgivings concerning the dignity and importance of his work... His power for good and evil is almost unlimited... He is a member of

an official aristocracy, owning no social superior; bound to no man; fearing no man...

There is no career which holds out such certain and splendid prospects to honourable ambition. But, better far than this, there is no career which so surely inspires men with the desire to do something useful in their generation – to leave their mark upon the world for good, and not for evil. The public spirit among the servants of the Government at home is faint compared with the fire of zeal which glows in every vein of an Indian official.[36]

About a hundred years later Philip Mason, who served in the ICS in the decades before India became independent, wrote in his history, *The Men who Ruled India*:

[By 1798] pride in the service is born but in its infancy... But the time is coming. The period of corruption is over; the period of experiments is coming to an end and will be done with when all executive power is back in the Collector's hands. Then comes the flowering, the highest peak perhaps in the lofty range of what the English have done, when a handful of our countrymen, by the integrity of their character and with not much else to help them, gave to many millions for the first time for some centuries the idea that a ruler might be concerned with their well-being.[37]

The hyperbole is extraordinary. But one can see how it came about. The ICS men felt that they were saving the Indian people from disorder, famine and ignorance. Their job was paternalistic. Early in their careers they were given responsibility for ruling huge areas. They were so thin on the ground (when Britain left there were fewer than 1,500 British ICS men ruling more than 300 million Indians) that they always needed to be efficient and vigilant – in other words dutiful – if British rule was to be maintained. They felt themselves to be an incarnation of Plato's guardians, those men who were to be set aside from the start of their education to be trained to be the wise rulers of Plato's ideal society. Indeed Philip Mason gave the second volume of *The Men who Ruled India*, the sub-title *The Guardians*.

As the nineteenth century progressed, the education that ICS men received in their homes, at school and at college, increasingly imbued them with a Christian sense of mission and duty, and the open competition brought in men with a more austere social background than the patronage-cum-Haileybury system it replaced. In the last five years of the old system, no less than 45 per cent of recruits had Indian connections, meaning that their fathers had been in the ICS, the Indian army or at India House; and a further 27 per cent were classified as 'aristocracy and gentry'. With the democratic regime of open competition those categories were greatly reduced. The great winners were the clergy and the professional classes. In the mid-1870s no less than 27 per cent of recruits were the sons of clergymen, ministers of non-established religions or missionaries; the rest were mostly the sons of men who were in the military services, the ICS and the learned professions; a few were sons of men of inferior occupations.[38] The high proportion of Haileybury men who followed their fathers into service in India is not dissimilar to the proportion of Roman consuls who were descended from consuls, or the proportion of early Chinese civil servants who were descended from civil servants: 33 per cent and 40 per cent.[39] In the mid-twentieth century the proportion of members of the top (administrative) class of the British civil service whose fathers were civil servants (of any non-industrial grade) was 21 per cent.[40] Nothing conditions a person for a profession, or has helped them to get the requisite education and entrée, like having a father in that profession.

The academic standard of the competition wallahs never reached the heights Macaulay had dreamed of. After a fairly good start, the number of university candidates declined until they were in the minority in the years 1865–88. The main causes of this decline were the unexpected success of crammers in preparing men for an exam designed for Oxford and Cambridge graduates; snobbish prejudice against the competition wallahs who came in through the new system, on the grounds that some of them were not gentlemen nor sufficiently sporting; and, partly in reaction to these two developments, the reduction in the upper age limit for candidates. This was set at an age designed to catch public school boys who were then sent to Oxford and Cambridge for two years on specialized courses – an unsatisfactory arrangement under which they seem to have passed their days on the fringes of normal undergraduate life.[41] At last, in 1889 the age limit was raised so as to permit Indian candidates, who had always been eligible since the exam was open to all Her Majesty's subjects, to sit the exam after first attending a British university; and a few years later the exams for the ICS and for the home civil service, which had adopted competitive entry in 1870, were combined. Thereafter nearly all recruits came from universities. But the attractions of the home civil service, together with the decline in the status of the ICS and a worsening in its remuneration, meant that the ICS was rarely the first choice of strong candidates. Macaulay's high flyers with firsts typically went for the home civil service, the seconds for the ICS. But this does not mean that the ICS did not recruit men of ability, nor that its recruits lacked moral integrity. On the contrary, the typically austere social background of the competition men, and the paucity of men of the highest flair and originality, which is evident from their typical exam results, are likely to have been conducive to subdued rectitude in behaviour.[42]

Of course education and social background were not all that mattered. The Spanish bureaucrats of the seventeenth century Spanish American empire were relatively well educated, but they were ill paid, they were not frequently rotated from post to post, their Spanish attitude to sex was less inhibited than that of the ICS men of the late Victorian era, and they were stranded away from home for so long that they became *déraciné*; their standards of behaviour were not like those achieved two centuries later in the ICS. The ICS men, besides their sexual inhibitions, had good salaries, were transferred to new posts every three years or less and, after the opening of the Suez Canal in 1869, enjoyed frequent home leaves during which their consciousness of the standards of their home society was refreshed.[43]

If one considers whether there was any corrupt behaviour amongst the new ICS men, two points stand out. Firstly, there must have been some rotten apples in the ICS barrel. An instance is the case of Mr Crawford who, when he was suspended from duty accused of corruption, fled from Poona to Bombay wearing a false beard, yet was acquitted after a long but seemingly lenient enquiry which criticized 'his utter recklessness in money matters' and opined that 'his sense of duty had become enfeebled through the influence of an irregular life'. The official papers about the case ran to several hundred pages.[44] One supposes that other cases were dealt with quietly. Secondly, in order to run their Indian staff and keep the local people in order and loyal, the ICS men had to use, or condone, traditional Indian practices, which, by their standards, were corrupt and unacceptable. They frequently had to turn a blind eye to the bribery that was customary among the people they ruled and which they could seldom hope to nail down. And long after patronage had been abolished in favour of competitive entry to their own ICS ranks, they used patronage to obtain the political support of Indians, a matter about which Philip Mason is quite explicit in his discussion of the last years of British rule:

Until far into the 'thirties, the district officer in most parts of India could usually count on a good deal of support, quite apart from what he always received from the police. Some of this came from the landowners to whom the Congress radicalism seemed a threat; more came from men who were old-fashioned and simple, who saw only bad men opposed to the Government and were glad to do something to show their fidelity...

Altogether, then, there was backing available in most districts most of the time and the police and officials were unfailingly stead-fast. The bluff still held – though by now it was so thin that it was hardly a bluff at all. The district officer's power was already much less than it had been. There were still titles and gun-licences in his gift but patronage was dwindling. Once he had been able to reward a zealous official or a helpful landowner by making his son a patwari [a village accountant], a clerk or a tahsildar [a sub-inspector of police]. But now everything must be done by merit as a result of examinations; what had seemed the most natural thing in the world was now held up as corruption. In a sense of course it was corruption; it was part of the whole system of bluff and hikmatamali – judicious management – by which the country had been ruled.[45]

What is described here is of course inevitable when rulers come from a society with different values and practices from those they rule.[46] It is perhaps not fanciful to suggest that the unease that the ICS men, imbued with Victorian puritanical values, must have felt at having to condone and indeed exploit standards which they saw to be inferior to their own, caused them the more energetically to strive to be seen to be virtuous. That may have been another ingredient in the making of their high reputation for public service.

In the home civil service the spirit of public service became at least as high as that in the ICS once the effects of competitive entry, introduced in 1870, had permeated the service. Comparison of the two services is not easy because the home civil servants were so much less visible and audible than their counterparts in the Indian service. The ICS men were direct rulers of subject people, taxing them, judging them, watching them, listening to them, calling in the army if there was trouble; they had a considerable measure of discretion to interpret the law and the policies handed down to them – though this diminished in the last decades of British rule. They had to be seen to exercise authority; they had to be visible in order to earn the respect of the people they ruled. So they proclaimed their values, acknowledged their power, kept diaries and wrote memoirs about their part in the ruling of the raj: what they thought and did got a good deal of publicity.

In the home civil service behaviour was very different. The job of the administrators (the title of the top elite selected by competitive entry) was to advise ministers and to organize and run the departments that implemented the policies adopted by ministers. They acted in the name of ministers, attributing every decision and all responsibility for what was done to ministers (except when it came to accounting to Parliament that the money voted to their Department had been spent according to the directives of Parliament). The tradition developed that home civil servants kept in the background, invisible, emphasizing, sometimes to the point of exaggeration, that they had no power, that their job, which was permanent, was just to interpret the will of ministers as they came and went. They were severely discouraged from keeping diaries and writing their memoirs. But like their ICS counterparts they felt themselves to be Platonic guardians. They were a proud but silent elite.[47]

The Evolution of Independent Judiciaries

In order that public corruption should be kept in check, a judiciary is required that can bring the corrupt to book and is itself resistant to corruption. The fulfilment of this requirement is inherently problematic for the reason captured in the Latin tag *Quis custodiet ipsos custodes*? (Who will watch over the watchers themselves?). The persons whom the judiciary must help to keep in check include the politicians, yet the judiciary is the creation of the politicians: the creation of an independent judiciary requires that at some stage in the evolution of a nation its rulers (or ruler) should have been persuaded that it was prudent to have their power circumscribed by law and to that extent handed to the judiciary. And the survival of an independent judiciary implies that subsequent generations of rulers have felt it was in their interest to respect those inherited constraints.

How, and how far, the judiciary in our four countries achieved independence, and hence an ability to check public corruption from the top, is the main question to which this chapter is addressed. I shall also look at corrupt behaviour by the judiciary towards those seeking favours from below, i.e. from other members of the profession and those to whom the judiciary administers justice. The two types of reform – the achievement of independence from above and the stopping of corruption from below – often went together, but not always.

The notion of justice that informed the process of reform, and which still prevails today, comes directly from the beliefs of the Enlightenment:

> ...the judges should be independent of the government in the sense that the government cannot dismiss them and is itself answerable to them if its actions are in breach of the law; they

should be skilled in their profession, and immune by virtue of their professional standards and the salaries paid them by the government from the temptation to accept bribes or other inducements to modify their judgements; torture should be prohibited and punishments should be humane and proportionate to the offence committed; there should be equality before the law in the sense that no one should be subject to special courts, laws or punishments by virtue of birth, creed or race.[1]

Our four countries fall into two groups, France and Germany in one, England and America in the other.

France and Germany

France and Germany differ from England and the United States, as regards the history of their legal systems in the eighteenth and nineteenth centuries, in several respects. They belong to the civil law tradition of Western law, as distinct from the common law tradition. Though it is an over-simplification, it can be said that the civil law derives in large part from Roman law, which in the Holy Roman Empire and in other parts of the Continent was drawn upon in the Middle Ages to provide a coherent corpus of law and legal procedure. Roman law did not wholly displace local customary law, but two tenets on which it rested – that the making of the law is the responsibility of the ruler or legislature and that the law should be codified – had an enduring effect; and they came to be the qualities that primarily differentiate the civil law countries from the common law countries. Further, the idea that the government is responsible for making and applying the law has meant that, in the process of reform, the application of the law was made the responsibility of a state-appointed body of judges who spend their lives on the state payroll as public servants. This stands in contrast to the practice in common law countries where the application of the law is the responsibility of judges selected from successful private practitioners of law, and of laymen acting as magistrates.

Until the reforms of the eighteenth or nineteenth century, France and Germany consisted of regions that had their own mixtures of Roman law and local customary laws, in which there were many types of law court – seigneurial (where the landowner settled disputes between peasants) ecclesiastical, municipal and the like – with royal courts above them. One motive for reform was to introduce national codes so as to help unify the nation. This can perhaps be regarded as an element in the process of nation-building which, in turn, was partly driven by military competition.

Reform of the law was also central to the post-Enlightenment aim of ending privilege and introducing social justice. France and Germany, it must be remembered, were countries where society in the eighteenth century was still formally divided into three Estates – in Catholic France, the Church, the nobility and the rest; in Protestant Prussia, the nobility, the bourgeoisie and the peasants. The Estates were legal entities whose members had different standing before the law.

The absolutist monarchs of France and Germany were not well placed to meet reformist pressures. One of the principal tenets by which absolute kings justified their grip on power was that it was their duty to provide justice for their people; it was their right and duty to be judge of last resort, able to override the courts. It was hard, if not impossible for them to recognize the notion that justice required that they should cease to have that power, and that the whole system of privileges before the law for persons of the superior estates, at the peak of which they sat, might need to be ended. The absolute king might see injustice, he might see fault in others, but it was hard for him to recognize that his own position and the social structure on which it rested might be untenable. In his wonderfully lofty way Louis XIV wrote in his memoirs:

> *Ce précieux depôt (la justice) que Dieu a remis entre les mains des rois comme une participation à sa sagesse et à sa puissance...*[2]
>
> [Justice, that precious gift that God has put into the hands of kings as if endowing them with a share of his wisdom and his power...]

France

Before the Revolution the process of codifying the law, which eventually led to the *Codes Napoleon*, had been started. In the reign of Louis XIV codes covering parts of the law, in particular a commercial code, were introduced on the initiative of Colbert.[3] And in the reign of Louis XV further codification was undertaken by d'Aguesseau. But codification, however desirable it might be, could contribute little to the production of better justice (as we understand it) so long as the courts in France were unreformed.

In pre-revolutionary France there were a jungle of courts from which appeals could in many cases be made, often via intermediate courts, to the *parlements*, the highest of the royal courts, which consequently were always flooded with work. The judges who had purchased or inherited their jobs were greedy and often incompetent; the salary they received in exchange for the purchase of their venal office was small, sometimes non-existent after it had been trimmed and taxed at source by the government; but by prolonging cases they could charge the litigants more by way of fees and charges. Suspected criminals might be kept in prison for years before they were brought to justice, and civil cases could drag on for decades, lives and even generations, until, as d'Aguesseau put it, they became 'immortal'.[4]

There were special courts for financial matters, from which there were rights of appeal in most cases to the *Cour des Aides* (another sovereign court). And every administrative body, for example, the *Eaux et Forêts*, the *Cour des Monnaies* (the mint), and many more, had its own court. Disputes between the courts over their rights of jurisdiction were so frequent that in 1763 an eminent lawyer observed that 'one could be forced to plead for two or three years merely to discover before which judge one had the misfortune to be heard.'[5]

That this system produced awful injustices, and therefore created desire for reform, is clear from the damning judgements of the system made by French critics and also foreign critics, for example, Arthur Young. How bad the injustices could be one learns from the tiny fraction of cases that were challenged and became public scandals. For example, there is the case of Monnerat, a merchant of Limoges, who in 1767 was arrested by the officials of the tax farmers cartel (the General Farm) and was accused of being a salt smuggler called Comtois, alias La Feuillade. Having protested his innocence, he managed, after six months in gaol, to get a perfunctory hearing before the special court that dealt with the tax cases of the General Farm. Condemned to imprisonment, Monnerat was sent at first to a dungeon devoid of light where he was tied to the wall by a chain weighing 50 pounds, attached to his neck. After a total of 17 months in prison he was released as a result of powerful intervention. Once free, he brought a case against the General Farm and was awarded compensation, but the members of the General Farm were so powerful that they obtained an order annulling the judgement.[6] Besides being tax collectors, they were, it will be remembered, lenders of badly needed money to the Crown.

Attempts were made to reform the system in the 20 years before the Revolution. These included steps that would have substantially improved the system of justice, notably by a reduction in the variety and number of courts, but they had come to nothing by 1789.

With the Revolution the *parlements* and other courts were replaced by a new system of district and departmental courts subject to a single court of review (*tribunal de cassation*); all judges and other officials were to be elected; and it was resolved that the changes in the law should be consolidated in a set of codes. But the subsequent political turbulence was such that codification had not been brought to fruition when Napoleon came to power.

Napoleon gave the system distinctive shape by unifying the French civil law in a single code that incorporated many of the values of the revolution, and also by codifying other branches of the law. He subscribed to the notion that the judiciary should be independent but, knowing the troubles the *parlements* had caused the *Ancien Régime*, he limited the independence of the courts so as to guard against any challenge to his personal power. His way of achieving this was to provide on the one hand that all judges, rather than being elected, should be appointed for life and instructed to follow their conscience; and to ensure on the other hand that the government controlled promotion of judges and named who was to preside on the bench. And he circumvented the regular courts by using special courts that introduced an element of political and military justice.[7]

This design is still almost intact today, apart from the intrusions of EU law. The present constitution, which was produced in 1958 to the order of President de Gaulle, affirms the principle of the independence of the judiciary, but it makes the president, who is both head of state and head of the executive, responsible for that independence. The consequences are predictable: de Gaulle violated the independence of the judiciary when it did not do what he wanted in a case he cared about. When an attempt was made on his life which, much to his indignation, put at risk the life of his wife who was in the car with him, he set up a special criminal court to try those accused of the deed. When it failed to condemn them to death he set up a special military court, which passed the death sentence on them. But the *Conseil d'Etat* reversed that judgement on the grounds that the procedure of the special military court did not give sufficient rights to the accused. Undeterred, de Gaulle put legislation through Parliament retrospectively validating the death sentence of the special military court.

After recounting this story, an expert observed:

> If this piece of history refers to rather exceptional events, it shows, nevertheless, that the executive has attempted to impose its will on the judiciary in this instance as well as in many others. It also shows, however, the degree of resistance by the courts and by individual members of the judiciary, which even a strong executive may have to face.[8]

That the president has so much power is an expression of the intention of de Gaulle, following in the footsteps of Napoleon, to keep ultimate power in his own hands as head of the executive, and also of the willingness of the French people to accept that degree of autocracy. The horrible experience of life under the revolutionary governments and their later experience of weak republican regimes have left the French people with the understandable feeling that unconstrained democracy may lead to anarchy, that autocrats such as Napoleon and de Gaulle have their merits.

The issue of political interference with the judiciary has been very much alive recently. After a series of major scandals in which top politicians accused of corruption had not been brought to book, a proposal to amend the constitution was brought forward by the government of Monsieur Jospin with the backing of President Chirac. This bi-partisan amendment would have prevented the minister of justice taking magistrates off cases when it looked as if their enquiries would embarrass the government; and it would have increased the number of independent members on the committee that picks judges and magistrates. But in January 2000 the proposal was scuppered when the president's party, the RPR, withdrew its support. The Napoleonic tradition is not dead: Valéry Giscard d'Estaing, a former president, himself rumoured to have been guilty of corruption when in office, argued that the power of the government to veto appointments of judges and prosecutors should not be reduced. What other professional organization, he asked – the diplomatic service, for example – would be run by a body of amateurs?[9]

Nevertheless, Monsieur Jospin's government has continued the policy of non-interference with the magistrates, which was adopted by Elisabeth Gigou, his first minister of justice, when she took office. That, together with the earlier rise of some crusading young magistrates who would not be deterred from exposing corruption in high places, has meant that investigations have been more searching than before. The result, also influenced by the enormous scale of the corruption that has been unearthed, has been a spate of extraordinary scandals. Damning evidence has been found against the late President Mitterand and against his successor, President Chirac. The latter, whose misdeeds were committed when he was Mayor of Paris, has been exempted from further investigation on the grounds that he is above the law while he is President. But Monsieur Dumas, foreign minister under Mitterand and once head of the Constitutional Council, the highest court in France, has been sent to prison for six months, his mistress for 18 months, and many seedy practices have been exposed. For the moment at least, the French judiciary seems to have broken loose from the reins of the politicians.[10]

Prussia/Germany

Because Prussia at the beginning of the eighteenth century had recently acquired substantial new dominions each with its own institutions, it contained an even greater diversity of justice than France. Overall, the most important institutions were seigneurial justice applied by lords of the manor and, at the higher levels, royal justice. The problems and complaints to which the system gave rise were essentially the same as in France – injustice, incompetent judges, interminable delays – caused partly by disputes as to the jurisdiction of rival courts and by the judges spinning out cases so as to increase their fees. But two differences between Prussia and France stand out. The first is that the main courts for the administration of ordinary royal justice, the *Regierungen*, which were the equivalent of the French *parlements*, had been shorn of their legislative and administrative functions and so, unlike their French counterparts, could not obstruct the will of the ruler by questioning legislation and similar antics: they had purely judicial functions. The second is the strong influence of the military on justice, as on everything else in Prussia. This was partly informal. In the words of Betty Behrens:

> The power and prestige of the army were such that, even in the second half of the eighteenth century when arrangements were more orderly than they had been under Frederick William I, the military commanders, with the tacit approval of the king, were able to bend or defy the law to their own or their service's advantage.[11]

There were also formal arrangements that gave the military extraordinary powers. Under the General Directory created by Frederick William I, a board was established in every province that not only had responsibility for military affairs and for the administration of the royal estates, but also was empowered to administer justice within its field of operations. In 1749 the mandate of these boards was defined as covering no less than 'all disputes concerned with political, economic and other questions affecting the public interest'.[12]

Frederick William I received numerous petitions from his people against unjust treatment that they claimed to have suffered under this judicial regime, but he responded perversely. He cursed the judges, reduced their salaries in the name of economy (which increased their dependence on fees) and was even known to physically batter judges who had made decisions he disliked. He would not change the system.

Reform came with Frederick the Great. Early in Frederick's reign, Samuel von Cocceji, the great legal reformer, tried to persuade the king to abolish the separate boards for military affairs. In this he was unsuccessful, but he had considerable success in reforming the regular system of royal justice: the number of courts was diminished, the pay of judges was increased and fees abolished, and the training and quality of judges improved. In short, the foundations of a decent court system were established, albeit in a circumscribed area. Some steps were also taken to improve the imperfect justice administered by the seigneurial courts.

The main achievement for which Frederick the Great is remembered is his codification of the law of Prussia, an enterprise that was started in 1780, late in his reign. The new code, which came into force eight years after his death and five years after the storming of the Bastille, was a compromise between the desire of the king and his advisers, inspired by the Enlightenment, for 'a masterpiece of the human spirit' resembling a clock 'in which all the gears have one purpose,' and their conservative desire to preserve entrenched rights and respect sectional interests.[13] The new code introduced the concept of the 'citizen', but social inequality was not removed since the three estates (the nobles, the burghers and the peasants), membership of which depended on birth, were maintained. Moreover the king was not constrained by law. In criminal cases he could override the judgements of the courts; and in civil cases, where this was not the case, he intervened nevertheless in the belief that it was his duty as an absolute monarch to see that justice was always done. The results could be capricious misjudgements – how many we do not know – of which the most notorious was the Müller Arnold case.

Briefly, Arnold was a miller who refused to pay rent to the land-owner on whose land his water mill stood, on the grounds that a neigh-bouring landowner had built a carp pond which deprived him of water from the stream that flowed through both properties and drove his mill. Arnold's landlord had him up before his manorial court which dismissed Arnold's story as invalid. Arnold appealed and was turned down, apparently rightly, since it seems to have been clear that he and his wife were liars. But he managed to bring the case to the attention of the king. When the Supreme Court in Berlin, to which the king eventu-ally referred the case came down against Arnold, the king, who was convinced that the judges were in league with the nobility to oppress the peasants, exploded. He summoned the Grand Chancellor and the judges of the appeal court and hurled abuse at them, calling them 'scoun-drels, rogues and swindlers'; he sacked the Grand Chancellor, three judges from the appeal court and four from the provincial court, and also dismissed Arnold's landlord from his position in local govern-ment (as *Landrat*). Worse than that, he imprisoned the seven dismissed judges for a year and ordered them to pay compensation to Arnold for the losses he had allegedly suffered. When the king offered to free them if they confessed guilt, the judges, courageously, stood firm. The judge-ment in the case was reversed as soon as Frederick died. The direct consequence of the affair was a flood of petitions from peasants trying their luck with cases against landlords. 'Social conditions as well as the course of justice suffered considerable disruption.'[14]

Nevertheless, Frederick the Great gave the Prussian–German legal sys-tem its enduring characteristics, codified law administered by an expert permanent judiciary. It took time for the large feudal enclaves in the system to be removed. The biggest change was made in response to the uprisings of 1848. The court system was reformed and qualifications for legal officials were raised and standardized. This rationalization of the system produced an expanded, highly trained professional judici-ary and a legal profession of enhanced status. But it also reduced the autonomy of the judicial process. The number of positions directly appointed by the Ministry of Justice was substantially increased with the result that the Minister of Justice, who was a political appointee, had greater say than before in the naming and promotion of judges; and the creation of the State Prosecutors' Office meant that the cases brought before the courts were dependent on the will of the administration.[15] The Prussian tradition of absolutism lived on, not least the tradition that public servants, including judges, were subservient to royal authority.

It is easy to forget that Prussia and the united Germany to which it gave birth remained a monarchical state until 1918 when democracy was introduced. As a result of the deep tradition of respect for authority, together with the relative ease with which the constitution of the Weimar republic could be amended, 'the Nazi regime could do away with judicial independence without even being faced with any considerable resistance'.[16] Measures protecting judges from the disciplinary law that kept other civil servants subservient were abolished by Hitler; he cut back the power over appointments of the judges who, cherishing their status and independence, mostly yielded to him reluctantly; and in 1942 Hitler had himself made the highest court authority with power to dismiss judges at will.

After 1945 the western allies, dominated by the United States, insisted in imposing on western Germany a constitution that would establish the rule of law in Germany and help prevent another Hitler seizing power. Montesquieu's ideas about the separation of powers, which had been espoused by the German liberal classes in the nineteenth century, were finally brought to bear. The independence of the judiciary was firmly written into the Basic Law of the Federal Republic. Further statutory provisions were later introduced to enhance judicial independence. Thus there are provisions which forbid the dismissal or transfer of judges except by a court, and also provisions designed to ensure that in appointing Federal judges the Federal minister of justice acts on the recommendation of an electoral council for judges, consisting of the ministers of justice of the member states (*Länder*) and an equal number of members of the federal parliament. The system for appointing judges to the lower courts varies from state to state but generally safeguards their independence.[17]

The Germans, anxious to break with their shameful experience of autocracy, seem to have become strong supporters of judicial independence. In the rather guarded words of an expert from Israel comparing the experience of different countries, '...contemporary German law, both the Basic Law provisions and the statutory provisions, provide significant protection for judicial independence, and one might say that the public awareness of the importance of an independent judiciary has increased.'[18]

The contrast is striking between the constitutions adopted by France and Germany after the Second World War, each influenced by its prewar experience. France, reacting to its experience of weak democracy, gave the head of state an unusual amount of power; West Germany, reacting to its experience of tyranny, introduced provisions to neuter the head of state.

England

Although there was much that was wrong, as we shall see, with the way the law was administered at the beginning of the eighteenth century, England, an evolutionary pioneer, had advanced much further towards our modern notions of justice than France or Prussia.

The law of England was unified. The Normans imposed central military-cum-political rule on England long before the Bourbons imposed it on France or the Hohenzollerns on Germany; and, in doing so, they largely unified the law in England. The development of the common law was the means by which they achieved this. When they had conquered Normandy, the Normans, rather than adopt the Roman law, had developed the local customary law of that area of France. In England they repeated the process, following a policy rather like that of those colonial powers of modern times which found it better to enforce the local customary law of the people they conquered than impose on them Western laws that were at odds with local custom.[19] One of the very few legislative acts of William the Conqueror that we know for sure is that he endorsed the English laws. His words were these:

> This I will and order that all shall have and hold the law of king Edward as to lands and all other things with these additions which I have established for the good of the English people.[20]

Royal emissaries were sent from London to supervise justice in the kingdom. As they did so, they noted the common elements of the local laws they found and applied them across the country. So began the evolution of the royal courts touring the country, and the evolution of the common law, derived from custom, built up by precedent and embodied in written reports of decided cases. Statute law was added to the common law, mainly in bursts at times when the scope of government was being expanded, for example, the Tudor period when statutes were introduced regulating trade and apprenticeships, creating trading monopolies and establishing the Poor Laws.

The English people were formally equal before the law, not divided into estates with different legal rights. Which is not to say that England was not a class society in which there were gross economic and social inequalities and much injustice.

Most important, the judiciary had achieved independence. This was the result of political developments starting with the clash between the king and the barons that led to Magna Carta (1215). For long periods the judiciary, while under royal control, was not used as an instrument in political struggles, but the resulting harmony was broken in the seventeenth century when parliament and king clashed and both demanded the backing of the courts in arguments over their respective powers. It was out of that struggle, in which the judges were assailed from both sides, that the judiciary, led by Chief Justice Coke, asserted itself and eventually achieved the remarkable kind of independence it enjoys today. The written basis of that independence rests firstly in the Petition of Right (1628), written by Coke, the violation of which by Charles I was the beginning of the sequence of actions that led to the Civil War. It lies secondly in the Bill of Rights (1689) and the Act of Settlement (1701) which were imposed on William and Mary after the Glorious Revolution, by which time Parliament was powerful; the Act of Settlement provided *inter alia* that judges be given security of tenure.[21] The result was to prevent Crown and Parliament from intervening in the administration of the law by the judiciary.

Malpractice in the Courts

That the English judiciary was independent was in no way a safeguard against corrupt behaviour by its members towards those to whom they were meant to be administering justice. Rather, the standard of conduct of the judiciary seems to have followed the same path as the conduct of politicians and civil servants, falling to a low level in the eighteenth century before being cleaned up in the nineteenth century.

Malpractices were common in the courts both of common law and equity but the court of Chancery seems to have been the most notorious, judging by the attention given to its malpractices in histories of the law and in the novels of Dickens. It is the court to which cases could be taken to be judged (originally by the Lord Chancellor himself) by reference to considerations of equity, which might not be satisfied by common law judgements based on precedent, and to which the application of a wide range of legislation on property, succession, bankruptcy and many other matters was later entrusted. Its notoriety seems to have been occasioned by the quite extraordinary delays, obfuscation and extortionate charges to which its procedures gave rise. In the words of L J Bowen:

> A Bill in Chancery was a marvellous document which stated the plaintiff's case at full length and three times over. There was the first part in which the story was circumstantially set forth. Then came the part which 'charged' its truth against the defendant – or, in other words, which set it forth all over again in an aggrieved tone. Lastly came the interrogating part, which converted the original allegations into a chain of subtly framed enquiries addressed to the defendant, minutely dove-tailed, and circuitously arranged, so as to surround a slippery conscience and to stop every earth. No layman, however intelligent, could compose the 'answer' without professional aid. It was inevitably so elaborate and so long that the responsibility for the accuracy of the story shifted during the telling from the conscience of the defendant to that of his solicitor and counsel, and truth found no difficulty in disappearing during the operation.

Having quoted this passage, Holdsworth comments that 'The system of equitable procedure might be well devised to secure complete justice in a world where considerations of time and cost could be disregarded – but in no other place... Dickens's pictures of 'Jarndyce v. Jarndyce' and 'Bardell v. Pickwick', of Doctors' Commons and the Ecclesiastical Courts, of the beadle, the local justice and the constable contain much real history.[22]

Before the Civil War twelve Masters and the six clerks who served the court of Chancery lived on fees and spun out the work to enhance their income and leisure. They, and their subordinates to whom they passed on much of their work, exacted additional gratuities by devious methods, such as taking money for accelerating the hearing of cases (a form of extortion known as 'heraldry') and charging excessive amounts for multiple copies of documents which suitors had to have made by the court officials even though they were unnecessary. Suits, it was said, had been known to last 20 years. Since the offices were venal, reform was opposed.

> ...while the actual work was badly done by underpaid deputies, the suitor paid enormous fees to sinecure officials. These officials naturally regarded their offices merely as property. They were

sold by the Chancellor or given to his relations. An attack upon one of these officials always appeared to those interested in the patronage, not as the act of dismissing a useless servant, but as the act of depriving a man of his freehold... It followed that all those who, from their experience of the court, were most competent to reform it, were most interested in maintaining it in its existing condition.[23]

Altogether England's courts seem to have rivaled the courts of France at this time as regards delays, over-charging and venality, and also in disputes about the jurisdiction of rival courts.

Under the Commonwealth, the government had good intentions to reform the judiciary but its leaders did not match the ranks of obstructive lawyers. Such reforms as were introduced, notably steps to reform the court of Chancery by setting fees and time limits, came to nothing. With the restoration of the monarchy, the old system was brought back in its entirety and the abuses became worse. There was more business for the court of Chancery but no increase in its judicial strength. For almost 20 years the Lord Chancellor was Lord Eldon, a meticulous person who, though he tried his hardest to work a system he thought it dangerous to change, was hampered by remarkable powers of indecision and procrastination. It was said of him that he often expressed a clear opinion after hearing a case and then expressed doubts – reserved to himself the opportunity for further consideration – took home the papers – never read them – promised judgement again and again – and for years never gave it – all the facts and law connected with it having escaped his memory.[24]

Delays were aggravated by the system of re-hearings and appeals, which could be pursued upon the most trivial points by a determined litigant, if he had the money. Any point arising in the course of a suit might be discussed – (1) before the Master of the Rolls; (2) before the same person by way of rehearing; (3) before the Lord Chancellor; (4) before the Lord Chancellor by way of rehearing; (5) before the House of Lords.

The Impeachment of Lord Macclesfield

Venality became worse in the eighteenth century and was given prominence when Lord Macclesfield, the Lord Chancellor, was impeached for corruption in 1725. The son of a country attorney, Macclesfield (then Mr Thomas Parker) was admitted at Trinity College, Cambridge, in 1685, aged 18, but without staying to graduate he went to the Inner Temple to train as a barrister, at which calling he was so talented that he became known as 'the silver-tongued counsel', and went on to be a distinguished judge. He seems to have been as little modest as he was honest. It is recorded that a country house he acquired, Shirburn Castle, contained five portraits of himself, three by Kneller, and that 'owing to his uncourteous manners he was exceedingly unpopular at the bar'.[25] But he obviously knew how to get rich and how to get on. A monumental set of silver for serving wine – a fountain, cistern and cooler – that was made for him was acquired in 1998 by the Victoria and Albert Museum, which reports that it weighs 2,300 ounces and cost Macclesfield £1,200, compared with £35 for a full-length Kneller portrait.[26] Macclesfield became a Whig Member of Parliament, a Fellow of the Royal Society, Lord Lieutenant of Warwickshire and Oxfordshire (in both of which counties he had acquired property) and Lord Chief Justice, which position he held when George I came to the throne in 1714. He quickly became a favourite of the new king, showing in a marvellous manner, according to one of his biographers, 'the versatility of his powers, by making himself agreeable to George I and the German attendants who accompanied him, male and female'.[27] In particular, he pleased the king by giving the opinion, as Lord Chief Justice, that the king had sole control over the education and marriage of his grandchildren, not their father, the Prince of Wales.

In 1718 he enjoyed what appears to have been an *annus mirabilis*; the king appointed him Lord Chancellor and on so doing gave him a present of £14,000, a salary of £4,000, and a life pension of £1,200 a year for his son; and he called on Macclesfield to read the king's speech to Parliament, his own English not being up to the task. From this great height he was to fall mightily. In 1725, shortly after the South Sea Bubble had burst, there were rumours that all was not well with the suitors' money held by the Court of Chancery, over which the Lord Chancellor presided. An inquiry by a committee of the Privy Council was ordered.

It was then the custom that money in court was under the absolute control of the Master managing the case; he was allowed to lend it and earn interest on it for himself, just as government ministers lent and earned interest for themselves on the money held by their departments. But someone had been tempted to speculate in South Sea stock. The inquiry found a deficit of over £80,000; and it reported that there was a case of grave suspicion against the Lord Chancellor. A little later, a petition was presented to the House of Commons by the guardians of the Dowager Duchess of Montague, a lunatic, stating that large sums belonging to her estate in the possession of the court were missing and asking for relief.[28] Shortly afterwards impeachment proceedings were started against Lord Macclesfield.

For 13 days the House of Lords heard the case. Macclesfield was charged with selling masterships in Chancery; receiving bribes for agreeing to the transfer or sale of offices; admitting as masters persons who were 'of small substance and ability, very unfit to be trusted with the great sums of money and other effects of suitors'; with making use of suitors money for his own private service and advantage; and many other misdeeds. The charges came to 21 in total. After his counsel had been heard, he addressed the House of Lords 'in most masterly manner'. Disclaiming all corruption, he relied on law and usage, maintaining that the taking of money for masterships had long been practised without blame. After deploying a mass of evidence he argued that he had not amassed as much wealth as he might have done. It is a defence that always comes naturally to those accused of corruption. Robert Walpole used it to answer accusations of corruption in the House of Commons in 1730;[29] and later in the century (1773) Clive famously declared during parliamentary cross-examination, 'By God, Mr Chairman, at this moment I stand astonished at my own moderation.' But it did Macclesfield no good. He was found guilty unanimously by the 93 peers, fined £30,000, and imprisoned in the Tower of London until he raised the money. This took him six weeks. When released, he retired into obscurity and soon died.

The trial produced fascinating evidence of the barefaced way in which venality had been practised. The account given by Master Elde is particularly illuminating, but he is just one of several who described how they had bought their masterships from the Lord Chancellor and how the Lord Chancellor directed them to negotiate with his man, Mr Cottingham. Elde told how, upon the death of a master named William Fellowes, some of his friends 'put it into his head that this Office might be a proper Office for me'. After considering the matter for two days he went to 'my Lord himself'. He was questioned about what then happened:

> I told his Lordship an Office was fallen by the death of Mr Fellowes; if his Lordship thought me a proper Person. And I

should be glad to have it. I was come to wait upon him about it. His Lordship said, he had no manner of Objection to me, he had known me a considerable Time, and he believed I should make a good Officer.

Mr Lutwyche. What further Discourse was there?

Mr Elde. My Lord at that time desired me further to consider of it, and come back to him again: And so I did… I came again in a Day or two…and told him I had considered of it, and desired to know if his Lordship thought fit to admit me; and I would make him a Present of £4 or 5,000. I cannot say which of the two I said, but I believe it was £5,000.

Mr Lutwyche. What Answer did my Lord return, when you made him that Proposal?

Mr Elde. My Lord said, Thee and I, or You and I, my Lord was pleased to treat me as a Friend, must not make Bargains…

Mr Serj Pengelly. After this Answer of my Lord Macclesfield, that they must not bargain, what further Application did he make?

Mr Elde. I made no further Application at all, but spoke to Mr Cottingham [Lord Macclesfield's man], meeting him in Westminster Hall, and told him I had been at my Lord's, and my Lord was pleased to speak very kindly to me, and I had proposed to give him £5,000. Mr Cottingham answered, Guineas are handsomer.

Mr Lutwyche. We desire to know what he paid, and in what Manner, and in what specie?

Mr Elde. Upon this I immediately went to My Lord's: I was willing to get into the Office as soon as I could. I did carry with me 5,000 Guineas in Gold and Bank Notes: I am not certain whether there was 3,000 Guineas in Gold or two, but I think there was three, and the Residue of the Money was in Bank Notes. This I brought to my Lord's House.

Mr Serj Pengelly. My Lords, we desire he may be asked what they were put into, or in what they were carried?

Mr Elde. I had the Money in my Chambers. I could not tell how to convey it; It was a great Burthen and Weight, but recollecting I had a Basket in my Chamber, I put the Guineas into the Basket, and the Notes with them; I went in a Chair and took with me the Basket in my Chair. When I came to my Lord's House I saw Mr Cottingham there, and I gave him the Basket, and desired him to carry it up to my Lord.

Mr Serj Pengelly. What Answer did he return?

Mr Elde. I saw him go up Stairs with the Basket, and when he came down he intimated to me that he had delivered it.

Mr Lutwyche. My Lords, we desire he may be asked whether he acquainted Mr Cottingham with what was in the Basket?

Mr Elde. I did not.

Mr Serj Pengelly. After Mr Cottingham came and acquainted you he had delivered the Basket, how long was it before you saw My Lord?

Mr Elde. I did not see My Lord after that, till I was sworn in...either the same Day, or if not, it was the next day after.

Mr Serj Pengelly. And when he was admitted, was he admitted in the Closet or in what Room?

Mr Elde. When I was admitted, my Lord invited me to Dinner, and some of my Friends with me; and he was pleased to treat me and some Members of the House of Commons in a very hand-some Manner. I was after Dinner sworn in before them.

Mr Serj Pengelly. I desire to ask whether he had the Basket again?

Mr Elde. Some months after, I spoke to my Lord's Gentleman, and desired him if he saw such a Basket, that he would give it me back; and sometime after he did so.[30]

When a hundred years earlier a previous Lord Chancellor, Francis Bacon, was impeached and sacked, perhaps unfairly, for taking bribes, no reform of the system was introduced. After Macclesfield's impeachment, a small move was made: the law was changed so that masters no longer had control of money in court. But the purchase and sale of judicial offices was not stopped. Indeed when nearly a hundred years later an act the 'For the Prevention of the Sale and Brokerage of Offices' was passed in 1809, after the scandal over alleged sale of offices by the Duke of York's mistress, judicial offices (and commissions in the army) were exempted, as they had been under the pre-existing act 'Against buying and selling of Offices' of 1653. The government held that since judicial offices had been exempt so long it would be wrong to abolish their exemption without due consideration and 'adequate equivalent', meaning presumably compensation by means of higher pay or a capital sum.

Radical reforms of the courts, sufficient to end corrupt behaviour by the judiciary, came only after 1832, that turning point of the political tide in England. In 1833 the appointment of masters was transferred to the Crown; they were to be paid a fixed salary; and the taking of any fee or gratuity was made an indictable offence. In the following year a select committee on sinecure offices, which recommended the abolition of a number of anachronistic offices that still survived – for example, the post of Grand Falconer of England – came across old-fashioned peculation in another corner of the judiciary. They found that the Chief Clerk of the Court of King's Bench, Lord Ellenborough, counted as part of his income the interest on £5,000, which, as custodian of money paid into court, he held in Exchequer Bills. Remarkably, his father, Lord Chief Justice Ellenborough, had appointed his son to be Chief Clerk and had arranged that these interest payments should go to his son in part payment of the fixed allowance he made to him. The son denied any wrongdoing, voluntarily gave up the arrangement and was exonerated by the committee; but the committee recommended new arrangements for the future.[31]

These episodes are a reminder of how important, at the very top of government and judiciary, had been the tradition that public offices were private property from which profit was to be extracted, and how slowly this notion was rooted out by piecemeal steps until, in the middle of the nineteenth century, the Victorian notion was embraced that public offices should be held by salaried persons who serve the public. The final cleansing of the judicial system came in 1852. A severe penalty was imposed 'if any officer of the court of Chancery or any of the judges thereof shall for anything done or pretended to be done relating to his office situation or employment wilfully take any fee, gift, gratuity, or emolument.'[32] At the same time, the courts were reorganized and procedure was reformed. In short, the administration of the law was remodelled and cleansed; the extortionate costs and the delays in obtaining justice were swept away. The substance of the law was retained, but procedure was now designed to ensure a clear statement of the issues of fact and law in a case and prevent a suitor with a good case losing it merely by a fault in its presentation. This aim appears in great measure to have been fulfilled.

The Basis of the English Judiciary's Independence

The independence of the English judiciary owes much to the evolution of private elites – the changing social elite from which the magistrates have been drawn and the legal elite from which the judges have been drawn.

The magistrates or 'justices of the peace' are unpaid lay persons who, advised by a clerk knowledgeable in the law, preside over local courts judging minor criminal offences. Today there are about 30,000 of them in England and Wales. They deal with a huge number of cases and settle 98 per cent of them; others they pass on to higher courts.

The system, which has feudal origins, was built up by Henry VII as a means of restoring order and of establishing effective government after the power of the barons had been broken in the Wars of the Roses. The magistrates were drawn largely from the landed gentry, an emerging class less arrogant than the old nobles. As new tasks were given to them – the administration of Elizabethan Poor Law and regulations concerning trade and labour, the maintenance of roads and the setting of the rates (the local property tax) – they became the agents through whom the Crown kept the peace and ruled the country.[33]

At the end of the nineteenth century almost all their administrative and executive functions were transferred to new, elected local authorities; and in the eighteenth century, full-time professional magistrates had been created to help meet the needs of the growing towns. But subject to these changes, the task of presiding over local courts remained with the lay magistrates. That this was possible depended upon the existence in England of an expanding middle class as a source of responsible persons ready to do unpaid service.[34]

The method of appointment of the magistrates (which strongly determines their independence) is seemingly anachronistic. Appointments are made on behalf of the Crown by the Lord Chancellor, acting on the recommendations of the Lords Lieutenant, the Crown's traditional representatives in the counties who are selected from the local gentry.[35] Until the twentieth century the Lord Chancellor never queried the recommendations of the Lords Lieutenant unless there was something fishy about them.[36]

When the Liberals came to power in 1905 their supporters, who objected to the over-representation of Tories amongst the justices and to the methods of selection, pressed the Lord Chancellor, Lord Loreburn, to pack the courts with Liberals and also to hand over the task of appointing justices to the elected local authorities. Lord Loreburn resisted the pressure until in 1909 the government appointed a Royal Commission, which recommended that the existing system should stay put but that the Lord Chancellor should establish local committees to advise the Lords Lieutenant.[37] That was done, but since the committees were overwhelmingly political, and the conservatives were in power most of the time, the political imbalance in appointments was not redressed before the Second World War.

After 1945 the Labour Lord Chancellor, Lord Jowitt, came under pressure to correct the imbalance and again a Royal Commission was appointed. This time the commission was more effective. It recommended that while personal qualities should come first, attention should be paid to the political affiliations of candidates so that an unfair preponderance was not given to any particular party.

As a result of this reform and the day-to-day efforts of successive Lord Chancellors, the composition of the justices has changed remarkably since 1909. In January 1990, 44 per cent of justices were women (who became eligible to serve in 1919). The proportion of black and Asian justices was still far less than their proportion of the population, but the number newly appointed has been catching up: in 1987 4.5 per cent of newly-appointed magistrates were black or Asian persons, an ethnic category that comprised 5.5 per cent of the population recorded in the 1991 census.

The Judges

All English judges have come up as private practitioners at the Bar. Their professional home is the Inns of Court, those club-like institutions, originally law schools, that still control entry to the Bar. As they hear cases, the judges bear responsibility, along with those still at the Bar who plead before them, for the interpretation of the common law and hence its evolution. They have long enjoyed high status in English society. In Halévy's words, describing England in 1815, 'A legal career was open to the ambition and talent of the poorest, and led to the highest positions in society'. On the lowest rung were the attorneys, now called solicitors, the Tulkinghorns and Jaggers, who could become rich by making themselves useful to landowners but who as a body lacked prestige and were separated from the barristers by a social abyss. They were comforted by the knowledge that they might win for their children the standing they could never obtain for themselves:

> A solicitor's son called to the Bar possessed the most favourable opening for a brilliant career. His father recommended him to his clients and his fellow solicitors. He had learnt his profession in his father's office, and his fellow students, when in due course

they became solicitors, brought their cases to him. Three of the most eminent Lord Chancellors of the eighteenth century were the sons of solicitors...[Lord Macclesfield is one of them] And the moment the solicitor's son began to practice at the Bar he felt himself a member of the governing class and shared its snobbery.[38]

The ladder upwards led to the Bench and now finally to the House of Lords. Since the Lords is the ultimate court of appeal it is necessary to elevate to its ranks selected judges to whom the task of hearing appeals can be delegated.

England is more egalitarian today. For the young person filled with financial and social ambition there are other routes to the top. Moreover, membership of the House of Lords has been devalued. But the law lords stand apart from other peers.

The appointment of judges, like the appointment of magistrates, is the responsibility of the Lord Chancellor, but in selecting judges he is guided only by informal advice from the legal elite to which he belongs, not by any formal machinery for consultation or by guidelines. He is a lawyer chosen and appointed by the political party in power, who is expected by force of custom to refrain from exercising that power to the advantage of his party. In 1985 Lord Lane set out the position admirably:

> The Lord Chancellor occupies a totally contradictory position – or to put it more accurately – 4 or 5 contradictory positions. He comprises functions which in theory should be widely separate. It is largely on his advice that the Queen, or the Queen advised in her turn by the Prime Minister, appoints the higher judiciary. He sits in his own right as a judge in the highest appellate court in the land, the House of Lords. He is at the same time head of the administration that provides services for the courts. He is finally a political animal, a member of the government of the day, who will lose his job upon the defeat and disappearance from power of the party of which he is a member. Just as the bumble-bee is said to be an aerodynamic impossibility, so the Lord Chancellor is a constitutional impossibility.
>
> Given a Lord Chancellor of integrity, and in the past half century at any rate they have left nothing to be desired at all on that score, they have managed to keep their various functions separate and apart. They have never worn their political hat when sitting as judges, nor have they consciously allowed their administrative powers in

any way to impinge upon the judiciary. The independence of the judges depends upon the ability of the Lord Chancellor to perform this impressive balancing act without falling off the tightrope.[39]

Lord Lane's concern at this time was that the traditional system, whereby judges travelling the country with their own staff were very much in charge of the courts and determined such matters as the order in which cases came before them, was being displaced by a new bureaucracy:

> Inevitably, as the bureaucratic machine becomes larger and larger, those who operate it will cease to have, as the staff did in times gone by, loyalty towards the judge and the court; they will unconsciously have their first loyalty to what they regard as the service which is the bureaucratic machine...in that division of loyalty, however understandable it may be, lies the danger. It is essential that the judges remain in control of the courts, in control of the their listing, in control of the allocation of judges. Any serious encroachment by the executive on this territory can spell the end of independence...one must be eternally vigilant.[40]

It is instructive to see how sensitive is Lord Lane to any encroachment on the autonomy of the judges and how uninhibited in speaking out. That is in the English tradition. English judges fought for independence. Since they make their way to the top as a private practitioners of law they may be less inhibited about speaking out in public than foreign judges who have made their careers as government employees and are not permitted to give their personal opinions.

The United States

At the start of the War of Independence the thirteen American colonies that revolted against English rule each had its own legislature and its own statutes, which had added to or modified the English law. In eleven of the colonies the superior judges were appointed by the governor, a Crown appointee, and in most states appointed for life, as they had been in England since 1701.[41] Local lay justices, the colonial replicas of English justices of the peace, were appointed by the governor or were elected locally.[42] In all the colonies, appeals against the judgement of the colonial courts were to the Privy Council in London. There was no political or legal connection between one colony and another until they united against English rule; each had derived from England the common law and its own version of an independent judiciary.[43]

Upon independence the United States needed to create new courts to interpret and apply the new Federal law and to deal with international legal matters, and they needed to find their own autonomous way of ensuring the independence of their new judiciary. Influenced by the legacy of English legal history and by Montesquieu's interpretation of that history, they embraced the notion of the separation of powers and set about writing it into their constitution. In Bryce's words, 'The Fathers of the Constitution were extremely anxious to secure the independence of their judiciary, regarding it as a bulwark both for the people and for the States against aggressions of either Congress or the President.'[44] The result was the creation of the United States Supreme Court, the independence of which was provided for in the constitution. The Supreme Court was given both the task of interpreting congressional acts when their meaning is disputed, and the task of examining Federal and state statutes and executive actions to see if they conform to the constitution in cases that are disputed. Except in cases involving ambassadors and foreign states, it does not take the initiative: as an appellate court it considers only cases brought before it. A ruling by the court that an action or statute is unconstitutional can be overruled only by an amendment to the constitution (which it is very hard for anyone to get through) or by a new ruling if the court changes its opinion. The Supreme Court is by design the highest power, vested with authority to check the president and the Congress. The fathers of the constitution laid down that the justices should be appointed by the president, subject to the consent of the senate, and that they should have life tenure (removable only by impeachment, of which there has been only one case), 'because they deemed the risk of the continuance in office of an incompetent judge a lesser evil than the subservience of all judges to the legislature, which might flow from a tenure dependent on legislative will.'[45] Similar terms of appointment and tenure are enjoyed by the judges of the Federal circuit and district courts.

The power and independence of the Supreme Court were built up early in the nineteenth century under the leadership of the great Chief Justice Marshall, who presided over the Supreme Court from 1801 to 1835. The court has been through periods when it has been under attack for having made rulings that were widely held to be out of step with the tide of political opinion, notably a ruling in 1857 concerning slavery, and various rulings made between 1935 and 1937 which stopped the implementation of several major items of President's Roosevelt's New Deal legislation on the grounds that they were unconstitutional. Several presidents have made abortive attempts to abolish or modify life tenure so that they could pack the court with justices of their liking during their time at the White House. But the independence of the Supreme Court has survived, and Supreme Court justices are among the most highly respected persons in American society.

The court appears to have benefited from the high standing of lawyers in American society, from the strength of American legal tradition, and in particular from the fact that, as in England, the justices come from the Bar and want the respect of all those at the bar who will scrutinize the judgements they make. Bryce observed at the end of the nineteenth century that although presidents appoint only men from their own party, no member of the Supreme Court has ever been suspected of corruption:

> The Federal judge who has recently quitted the ranks of the bar remains in sympathy with it, respects its views, desires its approbation. Both his inbred professional habits, and his respect for those traditions which the bar prizes, restrain him from prostituting his office to party objects. Though he has usually been a politician, and owes his promotion to his party, his political trappings drop off him when he mounts the Supreme bench. He has now nothing to fear from party displeasure, because he is irremovable (except by impeachment), nothing to hope from party favour, because he is at the top of the tree and can climb no further. Virtue has all the external conditions in her favour...the new-made judge has left partisanship behind him, while no doubt usually retaining that bias or tendency of his mind which party training produces.[46]

Below the carefully designed Federal judicial system for the appointment of judges there is what, by comparison, can only be called a mess. I refer to the systems for appointing judges in the member states and their cities and counties. After the War of Independence, the colonial system, whereby state justices were appointed in most states by the governor, usually for life, and so enjoyed a high measure of independence, was at first largely undisturbed: the power of appointment of state justices simply passed to the elected governor when he replaced the crown-appointed governor. But continuity was soon disturbed. In the period 1812 to 1860, when the United States experienced a wave of populist democracy, of which President Jackson was the most conspicuous practitioner, some of the former colonies transferred responsibility for selecting judges to the people, whose choice was then to be expressed through regular popular elections. As a corollary of the change, the tenure of state judges was limited to the period between elections instead of being for life. The state where the results were most notorious was New York, which in 1846 introduced popular election for all judicial appointments. But more important than these changes in the old states (i.e. the ex-colonies) was the adoption of popular election of judges for limited terms of office by many of the new states that were springing up to the west. This happened at the time of the influx into the old and new states of new immigrants, many of whom had little habitual respect for the law and its officers.

To this day, popular election is a common method of appointing judges in the states and localities. The position is not easy to assess since a wide variety of methods is used to select state judges; almost no two states are alike, and many do not employ the same method for choosing judges at all levels of their judiciary. In 1985, the position was this:[47]

1. The governor, advised by a commission,
   selects some or all of their judicial officers............. 31 states
2. The Governor appoints judges without
   using a nominating commission.......................... 3 states
3. The legislature appoints or elects most,
   if not all, of the judges.................................... 4 states
4. Partisan elections are held to select
   a. most or all judges.................................... 13 states
   b. some judges.. 8 states
5. Non-partisan elections are held to select
   a. most or all judges................................... 17 states
   b. some judges.. 8 states

It is hard to judge how bad are the effects of appointing judges by popular election. I have only fragments of evidence. In New York at the end of the nineteenth century, the party apparatus at Tammany sold judgeships and other government posts on the excuse that the price served to pay for the election expenses incurred in getting the candidate elected. The price of a judgeship was then estimated at $15,000.[48]

In the United States, concern about the integrity of state judges has been sufficiently strong to have moved many states to introduce improved machinery for investigating the conduct of judges, usually in the form of commissions of seven to nine members comprising lay persons, judges and attorneys who operate with a mandate from the state legislature.[49] But there is no unanimity of opinion about the pros and cons of choosing judges by popular election. The spirit of Jacksonian democracy, which led to the introduction of short-term elected judges in so many states on the grounds that the judges should be closely accountable to the people, lives on and is roused whenever there is a populist reaction against government, as there has been recently. In 1996, Justice Stevens of the Supreme Court spoke out, declaring that electing state judges is a 'profoundly unwise' practice. A newspaper report of his speech set out the nature of his concern.

> Persons who undertake the task of administering justice impartially should not be required – indeed they should not be permitted – to finance campaigns or to curry the favour of voters by making predictions or promises about how they will decide cases before they have heard any evidence or argument.

Stevens told lawyers at an American Bar Association convention. Stevens urged the ABA to continue screening candidates for the federal judiciary, a practice conservative Republicans want to end.

> In those jurisdictions that continue the most unwise practice of electing their judges – a practice that in my judgement is comparable to allowing football fans to elect the referees – an impartial appraisal of the integrity, the temperament and the competence of the prospective judge is an essential guide to informed voting... A campaign promise to be 'tough on crime' or to 'enforce the death penalty' is evidence of bias that should disqualify a candidate from sitting in criminal cases.[50]

Thus, in the United States the pursuit of democracy by politicians writing constitutions has produced an independent and uncorrupt judiciary at the top but lower down produced results that vary from good to rotten.

Conclusion

In the European countries we have considered, two developments have been necessary to the development of an independent judiciary. The ruler or rulers must have been persuaded to surrender power over the judiciary, and a legal elite must have evolved which, through its efficiency and integrity, has gained the respect of society and is able, if necessary, to stand up to government ministers. To establish and maintain the required elite, judges have been given security of tenure; and the selection and promotion of judges, or the provision of advice on those matters, has been largely entrusted to the judiciary (including, in England, the Bar, from which judges are drawn). This practice makes sense, just as it makes sense to leave the selection and promotion of doctors, accountants, soldiers and other professionals to their peers and superiors, sometimes with an admixture of outsiders to see fair play. All our three European countries have an established legal elite; the independence of the judiciary is rather well established in England and Germany; in France a struggle is now taking place in which the judiciary, for the moment at least, has gained ground.

The United States is rather different. It is a democracy that came into being through an act of creation, rather than a process of evolution; limits on the powers of the executive were written into its constitution from the start. Under the provisions of the Federal constitution and the various state constitutions, the legal elite's influence on judicial appointments is less than that of the European legal elites, particularly at the state level, and the influence of the politicians and the electorate greater. All the same, the United States has a highly respected and vocal legal elite, centred in the American Bar Association and the universities.

Aside from the special case of the United States, the evolution of an independent judiciary has come about slowly and in different ways in the four countries I have looked at; and one knows it has rarely occurred on an enduring basis in other parts of the world. Competition for power, which shapes the evolution of society, has not often produced surrender of power to the judiciary.

9

The Twentieth Century

The Start of the Century

At the beginning of the twentieth century conditions in the United States were different from those in Europe. Corruption had burgeoned after the civil war. It was being exposed by the 'muckrakers', but reform had scarcely begun.

In the three European countries, the public services – the civil service, the armed forces and the judiciary – had become modern professional elites. Of course these elites differed: in each nation, the public services were cast in a particular mould derived from its political and cultural history. But they had much in common: as a rule (to which there were exceptions) selection was by open competition; the successful candidates were given a secure career, relatively high status and the exercise of considerable power; and the services of which they became members, particularly those of Britain and Germany, had achieved a reputation for high standards of honesty. In these conditions the perpetuation or enhancement of the elites depended importantly on its members being seen to be honest; and their careers as individuals depended on their being honest. There was an incentive to be honest that tended to be self-perpetuating; the elites could live on – so long as the politicians found that they were well served by them and not obstructed in the pursuit of their political aims.

The institutional setting in which politicians operated was different. The pursuit of power by a politician was not and is not a matter of being selected on merit and joining an institution where promotion depends on being well behaved. Since hereditary monarchies were swept away, it has been a matter of gaining public support, whether as an elected person or unelected ruler; of out-manoeuvring rivals; of buying supporters with promises of office; of raising funds for propaganda, particularly when elections approach; of gaining the support of the media by pleasing and rewarding media owners. There is an incentive to be corrupt.

Indeed a cynic might go further and say that, except in societies where corruption is so visible and so severely frowned upon that it does not pay, the pursuit of power by politicians is a competition in seeing who can get away with more corruption. Moreover, perhaps remembering the Latin tag *Quis custodiet ipsos custodes?*, he would note that it is a competition in which the rules, and their enforcement, are not independent of the players: it is politicians themselves who are ultimately responsible for enacting laws which define what is corrupt and which lay down how those rules shall be enforced; they are often responsible for deciding what should be done by way of establishing an enquiry when there is a scandal; and when they seize power by force, they suspend or bend the existing rules to suit their ends.

It is worth considering for a moment how this kind of competition in corruption between politicians works in a democratic system, thinking of it as a game. If one of two players (A) acts corruptly in a manner that gives him an advantage in gaining votes, for example, by secretly raising electoral funds by forbidden means, his opponent (B) risks losing votes if he does not do the same: corruption by one player induces it in the other. But if B can uncover what A has done and publicly denounce him, B may win if two conditions are satisfied: firstly, the electorate is not so cynical as to be indifferent to corruption and secondly, B is confident he can demonstrate that he has not engaged in any corruption which A can uncover, thereby making it quits. If the two players know that they have acted corruptly in what the public will perceive to be equal degree neither has an incentive to denounce the other – except in so far as one of them may believe that by taking the initiative and playing Mr Clean he may gain support, perhaps because he has greater influence with the media.

Of course political competition is not always as mean as that, but it often is.

During the twentieth century many factors that bear on the quality of government changed. I shall concentrate on a few: the increase in the scale of government; the change in social values; the change in nature of military competition; the effects of the Cold War; and the internationalization of government.

The Scale of Government

The creation of the welfare state and the growing involvement of government in the regulation of the economy caused a huge growth in government. In 1880 total government expenditure (by central and local government) averaged only 10 per cent of the total national output (GDP) in our four countries; in 1981 it averaged 44 per cent – or no less than 47 per cent if the United States is excluded:[1]

	1880	1913	1929	1938	1950	1960	1973	1981	1997
France	11	10	12	22	28	34	39	49	54
Germany	10	18	31	42	30	33	41	49	48
UK	9	13	24	29	34	33	42	44	40
USA	n/a	8	10	10	23	28	31	32	32
Average	10	12	19	26	29	32	38	44	44

Behind the figures for 1880 lies the nineteenth century world of untamed capitalism. The protection of workers against disease, insanitary surroundings, hunger, illiteracy and poverty in old age was in its infancy: the role of the government was still confined to providing armed forces to defend – or expand – the nation, to maintaining law and order so as to protect life and property, and to gathering sufficient tax to perform those functions, and also the few regulatory and social functions that had by then been introduced.

Germany led the field in the introduction of social spending at the end of the nineteenth century; Britain followed. In 1929 government expenditure in both Britain and Germany was well over 20 per cent of GDP; in France and the United States it was about 10 per cent.[2] Indeed the British figures provide some statistical support, for what it is worth, for Runciman's well-argued claim that British society underwent its most important recent evolutionary change during and after the First World War, rather than after the Second World War.[3] The figures for France and the United States increased between 1929 and 1938 when both countries took steps to relieve the distress of unemployment and France began to rearm.

After the Second World War the figures were driven up as health and other welfare services were made comprehensive in the European countries, and by the Cold War. Military spending took a substantial part of government expenditure in the 1950s in all of our four countries – though less in Germany, which had been disarmed, than elsewhere; military spending was reduced again as the Cold War became a military stalemate and then ended:[4]

Military Spending as a Percentage of GDP

	1954	1996
France	7.3	3.0
Germany	4.0	1.7
UK	8.8	3.0
USA	11.6	3.6

While military spending declined, civil spending was increased in the 1960s by the augmentation of welfare services and, after 1973, by changes in the numbers eligible for state services and benefits: the number of persons unemployed increased greatly and so did the number of old people requiring pensions, medical care and social care. Despite these pressures, Britain, by squeezing the standard and cost of social benefits and services – for example, by depressing public-sector pay and by freezing the real value of the state old age pension rather than letting it rise with real wages – reduced government expenditure as a per cent of GDP between 1981 and 1997.

On the tax side, the two world wars were occasions when citizens of combatant countries were persuaded to accept new and higher taxes and, in Britain at least, social needs were exposed and were met by the government as civilians were mobilized and attacked from the air.[5] When peace was restored, taxation was not reduced again to the pre-war level, but the importance of this wartime ratchet effect on tax levels should not be exaggerated: in all four countries taxation, including social insurance contributions, was greatly increased in peacetime to pay for welfare spending.

Changing Values

Since old men, of whom I am one, usually think the world has gone to the dogs, any opinion I could offer about how moral values and social behaviour have changed in the twentieth century would be of little value. I feel sure that in Britain respect for authority and moral restraint in behaviour have declined since the middle of the century, but I shall not say more in general terms. My particular interest is in how attitudes to the quality and scale of government have changed, and here something rather specific has happened. By the end of the nineteenth century the ideas of the Enlightenment were in a remarkable degree victorious. Political thought of many schools gave backing to demands for more government. In the words of Anthony Quinton, describing England, 'At the end of the Victorian age, for all the tenacity of natural-law liberalism, active political thinking at all levels was dominated by the presumption of the omnicompetence of the state.'[6] This presumption flowed on into the twentieth century through the period in which welfare states were created and expanded in response to the demands of the masses. But in the last part of the twentieth century there has been a reaction. The view that more government improves the lot of the citizen has been challenged. The challengers have played upon the unpopularity of high taxation and of welfare scroungers and have propagated market economic doctrines, according to which government should be reduced in scope as far as possible for the sake of liberty and efficiency; tax should be cut, the bureaucracy should be shaken up; competition and the pursuit of private interest should be encouraged; capitalism should be unbridled. The extreme slogans have been 'Greed is good' (Mr Ivan Boesky) and 'There is no such thing as society' (Mrs Thatcher). These messages have been embraced and pursued most energetically by governments in the United States and Britain, less so in France and Germany.

The Changing Nature of Military Competition

In the first half of the century the outcome of the two world wars depended in an unprecedented manner on the relative ability of the participants to mobilize, by taxation and by command, their industrial resources and manpower for use in total war against their enemies.[7] Britain, Germany and the Soviet Union each managed at the peak of the Second World War to divert about 50 per cent of its GDP to the military – admittedly helped by supplies from abroad amounting to about 5 per cent of GDP, which in the case of Britain and the Soviet Union came from the United States, and in the case of Germany came as plunder from the countries it occupied, principally its rich neighbours to its west. It was an astonishing performance. But it cannot be said that efficient or 'clean' government triumphed over the dirty, except perhaps in the case of the defeat of Russia, crippled by rotten government in the First World War. In the Second World War, Germany, for example, had an efficient system ruled by tyrants and so, in wartime, did the Soviet Union; one was defeated, the other victorious. There followed the Cold War, a climactic episode that lasted 40 years and brought about such great changes in military technology that military competition and warfare seem to have been radically changed. Several aspects of it merit attention.

First, there is the change in the nature of military competition. In the two world wars resources had been devoted for a few years to the mass production of weapons destined for mass destruction in battle; in the Cold War resources were devoted for 40 years to the scientific and technological development of ever more destructive weapons which mostly were never used. The development of nuclear weapons can be seen as the genesis of this change. Nuclear weapons discouraged aggression. And their extremely costly development was a precedent that encouraged the principal powers – the United States, the Soviet Union, Britain, China and France – to keep pouring scientific and technological resources into military research and development almost regardless of cost, in the hope of keeping up with or getting ahead of one another in new weaponry. At the height of the Cold War at least a fifth and possibly as much as two-fifths of all scientists and engineers engaged in research and development in the United States and Soviet Union were working for the military. Since the total number of qualified scientists and engineers was far greater than it had been before 1950 and was growing rapidly, the annual scientific and technological effort devoted to military ends was vastly greater than anything known before.[8] So intense, prolonged and technically successful was this cold arms race that destructive power has become superabundant and, compared with earlier times, cheap. Broadly speaking, the new destructive power has come in two forms.

1. There are minor weapons, meaning automatic firearms, explosives, land mines, mobile telephones and similar apparatus. These have become so efficient, so cheap to produce and so abundant that almost any dissident group in any part of the world wanting to assert itself militarily has been able to do so, usually with the economic help of sympathizers at home and abroad;

and it has become extremely costly, if not impossible, for the government of any nation to subdue a dissident minority or conquer another nation and rule it in peace – as distinct from driving out its people or slaughtering them. It has been estimated that there are now about 500 million small arms and light weapons in circulation in the world, one for every twelve people.[9] Gone long ago is the time when we Europeans could subdue other continents because we had firearms and the local peoples had not. In 1999 it was reported that an AK-47 assault rifle could be bought in Uganda for the price of a chicken.[10]

2. There are major weapons systems, the leading species of which are advanced aircraft, missiles and warships which, in combination with modern sensors, provide a capacity to bombard an enemy's armed forces and people with 'conventional' explosives and incendiary devices, or with weapons of mass destruction, i.e. nuclear, chemical and biological devices. These are expensive; they have been of limited use in overcoming military power of the first kind; they have principally served to produce mutual deterrence and to permit major powers to engage in punitive, but usually strategically rather unproductive, bombardment of nations that do not have the capability to retaliate. It has rarely, if ever, proved possible by remote bombardment to change frontiers or conquer and pacify a people. Recently, the greatly increased accuracy of long-range weapons and sensors now possessed by the USA but not yet possessed by other nations may have made it possible to 'decapitate' a weak and exposed nation from afar by destroying its leadership, for example, Afghanistan today. The long-run political consequences of such action cannot be predicted.

These developments have broken the old positive effect of military competition. For the cheapening of destructive power has meant that mobilization of a large part of a nation's resources by a relatively uncorrupt and efficient government is no longer a prerequisite of military power. That is an important change, but it is not all. Two other developments have made it less necessary than before, and in some cases wholly unnecessary, for governments in many parts of the world to raise tax revenue in order to acquire military power.

Firstly, there has been a shift from traditional wars to what Mary Kaldor has called 'identity wars'. These have been numerous in the former territories of the Soviet Union and Yugoslavia, and in the post-colonial states of Africa. In these wars, groups of people who feel bound together – or can be led to believe that they are bound together – by religious, ethnic or other social bonds fight to rid themselves of dominance by, or the presence of, rival groups. Many kinds of fighting unit – regular forces or the remnants thereof; paramilitary groups; self-defence units; foreign mercenaries and regular foreign troops under international auspices conduct these informal wars. The military aim of those seeking autonomy is not to fight battles but to make life unbearable for those people it cannot control with a view to driving them out; for this purpose they calculatedly commit rape and other atrocities; by far the greater proportion of the casualties has been civilian. The combatants intentionally destroy productive activity and orderly administration and rely for resources on predatory acts of many kinds – loot, robbery, hostage-taking, 'protection' and 'war taxes', partly extorted at checkpoints established by rival groups; and on foreign assistance from a variety of sources – sympathetic foreign governments, aid agencies whose supplies are subjected to 'duties' or are simply looted, and emigrants who send money back to their families or contribute it to fighting organizations, as Irish Americans have done to the IRA.[11]

Secondly, Third World countries with rich deposits of oil and minerals (for example, gold, diamonds, uranium and copper) have been able, by granting concessions to exploit these natural deposits to companies from the industrial countries, to obtain rich royalties with which they can buy arms and the services of military advisers and mercenaries from the industrial countries.[12] Sometimes there have been direct 'oil-for-arms' deals. Those who rule countries of this kind have had no need to develop the economy of their country and establish an administration capable of collecting and handling tax and public expenditure efficiently in order to acquire military power: they have not needed to build nation states in the European manner. They have needed only to grant a concession to a foreign company to make a hole in the ground and take away what they find. The foreign company pays royalties to the government, out of which remarkably large sums have often gone to the ruler's personal bank account in a safe haven. Which of course explains why in these countries persons of greed and ambition, including military men, compete fiercely for power and possession of their nation's royalty income, and why they commonly spend so much on buying arms and the services of mercenaries which they believe will help them stay in power and help them to defend their resource-rich territory. It also explains why many resource-rich countries, mostly in Africa, have lapsed into corrupt tyranny, strife and economic decay instead of achieving economic development and improvements in life for their people.[13]

The Effect of the Cold War in Advanced Countries

As between the main contestants, the Cold War can be read as the triumph of the less corrupt over the more corrupt: as the Soviet Union struggled to keep up with the United States in the arms race, its command economy became progressively more corrupt and ossified until the Soviet government gave up the race, released its empire in eastern Europe and fell apart. What has followed in Russia and the other members of the Soviet Union has commonly been extreme corruption and lawlessness. The collapse of society under the pressures of military competition and rotten government has not had positive effects such as occurred in France when, after the French revolution, a similar collapse brought to power Napoleon who radically reformed the system of government. There are of course all kinds of reasons for this difference, but the significant point here is that military competition was different in the two cases. France after the Revolution was threatened by defeat in 'hot' war and adopted a military autocrat who, by military victories, could rally the nation and make it accept reform. The Soviet Union, while it had experienced something of that kind in the post-revolutionary civil war, faced in the Cold War an economic test of the relative ability of the contestants to develop and produce new arms. Defeat took the form of economic failure, a demoralizing experience, not a lost battle to which there could be a positive military response.

The Cold War had damaging effects on standards of government all over the world. Unlike the two world wars, it did not induce – or did not induce for long – a willingness amongst the peoples of NATO or the Warsaw Pact to make personal sacrifices or put national interest before personal interest. Rather, as the Cold War dragged on for 40 years, it induced resignation, punctuated by protest when, as in the case of the United States in Vietnam and the Soviet Union in Afghanistan, many servicemen were killed, and also when decisions to add more nuclear weapons to the huge numbers already deployed seemed to many people to be more menacing than reassuring. (By the 1980s the two superpowers together had about 50,000 nuclear weapons.)

Governments on each side lowered their peacetime standards of conduct as they sought to do each other damage by means of illicit actions short of war. Of course governments have always done these things, particularly in time of war. But in the Cold War illicit practices were a substitute for war; they were conducted with a extraordinary intensity for an extraordinarily long time, leaving two legacies that have been conspicuous in corruption scandals since the Cold War ended – the use of falsehoods by ministers and officials to cover up what they have been doing, and the involvement of ministers and officials in arms deals made by corrupt means.

The Habit of Mendacity

The way that western governments were sucked into the habit of mendacity in matters related to 'national security' can be seen most clearly in the USA where many official documents have now been made public under their Freedom of Information Act.[14] As early as 1948, President Truman, following a proposal by George Kennan, the head of the State Department planning staff, signed an order which stated that 'taking cognisance of the vicious covert activities of the USSR, its satellite countries and Communist groups to discredit and defeat the aims and activities of the USA and other Western powers', the CIA should create an office to plan and engage in:

> ...propaganda; economic warfare; preventive direct action, including sabotage, anti-sabotage, demolition and evacuation measures; subversion against hostile states, including assistance to underground resistance movements, guerrillas and refugee liberation movements, and support of indigenous anti-communist elements in threatened countries of the free world.[15]

The same document adopted the principle of 'plausible deniability'. This ordained that covert operations were to be:

> ...so planned and executed that any US government responsibility for them is not evident to unauthorized persons and that if uncovered the US government can plausibly deny any responsibility for them.

Some such instruction is of course a necessary accompaniment to covert operations, but one marvels at this Jesuitical descriptor – the principle of plausible deniability.

Following this order, covert operations were conducted with remarkable frequency and vigour, but not always with success, by the United States all over the world. Of course the Soviet Union was doing the same things, and on both sides the allies of the super-powers were drawn into covert activities and the harvesting of intelligence. Britain and France with their imperial links in the Third World must have been quite heavily involved, but compared with the United States they are still secretive about what went on.

It is easy to feel critical of the ruthless way in which corrupt practices were used covertly in the Cold War by the West, but one must ask oneself what would have happened if they had not been used: how widely would communism have prevailed and how corrupt would it have been? How necessary was it to corrupt democracy in order to save it? How far did the politicians and the agencies that conducted covert activities run wild? Fortunately, these questions, which are unanswerable, are irrelevant to this study. What concerns me is what effect the intensive practice of covert activities during the Cold War had on the quality of government in our four countries and what their legacy has been.

In the United States mendacity and the use of covert operations seem to have reached a peak in the Nixon–Kissinger era with the secret bombing of Cambodia, the widespread use of covert operations abroad and eventually the use of covert operations at home for electoral purposes which brought Nixon's presidency to an end. The flavour of the period is conveyed by the manuscript notes that Dick Helms, the director of the CIA, took down when President Nixon, in the presence of Messrs Kissinger and Mitchell, instructed him to take action against President Allende of Chile before Allende had assumed office:

> One in 10 chance perhaps, but save Chile!
> worth spending
> not concerned risks involved
> no involvement of Embassy
> $10,000,000 available, more if necessary
> full time job – best men we have
> game plan

make economy scream

48 hours for plan of action[16]

A month later a CIA cable to the station chief in Santiago said:

> It is the firm and continuing policy that Allende be overthrown by
> a coup... We are to continue to generate pressure toward this end
> utilizing every appropriate resource. It is imperative that these
> actions be implemented clandestinely and securely so that United
> States Government and American hands be well hidden.[17]

Kissinger once joked, 'The illegal we do immediately; the unconstitutional takes a bit longer.'[18]

What matters is that ministers and government employees, civil
and military, acquired the habit of misleading the public on an extraordinarily large scale for an extraordinarily long time; and official
secrecy, which is used and abused to prevent the public knowing the
truth, became entrenched. In the words of Patrick Moynihan, writing
in 1998 about the USA, 'The Cold War has bequeathed to us a vast
secrecy system that shows no sign of receding'.[19] On the other hand, it
has become harder for governments to enforce secrecy laws since the
Cold War has ended and appeals to the interests of national security
have become less convincing to potential miscreants and to those who
enforce the law.

The Cold War and Competition for Natural Resources

Many Western covert and overt military operations were motivated, in
part at least, by the view, which may have been fearfully exaggerated,
that the West's supplies of raw materials and oil were threatened by
communist intrusion into Third World countries. A feeling of
vulnerability was understandable. The Soviet Union with its vast
territory and varied natural resources was largely self-sufficient in oil
and raw materials; the West, in need of increasing supplies for its growing
industrial production, depended heavily on imports from Third World
countries into which the communist countries, including China, sought
in fits and starts to expand their sphere of influence. Western

governments used diplomacy plus overt and covert military operations to counter the Communists.[20] Meanwhile western firms paid rulers to obtain concessions to extract oil and minerals.

The business of obtaining oil and mineral concessions has always been conducive to the use of bribes, commissions, gifts and favours, and remains so since there are huge 'rents' (i.e. windfall profits) to be shared by the parties to a deal. In principle, concessions of this kind, which nowadays normally belong to the state, can be auctioned and, if the auctions are honestly conducted, there should be no opportunity for the buyers to bribe the sellers. But Third World governments rarely use auctions. They commonly sell concessions by negotiation. For which there are some good reasons. It is often necessary for the foreign company that buys a concession to build infrastructure, such as ports, pipelines, roads and dormitory towns for their staff; to make this worthwhile, a whole oil field or major mineral deposit has to be given to one foreign company, rather than split between many competitors; and that one company, which will become the source of a significant, perhaps dominant, part of the nation's revenue, will acquire substantial economic power *vis-à-vis* the government. Hence strategic and diplomatic considerations enter the calculation: the government will want to give the concession to a company backed by a government which it believes will be helpful to it in its international relations – and in supplying it with arms and mercenaries. But alongside these reasons for using negotiation, there is the prospect of bribes. Those who run a government that has a concession to sell will know that negotiation creates a strong incentive to the potential buyers to offer them bribes: they will know that from the point of view of the buyers, a sum that will add only a small percentage to, say, a billion dollar deal, will be worth paying in order to win the concession. Once negotiation is adopted as the means of allocating concessions, the dominant incentive is for bidders to engage competitively in the bribery of local rulers and fixers. It can be argued that the legitimacy of their actions in paying rulers depends on the nature of the Third World regime. In the case of hereditary monarchies of a feudal kind, such as exist in the Middle East, it will be necessary and appropriate under local law to make payments to the ruler and for him to decide how much to spend on himself and how much on his people. If a ruler has come to power and rules under a modern constitution, payments to the personal account of the ruler, rather than to the national treasury, will be illegal. If a ruler has seized power and suspended a modern constitution, payments to his personal account have yet another kind of illegitimacy. In all these cases the payment of 'commissions' to members of the ruler's family or his entourage is commonly the price of access to the ruler.

But the aspect of the problem that concerns me most is the apparent tendency for bribery, which is intense in the business of seeking resource concessions and selling arms, to become a secret habit of western firms and politicians that infects their domestic political behaviour. Of this there has been considerable evidence in scandals that have occurred recently in Britain, France and Germany. Most of these scandals have been about bribery by arms traders, on which more later. There has, however, recently been a revealing scandal over bribery in obtaining oil concessions. This concerns Elf Aquitaine, the French oil company. In an investigation into the Elf's affairs, it was found (with the assistance of the Swiss legal authorities) that between 1990 and 1997, when Elf was state-owned, more than 600 million French francs (more than £60 million at today's prices) had passed through the Swiss bank accounts of Monsieur André Tarallo, a senior Elf manager of Corsican origin who was so influential in running Elf's African affairs and so close to some African heads of state that he was known as the 'Monsieur Afrique' of Elf Aquitaine. M. Tarallo explained that the money was for the execution of commitments made by the company (which they labelled 'contrats de souveraineté') under which secret 'rémunérations' were made to African presidents. He argued that such payments were normal in the oil industry and were needed to improve the chances of gaining concessions. Le Monde published an outspoken editorial commenting on the affair:

> For too long French policy in Africa has been neither moral nor effective. So much is vividly confirmed by the enquiry into the Swiss accounts of Monsieur Tarallo and the interview which this important manager of Elf has given to Le Monde...
>
> It would be wrong to deny that corruption is indispensable in the obtaining of drilling concessions, though that does not mean that one should not try to stop it. M. Tarallo is unfortunately right when he says that all petrol companies use it... But the sins of others do not absolve Elf. Added to which it is a special case. Created by the political authorities to ensure that France is supplied with petrol, Elf has used its money to keep in power dictators whose principal aim has been not the development of their country but their personal enrichment. In exchange, Paris

could count on their support in its diplomatic battles and could offer captive markets to French firms...

This 'neo-colonialism' was put in place during the presidency of General de Gaulle and has been maintained by subsequent governments regardless of party... No one can doubt that the payments made by Elf to the African leaders received the approval of the highest authorities in the French state...

Looked at today the picture is not glorious. A former colonial power has taught corruption to its African clients – who were willing pupils – and there is nothing to persuade us that they have not rewarded their friends in Paris...[21]

Colourful evidence of the use of bribes is to be found in biographies of Armand Hammer and Tiny Rowland, two buccaneers who challenged the established oil and mining corporations and obtained concessions in the African continent.[22] Periodically stories also appear about the antics of the big established corporations.

In one case at least, lack of natural resources has apparently been an incentive to anticorruption policies: the tough ruler of Singapore, Lee Kuan Yew, is reported to have said that he came down hard on the corrupt because his tiny country with no natural resources has to rely on its good name to remain a centre of banking and technology.[23]

Bribery in The Arms Trade

The arms trade and the corruption around it burgeoned in the Cold War. Of course, bribery in the arms trade is not new; there is convincing evidence of it in the late nineteenth century and the first half of the twentieth century, not to mention what Pepys's diaries tell us about the British navy in the late seventeenth century and what we learn about the skulduggery connected with Beaumarchais, the clock-maker turned rogue courtier and dramatist upon whose comedies the operas *The Marriage of Figaro* and *The Barber of Seville* are based. In 1801, two years after his death, Beaumarchais' heirs sued the American government for money due to his estate for arms and ammunition that he had secretly supplied on behalf of the French king to the American revolutionaries during the War of Independence; remarkably, the claims were settled 34 years later by a grant from the American Congress.[24]

The Cold War arms race enhanced the opportunities for corruption in the arms trade. Technical advances made major weapons systems more complex and costly, and consequently made contracts for them fewer and more valuable. The choices of buyers could be influenced, and could afterwards be justified, to an unusual degree by claims, fair or foul, about the performance of what was offered. The weapons might never be tested in war and were often still under development when they were being sold. Moreover, the decisions to buy are finally made in secret by one or two people at the top of government.

The evidence of bribery in the arms trade, like all evidence of corrupt goings-on, comes principally from scandals that were revealed by chance and were followed by public inquiries. The most important of these was in the United States. In what follows I have drawn freely on Anthony Sampson's excellent book, *The Arms Bazaar*.[25]

The American scandal occurred when, during the investigation into the Watergate scandal, word came out that Northrop, an aerospace company, had given $75,000 in cash ostensibly to President Nixon's election campaign fund but in fact for his secret fund for the defence of the covert operatives who, on his behalf, had burgled the Democratic Party's headquarters in the Watergate building in Washington. From this evidence the SEC, the regulatory body responsible for the financial conduct of US companies, perceived that a new field of illegal company behaviour was being uncovered and forced Northrop to make disclosures about what they had been doing in the way of bribery. The disclosures so shocked the chairman of the Senate Committee on Multinational Corporations, Senator Church, that in the 1970s he persuaded his committee to launch an enquiry that laid bare, in particular, the way two aerospace firms, Lockheed and Northrop, had competed with each another and with other firms, American and foreign, in the use of bribes to gain export orders.

Lockheed, which appears to have behaved most wildly, admitted they had paid at least $22 million, which they believed had gone to officials and political organizations in foreign countries. (The use of middlemen makes it difficult for bribers to know the true destination of their money.) They had paid no less than $106 million in commissions to Mr Khashoggi, the most colourful Arab middleman in the arms trade whose skills were such that he was also working for Lockheed's rivals, Northrop, and was being richly paid by them. Lockheed used in their defence the argument, which, as we have seen, is always invoked in defence of corruption: they were behaving no worse than others; they pointed a finger at the French.

One cannot know whether Lockheed's behaviour, as revealed by the Church Committee and by the subsequent enquiries in countries where persons had been bribed, was worse than that of its competitors. To the innocent it seems extreme. Thus Lockheed, using various rum Europeans as middlemen, corrupted Prince Bernhard of the Netherlands, who was on the board of many companies, Inspector General of the Netherlands Armed Forces and altogether a highly influential man, but allegedly a philanderer who needed money to sustain his louche way of life. After the Church Committee had revealed that he had been paid $1 million when the Dutch government bought the Lockheed Starfighter, a Dutch enquiry, before which he pleaded loss of memory, found him guilty, causing him to resign all public positions in disgrace. Another alleged recipient of *largesse* from Lockheed was Franz-Josef Strauss whose political party in West Germany was said, by a rather unpredictable witness, to have been paid $12 million as a reward for his decision, when he was minister of defence, to buy Starfighters. Despite an uproar in Germany, this was never confirmed; Strauss, who fought back, had removed the vital papers when he left the ministry of defence.

But it was in Japan that Lockheed's antics seem to have been wildest. In a most tangled campaign to sell their Tristar civilian airliner they made payments in three directions. A company called Marubini was the official agent and received about $3 million in commission payments on the sale. Also, Lockheed secretly employed a man called Kodama. He, having been jailed for war crimes, had risen, principally by dealing in arms, until he had become one of the most powerful men in Japan, operating as 'a shadow manipulator in right-wing politics' and known to the Left as 'the monster'.[26] He was paid $6.3 million, some of it purportedly to be passed on to others. Finally there was the prime minister, Mr Tanaka, to whom $1.7 million was paid via the managing director of Marubini. The payments to Mr Kodama and to the prime minister had to be made in cash. For this tricky task Lockheed used Deak and Co., a New York firm that had been set up by a Hungarian who had been in the OSS, the forerunner of the CIA, and specialized in discreetly transferring money around the world. It had 20 subsidiary offices abroad and is believed to have served the CIA. To pay Kodama, Deak's Los Angeles office sent the money to Hong Kong, whence it was carried to Tokyo by a former priest called José Aramiya. The $1.7 million for the prime minister was taken from Deak's Hong Kong office to Tokyo neatly stuffed in cardboard orange-boxes.[27] Not much had changed in the 250 years since Mr Elde placed his 5,000 guineas in a basket and carried them by sedan chair across London to Lord Macclesfied.[28]

It is not just the buccaneering arms salesmen of the USA or the *méchant* French who have resorted to bribery. The leading arms firms in virtually every major arms-producing country have been implicated, including reputable firms from most respectable countries, for example, Oerlikon of Switzerland and Bofors of Sweden, not to mention Rolls-Royce who were reported in 1997 to have agreed to settle out of court with a Panamanian-registered company closely linked to 'prominent Saudi nationals'. This company had issued a writ in the English High Court claiming that Rolls had reneged on promises to pay commissions, variously put at 8 per cent and 15 per cent, on sales of aero engines to Saudi Arabia under the huge A1 Yamamah arms deal negotiated by Mrs Thatcher, a deal with reference to which it had been claimed that there had been no agents and no commissions.[29]

Nor have bribes been paid only to buyers in the Third World, with respect to which it is commonly argued that bribery, overt or disguised, is normal and therefore necessary. Besides Prince Bernhard of the Netherlands, Mr Tanaka of Japan and Mr Strauss of Germany, who have already been mentioned, those who have been brought down by scandals connected with the arms trade include two Italian ministers of defence and several Belgian ministers, including Mr Claes, who became the secretary-general of NATO and, more recently, Mr Aitken in Britain and Mr Kohl in Germany – though the sum Mr Kohl received from an arms trader is far smaller than that which he is alleged to have received from M. Mitterand via Elf Aquitaine in connection with the purchase of an oil refinery in East Germany by that company.

Bribery in the arms trade has not subsided since the ending of the Cold War. On the contrary, as military spending has been cut back the arms firms have been seeking markets abroad more fiercely than before. According to the revelations of Mr Said Ayas, the Lebanese middleman who was Mr Aitken's partner in arranging commissions on arms deals on behalf of a Saudi Arabian prince, he negotiated the following rates of commission with British arms firms in 1993 and 1995: 3 per cent on a contract with GEC for frigates, 10 per cent on a contract with VSEL for submarines, 9.5 per cent on a contract with Westland for anti-submarine helicopters.[30] One recent estimate reckons that in the international arms trade 'roughly $2.5 billion a year is paid in bribes, nearly a tenth of turnover'.[31]

For our purposes the relevant feature of the arms trade is that, in the countries with which we are concerned, government ministers, civil servants and military officers have become so intimately involved in the arms export business that they must have been unable to avoid condoning bribery (for example, by turning a blind eye to it), if not encouraging it (for example, by providing advice when serving in embassies overseas about which members of the local hierarchy it was best to approach and how); or obtaining funds from it for the benefit of themselves or, in the case of politicians, for their political party.

The nature of the relationship of governments to their national arms firms is of course exceptional. Governments are the only legal customers for weapons in the home market, other than sporting guns, and side arms in countries with lax gun laws; and they also regulate, by export licensing, all legal sales to customers in foreign markets. Moreover, their actions have been unusually intertwined with those of the arms firms since the 1960s when the United States, followed by Britain and France, adopted the policy of vigorously promoting arms exports in the hope of recovering from foreign sales part of the escalating development costs of new weapons.[32] For this purpose, they set up special units in their defence ministries charged with export promotion. In these units persons from private industry, from the regular civil service and from the military services have been inter-mixed and the distinction between the public interest of the government and the private interest of the arms firms has become obscured. Since the development costs of major weapons systems have been driven so high that in most countries only one company produces them, governments are typically dealing with a monopoly, trying to prevent it robbing them when they order weapons from it, while at the same time helping to promote its exports and seeking to keep it going. In these circumstances the distinction between what is right and wrong is hard to define and easily forgotten.

The bribery of public persons abroad in order to obtain export contracts has burgeoned in sectors other than arms, notably construction. Indeed the construction and arms industries are seen to be the leading international bribe-payers.[33] Construction contracts, like arms contracts, are commonly large and are decided by persons high in Third World governments. Moreover, they tend to be unpredictable, though in a lesser degree than arms contracts, as regards cost overruns and the quality of the product.

The Internationalization of Government

I shall leave aside the effects of the great increase in freedom of movement of finance, trade, information and persons across national frontiers. They are elusive, and they impinge most directly on private corruption. But a development that is closely germane to public corruption is the internationalization of government.

Since 1945, all nation states have become members of the United Nations and most of its specialized agencies. Added to which most European states have become members of the European Union and many other organizations. By 1984, the number of inter-governmental organizations exceeded 350.[34]

In both the UN and the EU, politicians and officials from countries with high standards of public conduct, as judged from a modern Western standpoint, have found themselves engaged in running international agencies jointly with politicians and officials from countries where customary standards of public conduct are, by comparison, anything from low to downright rotten. This mixing of standards is inevitable if nations with different customs join together for the sake of international cooperation or, as in the case of the EU, for the sake of politico-economic integration. It may be a price worth paying. But there may come a point at which the achievement of the intended international objectives is so far compromised by corruption and inefficiency that the costs of participation outweigh the benefits. It is a matter that has received far too little attention.[35]

Consider how personnel are selected at the United Nations and its associated agencies. The Secretary General and the heads of the specialized agencies are appointed by representatives of the member states amongst whom there is political bargaining over whom to select, and there is lobbying by candidates. As regards the rest of the staff, merit cannot be the overriding criterion for selection since, if it were, the staff would tend to be dominated by persons from the countries with the best educated populations, largely the rich countries. To prevent that, selection is also guided by quotas or informal understandings that sustain the representation of the less developed parts of the world. The result is patronage, operated within, and in defiance of, a framework of bureaucratic procedures as regards qualifications, references and such things that are supposed to select merit. Nepotism and inefficiency, the normal evils of patronage, often follow. The different agencies have had their ups and downs according to the changing leadership they have experienced.

In these respects the EU is little different from the UN or any other international agency, except that its membership is limited to the nations of Europe. But in other respects the EU is different. It is now a halfway house between an international organization for cooperation amongst sovereign states and a federal government. In this transitional state, beyond which it may or may not advance, the EU has a combination of features conducive to corruption.

Having been designed to tie together, by stealthy economic steps, countries that recoiled from immediate political federation, a highly paid international bureaucracy was created to invent and promote steps towards integration, and was soon put in command of large budgets. Yet precisely because there is no federal government, the bureaucrats have not been subject to proper financial scrutiny and political control and, as they have played the game of 'building Europe', they have been debauched. As the number of member countries has been expanded the bureaucracy has been subdivided (regardless of considerations of efficiency) so as to ensure that there is a top job at the disposal of each member. The commissioners, who are often expendable national politicians put out to grass, appear to have encountered few constraints on their conduct when they reach Brussels. The national leaders who form the Council have cared little about EU corruption, being more concerned with bargaining with one another in pursuit of their national political objectives and their personal ambitions; the powers of the European parliament are by design limited, compared with those of the members' national parliaments. Not surprisingly, when an independent inquiry was at last appointed after many rumours of corruption, it produced a damning report in March 1999 which caused the emasculated European Parliament to use its single blunderbuss weapon vis-à-vis the Commissioners and threaten to sack them. Rather than face that humiliation, the president, Jacques Santer, and all the commissioners resigned.[36] In short, the system, which is dominated by a bureaucracy not subject to proper financial scrutiny and political oversight, has invited corruption at the centre and has suffered it. And it is likely to do so again. Mr Kinnock, one of the Commissioners, has proposed a set of reforms. But one waits to see how effectively the EU bureaucrats and their political patrons will apply them.

The second way in which the EU propagates corruption is through its system for disbursing subsidies. Consultants employed by the EU have exposed some disgraceful scandals over the disbursement of aid to non-member countries.[37] But the more serious and shadowy problem is that of subsidies paid to member countries. Member governments are committed to provide large amounts of tax revenue to be redistributed amongst their number for the purpose of financing agricultural subsidies and other programmes agreed in Brussels. Since there is no federal tax system and no federal bureaucracy that reaches into member countries and hands out money locally, the members hand over part of their national tax revenue to Brussels, which redistributes it to the national bureaucracies of the member states to whom the implementation of the EU programmes, meaning the handing out of the money, is entrusted. If all the member countries had equally clean government it would be one thing. But that is not the case. Most of the countries of northern Europe, for example, Denmark, have a reputation for being scrupulous in implementing the programmes, but some of the member countries of southern Europe which, being poor, are major recipients of EU money are also notorious for corruption. This may have direct and indirect effects.

Directly, EU membership may have caused an increase in the scale of corruption in, for example, Greece, where the people appear to regard EU subsidy schemes for agriculture, tourism, rural development and the like as large new honey pots into which to dip their fingers, abetted by venal Greek bureaucrats. Indirectly, there may be a bad effect on the standard of behaviour in the cleaner member countries whose inhabitants may become lax, rather than priggish, when they learn what goes on in the dirtier member countries, saying to themselves, since others break the rules, why shouldn't we?

The risk that corruption may spread in the EU, causing a lowering of standards in the clean countries, not necessarily accompanied by an improvement in the dirty countries, is a matter that seems never to have been mentioned in the political debates about the enlargement of the EU. If a reasonable standard of cleanliness in government had been a criterion for eligibility, Greece should surely not have been let in; nor, one supposes, should the promise of membership have been made to some of the countries now waiting to be let in.

The Position at the End of the Century

At the end of the twentieth century, all our four countries, including Germany, were capitalist democracies competing in a world in which, since the collapse of communism, American economic ideology had become dominant.

In the United States there appears in the middle of the twentieth century to have been an improvement in standards of the public services from the low levels to which they had sunk at the end of the nineteenth century. In 1942 Morison and Commager judged that the muckrakers, who had exposed corruption, had 'aroused public opinion to the point where it was willing to support men like Roosevelt and Wilson in their reform programs.'[38] The New Deal and the Second World War led to the extension of Federal government and to improvements in its standards. Indeed it may not be fanciful to suggest that the same forces – military competition and the expansion of social expenditure – that earlier had been associated with improvements in the quality of government in Europe may now in some degree have had a similar effect on standards in the public services of the Federal government of the United States. In Heidenheimer's volume of readings on political corruption published in 1970 it was claimed that there had also been an improvement in the standards and honesty of public servants in the cities in the previous 20 years but not in the states.[39]

In our three European states the standard of conduct in the public services (I shall come to politics in a minute) was probably not greatly different at the end of the century from what it had been at the beginning. In Germany, the tradition of the honest civil service had survived Hitler and had been reinforced in some respects in the laws of the Federal Republic, for example, the laws relating to the independence of the judiciary. What had changed in Germany was that ministers were no longer civil servants serving a monarch or dictator but were politicians competing for votes in a democracy. As early as 1970 a German observer expressed the fear that this change would bring with it corruption.[40] In France, the civil service had been modernized but retained much of its old elite structure. In Britain, the tradition of public service, which was the credo of the reformed public services established in the late nineteenth century, lived on unchallenged until, under Mrs Thatcher, the policy was adopted of introducing business ethics and methods into the public services in the name of efficiency. For that purpose, institutions were knocked aside which were the means of ending patronage and other forms of corruption in the nineteenth century. This remarkable change of policy, apparently in a perverse direction from the point of view of preventing corruption, is examined in Chapter 11.

In politics there has been a wave of scandals at the end of the twentieth century.[41] This has been a worldwide phenomenon but it seems to have been particularly severe in those countries, for example, Britain and Germany, where established standards were high and were perceived to be high. As is always the case, it is impossible to know for certain whether the wave of scandals has been caused by an increase in misconduct by public persons or by fuller reporting by the media of what they had been doing all the time. But it is the character of the scandals and of the response to them that is most indicative of the way standards are going: when scandals are exposed they may be glossed over and condoned, with the result that questionable conduct is legitimized and standards are allowed to slide; or they may be condemned and followed by punishment and remedial measures, in which case standards are likely to be maintained or raised.

The Character of Recent Scandals

The main characteristics of recent scandals in our four countries seem to have been these:

1. The most conspicuous persons against whom allegations have been made have been heads of governments, top ministers or party officers, and their counterparts in opposition parties. Their motive has been the gaining of money for their party (which will help them to gain or maintain political power) or economic benefit for themselves and their intimates. Leading instances are the scandals over the conduct of Monsieur Mitterand and Herr Kohl, and also the scandals in Britain over the political offices and Honours accorded by the leaders of the two main parties to men who contributed large sums to their party funds.

2. Members of Parliament without office seem increasingly to have been accused of taking rewards in kind (entertainment, trips, holidays, presents and the like) or cash in exchange for lobbying. The 'cash for questions' scandal in Britain is an example.

3. Many scandals have been about ministers failing to tell the truth; and many scandals have been connected with bribery in the making of contracts in the Third World for the supply of arms and for construction work. The two – falsehoods and bribery – often go together.

A special factor is the effect of the ending of the Cold War. While it lasted it provided politicians with a justification for taking illegal actions of almost any kind in order to counter communism, and an excuse for denying what they were doing. This way of thinking seems, understandably, to have become a habit with respect to foreign and military policy and to have spilled over into domestic politics. Thus the Christian Democrat parties in Italy and Germany were backed by the United States, in covert and overt ways, as bulwarks against communism to the point where their leaders seem to have felt comfortable in using corruption in order to try to keep themselves in power after the Cold War was over. In a comment on the Kohl scandal it was remarked that:

> Like the Italian Christian Democrats, the German conservatives may have been spoiled by the Cold War environment that made their presence so reassuring to Western allies. Just as their Italian cousins kept Europe's largest Communist party from sharing power, the German Christian Democrats enjoyed special status as a political bulwark against the Soviet-backed Communists next-door in East Germany.
>
> That privileged role is now seen to have encouraged Mr Kohl, who ran the party as his personal fiefdom for 25 years, to do everything he felt necessary – including the acceptance of illegal cash donations – to preserve the Christian Democrats' hold on power.[42]

The ending of the Cold War has made that kind of behaviour harder to justify and has made it less easy to guard secrets. It is true that the laws relating to secrecy seem not to have been much relaxed, but it has become harder than before for governments to stifle the Press and the judiciary in the name of national security. Perhaps the most conspicuous case is Italy where as the Cold War ran down the judiciary became active in the pursuit of corruption amongst politicians with turbulent results. In Britain one wonders, for example, whether the judiciary would have been as tough on the government's attempts to hide behind considerations of national security in the Scott enquiry into the arms to Iraq affair, and whether Alan Clark, the key witness, would have been so uninhibited in revealing what had gone on, if that enquiry had taken place at the height of the Cold War.

The Reaction to the Scandals

All the scandals I have referred to have been, or are, I think, the subject of official enquiries or legal proceedings. These have consisted in inquiries by legal persons under constitutionally prescribed procedures in some countries, under less formal procedures in others; and there have been a few bits of new legislation. One example is the 'Ethics in Government Act' of 1978 introduced in the United States after the Watergate scandal. It established an Office of Government Ethics to oversee the disclosure statements required of senior members of the executive and created the office of independent counsel, responsible for the criminal investigation and prosecution of senior executive-branch officials, including the president. Another is the Sapin Law, introduced in France in January 1993 following a scandal, which brought in new codes of conduct and created an agency to prevent corruption; though, as regards political corruption, more important has been the non-statutory step, described in Chapter 8, of allowing magistrates to investigate scandals with less political interference. In Britain, as we shall see in Chapter 11, many non-statutory mechanisms have been introduced following scandals and some new legislation is contemplated. It is too early to judge the efficacy of these various measures, distinguishing how far they have served temporarily to appease the public, how far to correct the behaviour of politicians. In the United Sstates, the legislators seem in the 1978 Act to have set standards so high compared with their usual political conduct that accusations of transgression have become a cheapened currency of political combat. But one cannot know what the long-term effect will be.

The national attempts to check the behaviour of the politicians have tended to bring the judiciary and the executive into conflict. In France, the present burst of scandals described earlier is the product of a struggle between the investigating magistrates and governments that obstructed the magistrates' ability to bring ministers to book. In the United States the special prosecutor in the impeachment of President Clinton, chosen by a parliamentary body dominated by the opposition, behaved in an apparently partisan and inquisitorial manner. Of course tension between the judiciary and the executive is in some degree unavoidable, since the judiciary's interpretation of the law will not always be to the liking of the government. But when corrupt behaviour by top politicians becomes the source of friction between ministers and judges, the independence of the judiciary, unless well rooted, is in contention.

Some international measures are now being introduced to stop bribery in foreign trade. The lead has been taken by the United States, the country where popular democracy so openly gives rise both to corruption and, aided by the independence of the legislature from the executive, to morally inspired initiatives to stop corruption. Following the Church Committee's investigations, the United States in 1977 passed a 'Foreign Corrupt Practices Act' making it a criminal offence for American companies to bribe foreign officials. Although there were many loopholes, it was a beginning and, since it put American companies at a disadvantage, it helped generate American pressure for action by other nations. Now the United States has persuaded 34 countries to sign an OECD convention that requires the signatories to make it a crime to bribe any foreign official and requires countries to help one another prosecute cases. It remains to be seen how sincerely the governments that subscribe to this convention will enforce it, if necessary stopping loopholes through the use of subsidiaries. A lot will depend on how far they and the World Bank can unite to bring into line multinational corporations, in particular those engaged in the extraction of oil and other minerals and those supplying arms.

It can be said that there now seems to be a significant international tide of concern about corruption, particularly corruption in the Third World and in Russia; the World Bank and other international agencies have been addressing the problem and urging reform.[43] Transparency International, a remarkable non-governmental organization founded by a former World Bank official, produces an annual listing of countries according to how corrupt their politicians and public officials are perceived to be by employees of multinational firms and institutions interviewed in many surveys. Of our four countries Britain comes 13th and the United States 16th in the 2001 survey; Germany 20th and France 23rd. Germany's ranking had dropped by eight places since the 1999 survey, influenced no doubt by the scandal over the conduct of Mr Kohl. The top twelve places go to the countries of Scandinavia; to three former British dominions New Zealand, Canada and Australia; to the Netherlands, Luxembourg and Switzerland; and (in 4th place) to Singapore. Britain would surely have come higher on the list alongside its dominions if there had been one of these surveys in the middle of the twentieth century.

Conclusion

The forces that I have suggested were important in fostering less corrupt government in the late eighteenth and nineteenth centuries in Europe were reversed in the second half of the twentieth century by various developments. Military competition, transformed by technical advances, became more productive of anarchy and corruption than uncorrupt government; the secret corruption and toppling of legitimate governments became a means of cold warfare; and standards of public conduct fell as popular support for more and better government was challenged by hostility to big government and esteem for private greed. Added to which, technological and social developments reduced the ability of nations to insulate themselves from corrupting influences coming from abroad. In our four countries and elsewhere there has been a wave of scandals.

There have been reactions against corruption. In European countries where the rule of law has some hold, scandals that might have been covered up during the Cold War have been brought into the open and investigated by judges apparently acting with less inhibition than before; and there is more transparency and exposure of corruption than before. At the global level the World Bank, the OECD and Transparency International have been attacking the problem of corruption. It will be fascinating to see how these opposing forces evolve, influenced as they will be by technological and social developments we cannot foresee.

I 0

Britain in the First Half
of the Twentieth Century

By the end of the nineteenth century the civil service, the military services and the judiciary in Britain had been reformed. Appointment by merit had become the norm; good salaries, security of tenure and good pensions had been introduced; the ethic of public service, implanted by the Victorian education system, had widely taken hold.[1] But in politics and business things were different.

At the turn of the century there was a spate of personal scandals in Britain. In 1884 the political career of Sir Charles Dilke, a leading Liberal, was brought to an end when he was cited, possibly wrongly, in a divorce case and was alleged to have been in bed with two women;[2] in the 1890s there was the case of Oscar Wilde; and then there was Edward VII who, when Prince of Wales, twice had to appear in court: in 1870 in connection with a divorce case, and in 1891 in connection with a slander case brought, unsuccessfully, by a man who had cheated at cards when playing with the prince and his friends. These personal scandals are peripheral to my concern with public corruption, but not irrelevant. Scandals about private and public affairs tend to go together; they are both indicative of the moral tone of the times.

In this period the landed aristocracy, whose rents were reduced by the agricultural depression, were being overtaken in economic power by new men who had made fortunes in trade and finance, at home and abroad. These new 'plutocrats' sought to enter society; they displayed their new wealth: they acquired country houses; they poured money into blood sports; they turned London into a centre for luxurious living – and good eating. American expatriates attracted to the social merry-go-round joined their ranks. These plutocrats were criticized from the left by the anti-rich, and from the right by the old rich. Nevertheless many members of the aristocracy sought to keep up with them in the scramble for money. To do so they joined in a spate of stock market speculation and dodgy company promotions. Edward VII 'was both victim and instigator' of this new world. He surrounded himself 'with a coterie whose sexual licentiousness, love of gambling, and taste for luxurious entertainments made for a prevailing tone of hedonism, which spread far beyond the court...'[3] He 'enjoyed a flutter on the Stock Exchange as much as he enjoyed a stroll along the Paris boulevards'.[4]

What happened in public life was summarized by Alan Doig, on whose admirable work I have drawn freely in this chapter:

> ...turn-of-the-century commercial morality generally was appalling. In 1899 Balfour named the Stock Exchange and the public contracts as the "two great sources of public corruption", the *Economist* talked of "an atmosphere of money" inside the Commons, while the *Times* referred in 1898 to the "ugly phenomenon" of men of high social position accepting directorships in doubtful companies. Government contracts officials spoke of a freemasonry of contractors, particularly in the armaments industry; a series of ministers and MP's got their fingers burnt in injudicious business interests; commercial plunderers like Ernest Hooley and Horatio Bottomley dined with royalty and dreamed of high political office, while at the other end of the scale the doyen of Victorian muckraking metropolitan magazines, *Truth*, had sufficient evidence on small-time con-men and petty crooks to publish a book listing their activities.[5]

The Hooley scandal is an example of corruption being accidentally revealed (by bankruptcy) and then condoned. Hooley was a Nottingham lace manufacturer who climbed the financial world and society as a company promoter so successfully that he acquired a country seat in Cambridgeshire, was nominated High Sheriff and Deputy Lieutenant of that county and, most shocking, purchased admission to the Carlton Club. In 1899 the Official Receiver's report on his bankruptcy showed that he had bribed titled men whose names would look good on his company prospectuses, and had committed various offences under the Bankruptcy Act and the Debtors Act. But the Director of Public Prosecutions decided against prosecution, apparently for fear of the social damage a court case might cause. Before the decision against prosecution was made, Hooley told the press 'Look here! I have not said one-fifteenth part of what I can say about the British peerage. I have still got a lot of cards up my sleeve'.[6]

Horatio Bottomley, who seems to have entwined fewer grand men in his dishonest schemes, was sent to prison for seven years for fraud.[7]

As regards government contracts, over which there were scandals during the Boer War, the law was obsolete. An act of 1782 to prevent Members of Parliament being beneficiaries of such contracts applied only to partnerships, not to directorships of limited liability companies. Hence 'MPs had a considerable freedom in combining their political careers and their business interests', and so too did ministers. In 1892 Gladstone's Cabinet bound itself to a self-denying ordinance that ministers should give up their directorships when they took office, but the Unionists under Lord Salisbury allowed the rule to lapse when they returned to power in 1895. By 1900 half Salisbury's ministers held directorships of public companies.[8]

The Sale of Honours and Electoral Reform

But perhaps the most notorious field for scandal lay in the sale of Honours to the newly rich. Until the latter part of the nineteenth century the British electoral system was rotten, judged by modern standards. The number of voters was narrowly restricted by property qualifications. Landlords dominated many constituencies. An aspiring politician could buy a seat by offering cash and entertainment, and it was worth having one for the sake of the influence it gave to its holder in obtaining patronage and bending legislation that touched local interests, for example the building of canals and railways, not to mention the status of being an MP. Political parties were loose affiliations of MP's. The party leaders had little hold over their members – hence the trading of patronage for votes by the whips. Party matters were decided at the great clubs in London. The parties had neither central offices nor significant central funds. It was still an aristocratic era.

In the last part of the nineteenth century these conditions were radically changed. In response to the pressure for electoral reform, the franchise was extended (it reached more than 2 million voters in 1867), and in 1872 voting was made secret, which meant that a briber could no longer know if his bribe to a voter was honoured. These reforms undermined the cost-effectiveness of bribery at the same time as the agricultural depression began to knock the wealth of the landowners who dominated the Conservative and Liberal parties. In these new conditions both parties in 1883 supported legislation that put a stop to electoral bribery at the constituency level. The new law, which was remarkably effective, set a limit to the election expenditure of candidates, and it required them to keep accounts and submit them to official scrutiny.

Elections now became interparty battles; and the political parties began to evolve into centralized bodies. They needed money to help poor constituencies (up to the permitted limit), to finance their headquarters staff, and also to finance national propaganda campaigns, which had been made possible by the growth of the national press and on which expenditure was not limited. As a source of money, they found around them plutocrats ready to pay handsomely for Honours, meaning titles and other decorations, which, though formally awarded by the Crown, were in the gift of the prime minister on whose advice the Crown now acted. Business men, bankers and industrialists were moving into politics and into the governing class, and the sale of Honours contributed to social mobility at these levels of society.[9]

Lloyd George is notorious for having sold Honours, but it was not he who started the game. In 1886, after the Liberal party had split over Home Rule for Ireland and had lost rich supporters, Gladstone agreed that the chief whip should promise peerages to an English linoleum manufacturer and a Jewish banker in exchange for donations to the party.[10] (Earlier, when he was Member of Parliament for Oxford University, he had successfully pressed the claims for a bishopric of a person who had been his election agent; though in these matters he was restrained compared with Disraeli.[11]) The Unionists, i.e. the party formed by the Conservatives and those Liberals who joined them over Home Rule, followed suit and by the late 1890s were receiving substantial donations in exchange for Honours.[12] Searle tells us that Salisbury 'regarded the whole Honours business with world-weary cynicism' and that Asquith, 'accepted the bestowal of honours as a tiresome and distasteful, but necessary, part of the political system.'[13] Although the chief whip handled relations with donors or their intermediaries, the prime minister had to be kept informed, since he had to defend his nominations if queried by the Palace.

Lloyd George's Excesses

When Lloyd George became prime minister in 1916, the war was producing millionaires, often condemned as profiteers, who were impatient for status and eager to buy Honours; 'the plutocratic era was at its height'; the opportunities for trade in Honours were great, and both parties took advantage of them when they could.[14] The trouble with Lloyd George was that his dazzling brilliance as a politician was combined with a singular lack of inhibition in personal behaviour. A J P Taylor described him as 'the first prime minister since Walpole to leave office flagrantly richer than he entered it, the first since the Duke of Grafton to live openly with his mistress.'[15]

Before 1914, when he was Chancellor of the Exchequer, Lloyd George had been one of three members of the Liberal government who, having been accused of profiting by insider dealing in Marconi shares, were exonerated by a select committee dominated by their party.[16] When he became prime minister, he was hailed as a dynamic war leader and his first Honours list was compared favourably with 'the jobbery and snobbery' of his predecessor's lists.[17] But that did not last. Soon Lloyd George went further than others had gone in using touts to sell Honours, in selling Honours to anyone with money regardless of party or character, and in failing to keep party funds separate from his personal funds. Admittedly, Lloyd George's position was unusual. On forming the coalition in 1916 and becoming prime minister, he had broken away from the Liberal Party and become leader of a personal party without formal organization; the money he raised by selling honours and other means he regarded as his own to be used for electoral purposes or his personal benefit as he chose. In defence of his conduct he obtained '...a high legal opinion that he was free to gamble the money away at Monte Carlo if he wanted to'. In the words of Robert Blake, 'Lloyd George kept a degree of personal hold over his fund as unprecedented as the method by which he raised it.'[18]

Nothing was done about the sale of Honours until 1922, even though there was increasing criticism of what was going on. For a time Lloyd George's popularity as a war leader protected him. Moreover, silence and inaction suited the Unionists as well as the Liberals. Both had sold Honours during the period of the coalition government, as well as before: Lloyd George had shared the spoils of office with his Unionist partners in the coalition.[19] But in the summer of 1922 Lloyd George went too far. He nominated to a peerage a South African financier and mine owner who had recently been fined £500,000 for fraud and whose nomination was not backed by the South African government. By now the post-war coalition government was unpopular and losing cohesion. There was outrage in the press and Parliament. After a good deal of shuffling by the leaders of both parties, who feared investigation of their past deeds and criticism from their ranks, a Royal Commission was appointed with the carefully restricted task of advising what procedure should be adopted in future 'to assist the prime minister in making recommendations of the names of persons deserving of special honour'. The Commission refrained from looking into the past; it invited present and past prime ministers and whips to give evidence, but no one else; it did not entertain the idea that Honours should not be a party matter. In a brief report, unaccompanied by minutes of evidence, it recommended that there should be a vetting committee of three privy councillors to look at the list of nominations for political Honours and offer advice, and that it be made a criminal offence to offer money for a title or act as an intermediary. The Commission's aim seems to have been to stamp out, or at least appear to stamp out, the worst abuses while leaving the existing system intact.[20] The Conservatives, who had came to power after the collapse of Lloyd George's coalition in October 1922 and were keen to dissociate themselves from the stain of the coalition era, at once adopted the procedures recommended by the Commission, and in 1925 they made them law.[21] In the same year Maundy Gregory, the most notorious tout in the Honours business, was brought to court under the new act. He was persuaded, by persons eager to shield the political parties, to plead guilty so that details of his deals should not be revealed in court, and to accept a pension that they had raised for him and settle quietly in France, after he had served a brief prison sentence. He honoured the deal and died in France. Lloyd George suffered only damage, albeit severe, to his political reputation.

The Inter-War Years

There soon followed the relatively scandal-free years in which the country was led by 'honest Mr Baldwin'. The tone of political life became more respectable. The sale of Honours, however, seems not altogether to have ceased; nor had the practice of rewarding press barons for their support, which had taken hold since the beginning of the century, and of which the most notable beneficiaries were the Harmsworth brothers, the pioneers of mass circulation newspapers in Britain: Alfred, 1st Viscount Northcliffe, was made a baronet in 1904, a baron in 1906, a viscount in 1917; Harold, 1st Viscount Rothermere, was made a baronet in 1910, a baron in 1914 and a viscount in 1919.[22] The most profligate dispenser of these Honours, as with others, was Lloyd George.[23]

The Conservatives turned to raising funds by appealing to business-men, who now felt threatened by the growing Labour Party, to make their companies subscribe to the party, directly or indirectly. There was thus a movement from individual to corporate giving, which fitted the tendency for family businesses to become public companies. But the pursuit of titles was not over. Pinto-Duschinsky concluded from an examination of how money was raised by the Conservatives for the 1929 election that:

> ...the desire for a title featured strongly in the minds of a consid-erable number of contributors. Although these hopefuls were now obliged to go through the motions of giving to charity and serv-ing the party in a voluntary capacity, it was recognized that the real objective was to create a presentable case for the award of a title or a peerage.[24]

Searle, having reviewed the evidence, concluded that:

> ...though the Conservative Ministries of the 1920s prudently avoided the "excesses" which had brought such opprobrium on the post-war Coalition, one should view with some scepticism the claim that Baldwin and his colleagues were living on a much higher plane than their predecessors.[25]

Such scandals as there were in the later inter-war years seem to have been dealt with firmly. There was a scandal in the City in 1929 involving a crooked company promoter, but politicians were not closely involved, and the culprit, Clarence Hatry, and his associates received prison sen-tences. In 1936 a budget leak caused the resignation from the Cabinet of J H Thomas, a former railwayman who, having come up through the Labour Party, had joined the national government; and in October 1940, just after the fall of France, a junior minister, Mr Robert (later Lord) Boothby, was censured severely by a select committee and forced to resign for having pleaded in Parliament on behalf of emigré holders of Czech financial claims, without declaring that he had an interest in the matter.[26] The high moral stance of the young Labour Party, which in these years became a force in politics, may have had some beneficial effect on standards, but for the most part the members of the Labour Party applied their energies to attacking what they saw as a rotten economic system, not the peccadilloes of individuals.[27]

Assessment

How then is one to judge standards in public life at the turn of the nineteenth century and afterwards? One's first instinct is to say – and it has often been said – that the turn of the century was a period rife with scandal. But the mere fact that there were scandals does not tell us what was happening to standards of conduct in public life. A scandal tells us two things: firstly, what behaviour was regarded at the time as corrupt. From which one may be able to judge, by looking back to earlier times, whether standards had evolved upwards or downwards – or had stayed constant. And secondly one can see whether the government instituted an uninhibited enquiry; and whether, if misbehaviour was found, it took action, in the shape of punishment or remedial legislation, to maintain or raise standards; or, on the contrary, it failed to do those things and let standards slip.

Let us apply these two criteria to the three types of scandal we have touched upon – dishonest company promotion, corruption over military contracts and the sale of Honours.

1. Dishonest company promotion

It looks as if behaviour at this time fell to a low level, though in some degree that always happens when there is a bout of speculative fever in stock markets. Government action seems to have been equivocal. Hooley was not prosecuted although laws existed under which he could have been brought to book; Horatio Bottomley was prosecuted and sent to gaol.

2. Scandals over government contracts

That there were scandals over military contracts cannot be taken as evidence of a decline in standards of conduct compared with earlier periods; military contracts have always been meat for vultures. But a lax attitude to standards is suggested by the failure to keep up to date the law preventing MPs from being beneficiaries of government contracts, and also by Lord Salisbury's conduct in allowing his ministers to be company directors after Gladstone had forbidden his ministers that luxury. Considerable remedial action was taken. In 1889 an act was passed to stop corruption in the obtaining of public contracts; this was extended in 1906 to cover corruption in private business, and was strengthened in 1916.[28] Under these acts public servants are treated more sternly than other people: they are deemed to have been guilty of corruption if they are found to have received money from a person holding or seeking a government contract, unless they can prove the contrary; and the courts, in addition to the normal penalties of imprisonment and fine, may punish public servants by making them hand over the bribe to the government, by disqualifying them from public office and withholding their pensions. Standards were being raised and the notion was in the ascendant that public servants were special people in a position of trust from whom the highest standards should be expected and exacted.

3. Sale of Honours

The sale of Honours is *par excellence* an example of the rules of permissible conduct being raised and new tricks then being found to circumvent the rules at the new higher level. It was electoral reform – the widening of the electorate and the limitation of electoral expenditures by candidates – that caused political leaders to turn their attention to the sale of Honours as a means of financing election campaigns under the new electoral regime. The selling of Honours was regarded as shameful but it was condoned until Lloyd George went too far. The remedial action then taken was weak. The sale of Honours has continued.

The reforms that were introduced in this period did not impose many formal restraints on politicians. The behaviour of politicians was very largely left to their sense of honour. In particular, they were expected voluntarily to disclose private interests that might conflict with their public duties.

The Mid-Century Peak

When Britain fought alone against Hitler, the British people were induced to make sacrifices on a remarkably egalitarian basis for the sake of the war effort; profiteering and corruption were frowned upon and were not conspicuous – which is not to say they never occurred; and to avoid a repetition of the war profiteering of 1914–18, an excess profits tax was introduced during the period of rearmament before war broke out.[29] The political parties combined in a patriotic coalition in which, for example, Ernest Bevin, a forceful working class trade unionist, worked in harness with Churchill; the civil service was greatly reinforced by the enlistment of outsiders, notably businessmen and academics, some of whom quickly rose to the top. The high standards continued for some years after the war.

One could caricature the politicians of the period after 1945 by saying that Conservative members of Parliament were typically Etonians, Labour members were typically Wykehamists or trades unionists who had been brought up close to the chapel. Victorian values had been drummed into all of them. They might misbehave, but if they did they knew it; they mostly had consciences and could be brought to apologize and resign if caught out. Misdemeanours in public life were not tolerated.

In 1947 Hugh Dalton, the Chancellor of the Exchequer, resigned immediately when it became known that he had foolishly told a journalist of a proposed tax change just before he delivered his budget speech. Two years later Mr Belcher, a junior Labour minister was found by an official tribunal under the chairmanship of a High Court judge, Sir George Lynskey, to be guilty of (a) having been given some cases of wine and whisky by a distiller, Sir Maurice Bloch, in return for helping him to obtain licences to import sherry casks (in which whisky is put to mature); and (b) having received several presents, including a suit of clothes, from Sidney Stanley, an alien and undischarged bankrupt who had escaped deportation by changing his name, and having befriended Belcher had claimed to his business associates that he had influence with the government and could bring them favours if they employed his services. For these misdemeanours, which today seem rather small, Belcher resigned from ministerial office before the tribunal's hearings were complete and soon afterwards resigned from the House of Commons. Sir Maurice Bloch's name was removed from the list of Justices of the Peace by the Lord Chancellor. When the House debated the Lynskey Tribunal's report in February 1949 there was uncompromising insistence on the highest standards of political morality. The prime minister, Mr Attlee, said 'where any individual is highly placed, a finding that he has in any way departed from the highest standards involves a very heavy penalty...public administration in this country and public life in this country stand unrivalled in their high standards of service and incorruptibility.' Churchill took the same line. The scandal attracted much publicity and shocked the public; there was no attempt to make party capital out of it.[30]

In 1954 there was the Crichel Down scandal in which some agricultural land, which had been appropriated as a bombing range but was no longer needed, was kept in public ownership and leased by the Commissioners of Crown Land instead of being offered back to the original owner. Following an enquiry in which some civil servants were criticized for mistakes and errors of judgement (not for seeking personal gain), their minister, Sir Thomas Dugdale, followed the honourable tradition that ministers should assume responsibility for the actions of their civil servants and resigned.[31]

What is remarkable today is that all these episodes were treated as major scandals, and that the ministers associated with them fell on their political swords so honourably. Standards are not like that now.

Britain in the Second Half of the Twentieth Century

As the Second World War receded, the standards of conduct of politicians began to slide. In 1957 when the Labour Party was in opposition, three important figures in that party – Aneurin Bevan, Richard Crossman and Morgan Philips – won a libel suit against *The Spectator* for reporting that they had been drunk at a conference in Venice. Their later admissions indicate that at least one of them perjured himself. (Their solicitor, who encouraged them to press their case, was Mr, later Lord, Goodman who rose to become an *éminence grise* close to Harold Wilson.)[1] This was not a creditable episode. More important, Britain's political leaders appear to have taken to burying scandals, rather than jumping on them and taking remedial action in the manner of Mr Attlee and his contemporaries. It is convenient to consider first the period up to 1979, when a radically new approach to government was introduced by Mrs Thatcher.

The Slide

In the 1960s there were rumblings about the way Members of Parliament were pursuing their private interests. In 1961 a young Labour MP, Francis Noel-Baker, wrote a prescient article saying that members were being asked to become allies of private businesses or other interests in exchange for fees, retainers or expenses, and that these arrangements were kept quiet, unlike members' traditional interests (as landowners, bankers, company directors or trades union leaders) which were known or declared. 'The door', he wrote, 'is wide open for a new form of political corruption, and there is an uneasy feeling in Parliament and outside, that its extent could be much wider than the known or public facts reveal...

The existing convention in the House of Commons seems inadequate to meet this situation.[2]

A case of the kind he foresaw occurred at the end of the 1960s. A public relations firm that had a contract to promote the cause of the Greek colonels took on a Labour MP, Gordon Bagier, as a paid consultant and then claimed, in a progress report to its Greek employers, that it had a British MP lobbyist working behind the scenes to influence other MPs. When this leaked into the press the PR firm denied that it had meant what it said, and the MP denied that he had acted as a lobbyist. But the case served to bring into the open the problem of relations between MPs and PR firms. Richard Crossman, according to his diaries, wanted a select committee appointed to consider the conduct of PR firms as well as the conduct of members, and advise Parliament. Harold Wilson agreed, but two ministers, James Callaghan and Richard Marsh, were against it, arguing, in Crossman's view not unreasonably, 'What do we get out of this? All we shall do is expose two or three other Labour MPs who may well have been working for PR firms. If we set up a Committee of Inquiry into this, don't we merely damage the Government at this stage?'[3] What emerged was a Select Committee on Members Interests with narrow terms of reference, which merely clarified the guidance to MPs about when they should voluntarily declare their interests. Although this report, produced in 1969, proposed so little, it was still shelved.[4] Its proposals were implemented only after a bigger scandal – the Poulson affair.

John Poulson was an entrepreneur-architect who in the 1960s, when public investment was being increased, won contracts for his firm by proposing grand schemes and lavishing bribes, hospitality and favours on public officials in order to get them. The contracts came mainly from Labour local authorities and other public agencies in the northeast, where Poulson enlisted a Mr T Dan Smith, a house painter who had come up through the Newcastle Labour Party. Smith in 1966 became chairman of the Northern Economic Planning Council and 'entered the wheeler-dealer world of business, Whitehall and public relations'. The major recipients of Poulson's gifts included Mr Pottinger, a senior civil servant in the Scottish Office who for seven years received gifts from Poulson the value of which in some years exceeded his salary; and Mr Cunningham, a senior trades union official who was a Justice of the Peace, a member of the Labour National Executive Committee and a person who served on many public authorities – the Newcastle Airports Authority, the Northumberland River Authority, Durham County Council, the

Durham Police Authority and others. These four persons – Poulson, Smith, Pottinger and Cunningham – each received a prison sentence of about five years. Lesser sentences were handed down to about ten other persons, nearly all of whom held positions with local government or nationalized industries.

In addition, three Members of Parliament – Messrs Cordle, Maudling and Roberts – were found to have been rewarded by Poulson, and their cases were considered by a Select Committee of Parliament in 1976–77. (Mr Maudling, a Conservative, had resigned from the office of Home Secretary in 1972 on the grounds that he could not hold that office while the police were investigating the Poulson affair.) The Select Committee criticized all three for conduct inconsistent with the standards expected of Members of Parliament. But the House 'showed remarkable reluctance to support the Committee's Report, criticizing its decisions, methods of examination and interpretation of evidence' and the three members showed only qualified repentance, or none. When a senior Labour member of the old guard, Mr George Strauss, urged the House not to whitewash the report and proposed a six month suspension of the two who were still Members of Parliament, his motion was overwhelmingly voted down in favour of a motion, supported by Mr Michael Foot, the Leader of the House, that the House 'take note' of the report, meaning they should do nothing.[5]

In two other responses to the Poulson scandal the politicians behaved no better. The rules guiding the voluntary declaration of interest were considered again in 1974, when it was laid down that members should in any debate or proceeding of Parliament or dealing with other MPs, ministers or civil servants declare any relevant (in their judgement) financial interest or benefit past, present or future. A register was established in which members were required to record their interests, plus a committee to watch over it. Immediately there was trouble, led by Mr Enoch Powell who objected to the registration of interests on the grounds that it was a departure from reliance on honour. After much shuffling, an incomplete register was published in 1980.[6]

The second response was the appointment in 1975 of a Royal Commission on Standards of Conduct in Public Life under a judge (Lord Salmon) that recommended various steps, including a strengthening of the Prevention of Corruption Act of 1916, which would reduce reliance on trust in public servants and improve the possibilities of detection and investigation. It recommended that bribery of an MP acting in his Parliamentary capacity should no longer enjoy exemption from the criminal law. But the House of Commons did not even debate the Salmon Report; nor did it debate another report that made suggestions concerning corruption in local government.[7] In the words of Alan Doig:

> The failure of the Commons to debate either Report – let alone act on their modest proposals – has reflected a comprehensive and consistent unwillingness to deal with the issue of corruption and misconduct, an unwillingness clearly reflected by both Labour and Conservative governments' replies to questions in the House on what they intended to do about the recommendations of the Salmon Report, and when they intended to act.

Alan Doig then quotes the blocking answers given by ministers to 12 parliamentary questions about the implementation of the Salmon Report that were asked between July 1976 and June 1980 – after which the subject appears to have been dropped. In answer to the eleventh of these questions, Mr (later Lord) Whitelaw, having been asked what proposals he had in mind to improve the standards of conduct in public life, replied, 'To set a good example to others'.[8]

In considering the Poulson affair and other scandals of this period, it is important to remember that what is indicative of the rise or fall of standards in public life is not so much the occurrence of scandals, which are usually brought to light accidentally (Poulson's corruption and the trail to his associates were discovered by chance during bankruptcy proceedings after his firm failed) but the response of the politicians to scandals. If the politicians jump on behaviour that is seen to be corrupt and introduce remedial measures, the probable effect of their actions will be to raise standards or at least maintain them. If, as happened in this period, they gloss over scandals and shirk action, the probable effect will be to let standards slide.

In the 1970s the press criticized various Members of Parliament for their business activities. The members came from all the main parties. They included Messrs du Cann, Sandys, Thorpe and Stonehouse (who ran into such severe financial difficulties that he shammed disappearance). And in 1976 there was the scandal over Harold Wilson's resignation Honours list which appeared so excessively to honour his cronies rather than people with a record of public or political service, that the Political Honours Scrutiny Committee, established under the 1925 Act, protested at some of the individual names. According to one of its members, Lady Summerskill, another member of the old guard who had served in the post-war Labour government under Mr Attlee, the committee 'could not approve of at least half the list', but the committee's recommendations, with one exception, were ignored by the prime minister; the committee were faced with a *fait accompli* that they had no power to upset. A row ensued in which, in addition to criticism from the Opposition, over one hundred Labour MPs recorded their objections. But no remedial action was taken. The incoming prime minister, James Callaghan, who no doubt would have found it awkward to set in train enquiries into the conduct of the person who had just handed the office of prime minister to him, said in answer to questions in the House of Commons that he was not at present satisfied that a committee should be established to review the system, or that additional powers were needed to strengthen the Scrutiny Committee; and, with reference to Wilson's list, he doubted whether those making accusations had read the whole list.[9]

How disreputable some of the persons on Wilson's 1976 list were soon started coming to light – and there may be more to come. Early in 1977 Sir Eric Peachey, a property developer whom Wilson had knighted, committed suicide after being accused of fraud. At the end of the year warrants were issued for the arrest of Lord Kagan, a manufacturer of raincoats who was a close buddy of Wilson's and had been ennobled by him, on charges of conspiracy to defraud the tax authorities and of falsifying his accounts; Kagan bolted to Israel, but when visiting Paris he was extradited to England and was sentenced to ten months imprisonment and a heavy fine.[10] Recently it was reported that Lord Goodman, the apparently dependable and cultured solicitor with whom Wilson regularly discussed the problems of the day and whom he ennobled, had robbed Lord Portman, one of Britain's richest hereditary landowners, of £1 million (equal to £10 million today) and had paid some of it to politicians, apparently including Wilson, with whom he gained power and influence. According to *The Times* obituary of Lord Portman, in which this was reported, Lord Portman had trusted Goodman, who was the sole trustee of his family's money, but became suspicious and, after being fobbed off with a string of excuses, sued him in 1993. By then, however, Goodman was dying and Lord Portman, rather than drag Goodman through the courts, settled out of court for half a million pounds; and – intriguingly – agreed in 1994 not to disclose information about what had happened until 2006, presumably on the grounds that by then the persons involved would be dead.[11] It is clear that Lord Goodman, who 'carried many things around in his head', handled the

Portman trusts in a remarkably casual way.[12] In June 1999 his old firm of solicitors issued a statement to Brian Brivati, who was writing a biography of Goodman, saying that after reviewing hundreds of files and thousands of ledger entries 'all funds were accounted for', on which basis they denied that there had been any wrongdoing by Goodman. Brivati took the view that 'The balance of the evidence suggests that Lord Portman's allegations are without foundation.'[13] But if that is the case, one wonders why half a million pounds was returned to Lord Portman and why he was persuaded to forbid disclosure of what had happened for 12 years. We must wait and see. It is inconceivable that Attlee would have had anything to do with men like Kagan, Miller or Goodman.

La Fin de Siècle

It took almost another 20 years before a rising tide of scandal unequalled since the beginning of the century induced some remedial action: in 1994 Mr Major appointed a new Committee on Standards in Public Life.

It was the cash for questions affair, when MPs were found to have been directly taking bribes as a reward for seeking information of value to business, which caused Mr Major to appoint a new Committee on Standards in Public Life in 1994.[14] By then the government was repeatedly being accused of 'sleaze'. There had been a wave of political scandals accompanied by a wave of scandals in private affairs, including financial scandals in the City, scandals over the sexual conduct of members of the royal family and politicians; all went together, as they had done at the beginning of the century.

There are two conspicuous features of the many scandals over the behaviour of ministers and Members of Parliament. Firstly, the government and Members of Parliament have shown increasing reluctance to confess and resign when accused of misconduct; they have often tried to get away with what they had done, using all the tricks of public relations for the purpose; they have been as amoral as Lloyd George was at the beginning of the century. Although Alexis de Tocqueville wrote *Democracy in America* more than 150 years ago, the observations he made about corruption are relevant:

> In aristocratic governments those who reach the top are rich men who want only power. In democracies they are poor and have

their fortunes to make. It follows that in aristocratic states rulers are not easily corruptible and have only a very moderate taste for money, whereas the opposite is true in democracies.[15]

Mrs Thatcher, it must be remembered, displaced the patricians amongst her ministers (who were called 'wets') by new men and women who were less restrained in their pursuit of power and wealth. And the Labour Party regained power in 1997 only after persons whose attitudes to government were little different from those of the new Conservatives displaced the upholders of its traditional values. In 1995 Peter Hennessy, in evidence to the Committee on Standards in Public Life, said of the new class of politicians in all parties:

> They start as would-be bag carriers to ministers, they have never held what one might call a proper job, they have always been in politically-related jobs and they rise on the basis of the worst kind of patronage...[16]

Secondly, many of the scandals, as in other countries, have been connected with the arms business – Westland helicopters, arms to Iraq, the Pergau dam, the unanswered questions surrounding the Saudi Arabian arms deal and Mr Aitken's perjury.

One can point to factors that apparently contributed to the decline in standards in public life in this period – the legacy of the Cold War, the new regard for greed, the emasculation of the civil service and arrogance of a political party that remained in power too long – but one cannot judge their relative importance. It might be said that the change is the consequence of an evolutionary development in society in which two populist leaders, Mrs Thatcher and Mr Blair, have gained power by leading the expanding middle class in revolt against high taxation and big government, and against the established elites that might stand in their way – against, that is, patrician politicians, civil servants and the House of Lords. The attack on the elites may have augmented the populist appeal of these leaders; it has certainly enhanced their unconstrained power when in office.

The new Committee on Standards in Public Life is to be permanent. Its first two chairmen, Lord Nolan and Lord Neill, were distinguished lawyers. Its third chairman, Sir Nigel Wickes, is a retired senior civil servant who served as private secretary to recent prime ministers. One wonders if a person of that background will be as critical of government as the lawyers. In its first report in May 1995 the Committee, having cautioned the reader about the difficulties of ever knowing how much corruption is going on, said two things that indicate how serious they felt the situation to be: first, 'There is no precedent in this century for so many allegations of wrongdoing, on so many different subjects, in so short a period of time'; secondly, it said, tactfully, that 'people in public life are not always as clear as they should be about where the boundaries of acceptable conduct lie.'[17]

The report did not question the market approach to government. Rather it enunciated 'Seven Principles of Public Life' that should be followed by all persons in public life – selflessness, integrity, objectivity, accountability, openness, honesty and leadership. They proposed that all public bodies should draw up Codes of Conduct based on these principles, and that internal systems for maintaining standards should be 'supported by independent scrutiny'.

The obvious difficulty with this approach is that first of the seven principles, selflessness, which was at the heart of the nineteenth century Northcote–Trevelyan, neo-Platonic conception of public service, stands in direct contradiction with selfishness, which is at the heart of today's espousal of competitive behaviour.

After its first report of May 1995, the committee published a number of specialized reports and then in January 2000 another report in which it surveyed the field.[18] I shall consider the main problems the committee has addressed and what has been done about them, dealing first with the law against corruption, then with problems that principally concern the conduct of politicians; and finally those that principally concern the conduct of public servants.

The Law Against Corruption

The laws against corruption enacted 1889, 1906 and 1916 are now to be updated, a step proposed by the Salmon Committee in 1976 and revived, with increasing urgency, in the reports of the new Committee on Standards in Public Life.[20] Pressure seems also to have come from the United States and other members of the OECD as they sought action against international bribery: Britain has not had adequate powers to enforce the OECD convention against international bribery referred to in Chapter 9 and has been conspicuously slow in doing anything about it.

The Government's proposals for new legislation, which were set out in a White Paper in June 2000, envisage that the present complex of laws relating to corruption should be tidied up and that for that purpose corruption should be redefined. Through the thickets of legal argument one can see three proposals for substantial changes that are of relevance to our analysis.[21] Firstly, MPs should no longer be able to avoid criminal prosecution for corruption by claiming Parliamentary privilege, the essential purpose of which is to maintain freedom of speech. Secondly, British courts should be empowered to prosecute Britons for bribery committed abroad. Thirdly, public servants prosecuted for corruption should cease to be treated more sternly than private persons: the presumption of corruption if they are found to have received money from a person holding or seeking a government contract should be abolished, and they should cease to be exposed to differential penalties.[22]

The first two proposals – those relating to the bribery of MPs and bribery abroad – look as if they should help to check corruption. But that cannot be said of the third. The stern laws against corruption by public servants may rarely if ever have been used, but they must have been a deterrent and, perhaps more important, they were a formal expression of the view that public servants were different from other people: they were privileged and respected guardians of the public interest; more was expected of them than of ordinary people. In the market-oriented policies of today that notion has been displaced by the notion that the civil service should be run on business lines and civil servants should be like businessmen. There is, I think, no disputing that, for the reasons discussed below, this approach is more vulnerable to corruption than the old. That being so, it is remarkable that the proposed legislation, instead of maintaining and bringing up to date the stern regime for public servants, has relaxed it.

As regards implementation, the government stated that these new rules were to be introduced as part of a Criminal Justice Bill in the session of Parliament that ends in October 2002. But at short notice the Government plucked out the rule against Britons paying bribes abroad and included it in the Anti-Terrorism Bill that it rushed through Parliament after the destruction of the World Trade Centre in New York in September 2001.[23] In the time-limited debate on that Bill, which became law in December 2001, Members of Parliament concentrated on the question of how far civil liberties should be taken away for the sake of security; the antibribery clauses were not critically examined.[24] Their introduction into law appears to be at least a gesture in the right direction. But it is questionable how effective they will be since they leave untouched bribery through foreign subsidiaries.[25]

It remains to be seen what will happen to the other two promised measures – the reduction of MPs' immunity from prosecution and easing of the anticorruption law relating to civil servants.

Corruption and Politicians

The principal areas of corruption amongst politicians that the Committee has addressed have been the taking of bribes by MPs, party funding and the sale of Honours.

I. The bribing of MPs

To stop MPs taking bribes or being suspected of doing so, a Parliamentary Commissioner for Standards has been created with the task of maintaining a fuller register of members' interests, providing advice and guidance to MPs on matters of conduct, and investigating allegations of misconduct. The Commissioner is to publish the conclusions of her investigations and report to a Select Committee of Parliament. The position of the Commissioner is awkward. She is something like an inquisitor, but instead of having powers of punishment she reports to MPs. Moreover her position, unlike that of a member of the judiciary, is not secure. The incumbent at the time of writing, Elizabeth Filkin, is not being renewed in office after her first term of 3 years, apparently because she was too vigorous in the performance of her duties for the liking of those who dominate the House of Commons.[26] But the fundamental problem is that, as regards misconduct over conflicts of interest, the conduct of MPs is to be judged by MPs. If this worked adequately in the past, it was because there was a sufficiency of MPs and ministers who had high standards and who, when it came to deciding how to judge their fellow members, were not coerced into toeing a party line that went against their consciences. If recent behaviour is anything to go by, standards in both those respects cannot now be relied upon – if they ever could. *The Economist* commented in 1996 that 'Lord Nolan, whose forthright investigations so far have done the public great service, would do even more good if he decided that regulation of MPs by MPs was fundamentally flawed.' Various proposals have been made, for example, that Britain 'should follow the model of a number of Commonwealth countries and establish an independent commission against corruption, not just to consider cases involving MPs but also ministers and civil servants.'[27] The position should in some degree be modified by the proposed anticorruption legislation under which Members of Parliament will no longer have immunity from prosecution in the courts for bribery.

2. Party funding

As we saw in Chapter 10, a limit was imposed in 1883 on the election expenses of each candidate but not on the national election expenditure of the political parties. That remained the position until 2001, and it has not been much criticized until recently. The tradition has been that the Conservatives raised funds from business, Labour from trades unions, while Honours were known to be given in return. There was some criticism by the odd radical maverick, for example, Willie Hamilton, but most politicians preferred to keep quiet.

Towards the end of the twentieth century several things changed. Mrs Thatcher's appeal to business was more energetic and overt than that of previous Conservative leaders, and then Mr Blair joined the pursuit of money from business when, under the flag of 'New Labour', he began to seek centre-right votes. In some conspicuous scandals, donors to both parties were seen to have given money in exchange for Honours, jobs in government or the promise of government policies that served their interests. The giving of money in exchange for policy favours is not new; Cecil Rhodes was a classic player of the game.

The most notable scandals on the Labour side concerned Mr Geoffrey Robinson (who was given a ministerial job but resigned after his financial support of Mr Mandelson and other financial matters were criticized), Mr Bernie Ecclestone (a motor-racing mogul who was alleged to have given £1 million to the Labour Party on condition that it did not support legislation to restrict tobacco advertising on racing cars, which sum was returned to him by the Labour Party after the story broke) and Lord Levy; and there is also the case of Mr Brian Davies, whose gift to the Labour party of £1 million from his animal rights fund is said to have fortified the government's opposition to fox-hunting.[28] On the Conservative side, there were scandals too, of which one – Mr Hague's dealings with Mr Ashcroft – dwarfs all others and is a reminder of the extent to which the rival political parties have acted together to keep the system going. In April 2000 Mr Hague put forward for a peerage the name of Mr Ashcroft, the Conservative party treasurer who had given £3 million to the party. The vetting committee raised objections but was prevailed upon by Mr Blair to withdraw them, which it did on condition that Mr Ashcroft took up residence in Britain and divested himself of his responsibilities to Belize, for which country (where his companies benefit from tax concessions) he was ambassador to the United Nations. The idea of a conditional peerage was denounced as a constitutional outrage by a number of senior Conservatives and others.[29] There was also strong criticism of the fact that Mr Hague was accepting foreign donations in the interregnum before the new legislation forbidding them was passed.[30] To this new legislation I now turn.

The Committee on Standards in Public Life in October 1998 had produced a report on party funding that tackled the problem with refreshing directness, proposing limits on what political parties are permitted to spend on elections (in addition to the amounts spent by candidates). Its declared aim was to encourage more openness about the source and use of party funds, greater public confidence that individuals and organizations are not buying influence with political parties, and more small-to-medium-sized donations to party funds. Specifically, it recommended open declaration of all gifts above £5,000, a ban on foreign donations, a ban on anonymous donations of more than £50, and prior approval by shareholders of gifts by companies; and, for enforcement, it proposed creation of an independent Electoral Commission with wide executive and investigative powers to act as registrar of political parties, to receive accounts and reports of disclosable donations from the parties and investigate discrepancies. The committee also proposed that, in order to reduce reliance on contributions from big donors, tax relief should be provided for private donations to political parties of less than £500.

The government accepted the proposals, apart from the proposed tax relief for donations of less than £500 and some recommendations regarding the financing of referendums. The new regime was passed by Parliament and came into force early in 2001. It remains to be seen how it will work.

The principal question is how far the upper limit on election funding and the required disclosure of donations will deter the political parties from selling policies, Honours and jobs for large donations. Unofficial disclosure through leaks did not stop these activities, though it did contribute to calls for reform.

The political parties are sure to look for ways of circumventing the new rules just as they did after the 1883 Act. Michael Pinto-Duschinsky has pointed to a potential loophole caused by European law: the government, he tells us, has been forced to accept the right of European-based companies to donate to British companies but cannot impose on them the obligation to adhere to British company law, with the result that as things stand it will not be necessary for them to obtain the consent of shareholders before making donations.[31]

3. The Award of Honours

The use and abuse of the award of Honours is being influenced by the reform of the House of Lords. This reform, which is being introduced in two stages, provides on the one hand for a substantial increase in the total number of peers to be appointed by patronage and, on the other, for some rather obscure and apparently feeble reinforcement of the mechanism for vetting nominations.

An interim regime was introduced at the end of 1999 under which most hereditary peers were removed and replaced by an unprecedented intake of life peers. The prime minister nominated most of these in the traditional manner, though a new non-statutory House of Lords Appointments Commission was established to appoint a limited number of non-party life peers.

The government's proposals for the final reform, published in November 2001, have provoked such an outcry that it is uncertain what will happen to them.[32] Indeed it has been suggested that the government so likes the interim regime that it has 'chosen an alternative which is so shameless that it has not the slightest chance of being accepted and enacted.'[33] The main objection is that only 20 per cent of the reformed House of Lords are to be elected; another 20 per cent is to be appointed by the Appointments Commission established under the interim regime; but the majority is to nominated by the political parties according to their strength in the previous election of the House of Commons.[34]

The scale on which successive prime ministers have exercised their patronage since 1958, when life peerages were introduced and the creation of hereditary peerages effectively ceased, can be seen in the following figures:

Rate of Creation of Life Peers by Successive Prime Ministers[35]

Prime Minister	Life peers	Months in office	Number created per 12 months in office
Harold Macmillan	90	65	17
Alec Douglas-Home	29	12	29
Harold Wilson	143	68	25
Edward Heath	48	45	13
Harold Wilson	83	25	40
James Callaghan	60	37	19
Margaret Thatcher	216	139	19
John Major	171	77	27
Tony Blair	248	54	55
Totals			
Conservative	554	338	20
Labour			
a. excluding Blair	286	130	26
b. including Blair	534	184	35

Two points stand out. First the greatest extravagance occurred under Mr Wilson in his second administration when he was much criticized for 'cronyism', and under Mr Blair, whose conduct has been similarly criticized. It can be argued that Labour needed to redress the Conservative domination of the hereditary peerage; and that when reform was introduced and most hereditary peers were removed, Labour had to undertake a large once-for-all injection of life peers. But there was no necessity for the choice of these replacements to be vested in the prime minister.

For the future, the White Paper proposes that the term of appointed members should be limited to 5, 10 or 15 years – the term of office is a point on which the White Paper invites the public to offer views – which would mean that the parties were making nominations on a recurrent basis, possibly at a high rate.

As for vetting, the interim regime gave the task of vetting the prime minister's nominations for peerages to the new House of Lords Appointments Commission.[36] The government's proposal for the final regime is that the commission should be made a statutory body and should vet all persons nominated for life peerages by the political parties. The words used to describe what the government envisages merit close attention. They remind me of the great American definition of weasel words: 'Why, Weasel words are words that suck the life out of the words next to them, just as a weasel sucks the egg and leaves the shell':[37]

> The Commission will carry out the propriety checks on those nominated by the political parties. This will be its only involvement in the individual nominations made by the parties. The Government does not accept the Royal Commission recommendation that the Appointments Commission should have the final say over the identity of party nominations. Parties of whatever persuasion must be able to decide who will serve on their behalf. The Commission will of course scrutinize nominations to ensure that those put forward are fit and proper candidates for membership of the Lords.[38]

For Honours other than appointments to the Lords the old vetting committee remains in place, still composed of three privy councillors appointed by the prime minister of the day. A long-serving loophole in its terms of reference has been closed. The 1925 terms of reference gave the scrutiny committee the job of looking at all peerages, and at lesser Honours only if they were given for 'political services'. Which meant that if an industrialist was nominated for a knighthood for 'services to industry' after his company had made a large donation to a political party, his case did not come to the attention of the committee.

Corruption and the Public Service

It has been said that Mrs Thatcher and President Reagan believed that the public service may not be devils incarnate, but they do represent something very wrong with the organization of political and economic life in their countries.'[39] Certainly Mrs Thatcher came to power on an antigovernment programme, and one of her aims was to cut down a large and strongly unionized public sector, led by civil servants whom she perceived to be wedded to an unenterprising notion of public service. She brought in men from business to give advice on how to reform the civil service so as to reduce its size and achieve efficiency of the kind they knew in business.

The main thrust of the new policies was to break up the machine of government and the unitary civil service, cultivate private competitive forces wherever possible and turn the civil service into something as close as possible to a private business. The spending of large amounts of public funds was handed to independent agencies under government departments and to QUANGOs (executive non-departmental public bodies and National Health Service bodies). The 'hollowed-out' central government departments were instructed to go in for market testing to see if services could not be bought from outside more cheaply than they could be produced by civil servants inside.

Politically-appointed advisers have been brought in on an increasing scale; and there has been a vast increase in the use of consultants employed on contracts to do all kinds of work, for example, to introduce new computer-based accounting systems, to make economic assessments, to recruit staff to departments and agencies. Performance-related pay has been introduced as widely as possible. The Civil Service Commission, which used to recruit staff, has been reduced by a series of Orders in Council to being a regulatory body that supervises the performance of the private firms to which recruitment has been sub-contracted.[40] The result has been a fragmentation of the civil service. Mr Blair, far from reversing these policies and practices, has kept pushing them forward.[41]

In 1968 the Fulton Committee on the reform of the home civil service (of which I was member) severely criticized the service for remaining stuck in the mould set by its nineteenth century reformers and strongly urged that it be made more professional and better at management; it also recommended that the hiving off of executive tasks to independent agencies on Swedish lines should be explored.[42] We believed that our proposals would modernize the civil service whilst preserving its unity and its dedication to public service. We never entertained the idea that the service should be broken up or that its public service values should be thrust aside in favour of market values. Nor did it cross our minds that under the British constitution – or lack of it – it would be possible for a government, by means of Orders in Council, to take apart the civil service without presenting legislation to Parliament and seeking its approval.

There have been many studies and expressions of concern about the destruction of the British tradition of public service.[43] An eloquent warning came from the late Lord Bancroft who, before he parted company with Mrs Thatcher and took early retirement in 1981, was the last head of the civil service to hold out for the established system and its values Speaking in the House of Lords in 1994, he referred to the 'dismantling of the public services by executive action subject to very, very limited parliamentary control and debate.' It has been done piecemeal, he said, on the hoof. What took a century and a half to build was in danger of being off-handedly demolished in a decade and a half.[44]

In 1993 the *Spectator* warned that:

> In sweeping the career bureaucrats aside, the Government may end up destroying the only thing which has prevented officials in this country from turning into the gangsters so frequently encountered abroad: the conviction that the Civil Service is not about private enterprise or personal profit, but public service.[45]

I shall consider the effect of the new policies on corruption in the public service and the remedies proposed by the Committee on Standards in Public Life under four heads: patronage; the diminished ability of civil servants to restrain ministers; the new inducements to civil servants to pursue their private interests; and the risks of fraud by firms to whom public work is contracted out.

1. Patronage

The problem has been not so much an increase in patronage. That had happened as government agencies proliferated in the years after 1945. Rather it is that the Thatcher government in abolishing Labour-created public agencies and manning new Conservative-created agencies sought believers in their new philosophy and accordingly chose persons with Thatcherite convictions. One can see the logic of the policy, but it was vulnerable to abuse and to the perception that jobs were being given to party supporters as a reward for their services. After 1945 the Labour government had faced the same problem when it needed to man the boards of the new public agencies and enterprises it was creating and sought persons who were sympathetic to their beliefs; but the behaviour of ministers was then restrained by the civil service – though the Poulson affair is evidence that appointments were not always immaculate. In order to find suitable candidates for the jobs to be filled at that time, Sir Edward (later Lord) Bridges in 1945 established at the Treasury a list of suitable persons for public jobs. Bridges, a godlike figure who had steered the civil service brilliantly through the war, solicited names for the list, which came to be known as the 'The Great and the Good', in confidence 'from all sources thought to be reliable' by him.[46]

Under Mrs Thatcher, ministers appear to have paid little attention to advice of the civil service and to have been uninhibited about political patronage. A Conservative junior minister who had responsibility in 1993 for many appointments was reported to have said, 'I can't remember knowingly appointing a Labour supporter.'[47] The persons chosen were mostly businessmen who were not normally familiar with the ethics of public service.

Some disgraceful misconduct came to the attention of the Public Accounts Committee of Parliament, so bad that the chairman of the committee, Sir Robert Sheldon, seems to have become intermittently apoplectic when telling the Committee on Standards in Public Life about it:

> ...the Welsh Development agency was a striking example... I mean the idea that there could be somebody recruited who had been in prison three times for fraud, recruited through a Government agency and entertains models in his hotel room on a Sunday afternoon paid for by the public purse – I mean it is something that was quite alien to anything we had come across before. There are a number of examples, not quite as serious as that, but very serious ones – the Wessex Regional Health Authority, the Development Board for Rural Wales and those sorts of things.

He went on to describe another new phenomenon, 'silence clauses' which he believed should never be associated with the spending of public money:

> There have been a number of cases where people coming in from outside – and of course they have not got the ethos of the public service and they feel that they are running their own show, and without those standards they have been buying off people that they disagreed with, but inserted into their dismissal have been "silence clauses" – they are not allowed to say anything.

The remedy proposed by the Committee on Standards in Public Life has been to create a Commissioner for Public Appointments to 'regulate, monitor and report on the public appointments process.' Ministers are still ultimately responsible for appointments to the agencies for which their departments are responsible, e.g. the Minister of Health is responsible for appointments to bodies within the Health Service. The Commissioner watches and reports on what ministers do. His first step was to lay down a 'Code of Practice for Public Appointments

Procedures' consisting of seven principles, including selection by merit, independent scrutiny, equal opportunities, and openness and transparency. Having established the Code, his and his successor's task has been to provide advice to ministers, to receive complaints and to monitor what goes on in all the many public agencies. He has a tiny staff and has employed a private accountancy firm, Ernst and Young, to audit government departments' appointment practices and report to him. (Market doctrine has been pursued to the point where a private firm is employed to enforce public standards in public agencies.[48]) At the start, the first commissioner, Sir Len Peach, a former chairman of the Police Complaints Authority, adopted the denial approach noted in Chapter 2 and declared that he had set himself three aims: to create and maintain a greater level of public confidence in the system; to create and maintain a greater level of confidence in the system amongst those seeking public appointments; and to make the public appointments process more effective.[49] He refrained from saying that he was there to stop political patronage and other misbehaviour.

A test of the efficacy of the new system occurred over appointments to the National Health Service (NHS) boards. The Thatcher and Blair governments, each in turn, appointed political sympathizers to these bodies, the total membership of which runs to some 3,000 persons, in a manner suggestive of the US spoils system. The Conservatives, seeking to introduce business ways into the NHS, put in their men and women. The reaction of the Labour government that came to power in 1997 was to push in their men and women by rarely renewing the appointments of incumbents and seeking nominations from Labour MPs and local authorities. These things they did despite the fact that the new machinery, designed precisely to stop political patronage, was in place. The result was a stinging report in March 2000 by Dame Rennie Fritchie, a formidable lady who had recently taken over as Commissioner and who, according to the press, had declared her intention to achieve a 'squeaky clean' system.[50] She concluded, after considering the advice of a scrutiny group that had analysed NHS appointments, that 'the process has become politicized in a systematic way' and that many of the principles in the code of practice laid down 'have either been, or risk being, breached in both their letter and spirit. 'The Department', she said – and she might better have said the minister, for it is ministers, not their civil servants who are entrusted with the power of making appointments – 'must ensure that in developing a new appointments process, it places my principles at the heart of the process.'[51] One waited to see whether ministers, having violated rules recommended by a monitoring body that has only advisory power, would bow to its strictures. They appear to have done so. Responsibility for making appointments to NHS boards was delegated to a new nine-member NHS Appointments Commission in April 2001.[52] It is of course a non-statutory change that can be reversed or modified by future ministers.

2. Civil servants and ministers

In the words of Sir Archibald Hamilton, chairman of the Conservative Party's 1922 Committee, giving evidence to the Committee on Standards in Public Life, 'Ministers are stopped from being corrupt by the Civil Service at senior levels.'[53] The civil servants' ability to perform this task has been an element in Britain's largely unwritten constitution. They have had one important statutory power to support them: it is the duty of the Permanent Secretary of a department to report to Parliament that the money voted to his department has been spent for the purposes for which it was intended; hence it is his or her duty to warn ministers against spending money for purposes for which it was not voted. But for the rest, their influence with ministers derives from the British tradition that ministers constitutionally act as advisers to the sovereign, and civil servants in turn act as advisers to ministers; ministers are responsible for what their civil servants do, and should take the praise or blame for it, as Sir Thomas Dugdale, did when he resigned over the Crichel Down affair in 1954. In contrast to the American tradition, there has been no perceived separation between politician and civil servant, with the latter taking responsibility for the implementation of policy:

> Among the advice a [British] minister must expect from civil servants is advice on the relevant facts of a case, relevant precedents and relevant law. Thus the civil service is likely to curb the exercise of any arbitrary power by ministers. In theory and largely in practice, civil servants are privy to almost all decisions ministers make, able and encouraged to advise them on every aspect of that discretion, not only in terms of their meeting of their own political objectives, but also as a safeguard against illegality and impropriety. Since the Northcote–Trevelyan reforms, this has been the cornerstone of the British administrative tradition.[54]

The argument for maintaining the tradition that ministers are responsible for the execution of policy has been that it preserved the accountability of ministers to Parliament: it permitted MPs to take ministers to task for the actions of their officials.[55] But as the work of departments expanded and became more complex in the twentieth century the implicit assumption that ministers could keep an eye on what their officials were doing became less and less realistic; the influence of civil servants over ministers increased. When ministers arrived at a department, where they would typically stay about two years or less, they often knew little or nothing about the subject for which they had become responsible; civil servants had to educate them and take care of things for them. As the scale of government was increased, civil servants increasingly had to take decisions in the name of ministers that ministers did not know about, and could not know about if they were not to be drowned in detail; and they mostly took those decisions under existing law that ministers could not change without legislation. Meanwhile the senior class of the civil service, the administrators, remained a quietly confident elite, a band of Platonic Guardians. As the number of cabinet ministers and junior ministers was expanded and the social classes from which they were drawn became less exclusive, the civil service provided general guidance to ministers on how to behave. This came in the form of a document, quaintly called 'Questions of Procedure for Ministers', that was kept by the Secretary of the Cabinet and updated from time to time by him, subject to the approval, and sometimes the instructions, of the prime minister. Lord Trend, who was secretary of the Cabinet from 1963 to 1973, described the document as 'tips of etiquette for beginners'.[56] In all these respects, civil servants exercised, by example, advice and the raised eyebrow, a restraining influence on ministers.

That tradition has now been severely kicked aside. Political commentators and young radicals used to complain that ministers were tamed and run by their civil servants, a phenomenon brilliantly caricatured in the television series 'Yes Minister'. Now one hears of ministers bullying civil servants and asking them to do questionable things.

It is impossible to find out precisely what goes on in the secretive world of Whitehall, but many fragments of evidence fit together. Two episodes are publicly known in which the Secretary to the Cabinet, who is also the Head of the Civil Service, was made by a prime minister to do things to protect the reputation of the government that he should never have been asked to do. Sir Robert (now Lord) Armstrong, rather than a minister, was sent to give evidence in the Spycatcher trial in

Australia and found himself having to admit he had been 'economical with the truth' in answering questions about events the responsibility for which lay with ministers. Sir Robin (now Lord) Butler was made to investigate and question Mr Aitken about the Ritz affair. Being unable, as a civil servant, to challenge the word of Mr Aitken, he wrote a report to the prime minister, which he had allowed Mr Aitken to amend in draft, and in which he accepted Mr Aitken's denial of wrong-doing. But the really objectionable point is that Sir Robin's verdict was made public for the purpose of quashing rumours of wrongdoing by Mr Aitken, thereby avoiding a scandal. Mr Aitken later admitted to perjury and attempting to corrupt the course of justice and was sent to jail. The Committee on Standards in Public Life concluded that, 'in many circumstances it is wholly appropriate for the Cabinet Secretary to "investigate" in the sense of collecting relevant material and infor-mation and advising upon it' but it is inappropriate for him to give a verdict. 'In other words, the responsibility for the answer given by any minister to an allegation must remain solely his or hers, and cannot be shared with a civil servant, however senior.'[57]

There have also been well-reported cases of ministers pushing their Permanent Secretaries to authorize dodgy expenditure. The most incredible has been that of 'Miss Whiplash', when the Permanent Secretary of the Treasury, of all people, was somehow persuaded to agree that the Treasury should pay from public funds a lawyer's bill that Mr Lamont, the Chancellor of the Exchequer, had incurred in evicting a lady of ill repute from property he owned. Then there was the Pergau dam affair, when Mrs Thatcher, in order to get an arms contract from Malaysia, used part of the British budget for aid to developing countries to finance the building of a dam that was favoured by the local ruler but regarded as an unacceptable project by the aid department in London. The Permanent Secretary of the aid department objected, the Commons Public Accounts Committee upheld his view, and the funds were found in another way; but the Permanent Secretary's career ended in a manner that looked rather punitive.[58]

A less visible problem is that ministers are now so obsessed with propagating favourable attention in the media, and so inclined to treat their civil servants as personal servants rather than as managers of their department, that, according to Foster and Plowden writing in 1996:

> One can already see civil servants being drawn into developing news-handling as their primary function and their presentational

skills as most likely to earn them ministerial respect. It is in this area that the dangers of the future politicization of the civil service are greatest.'[59]

The problem of ministers pushing civil servants to do improper things has been met by the introduction, on the recommendation of the Committee on Standards in Public Life, of a Code of Conduct for ministers and another for civil servants. Ministers are told they must not ask civil servants to do anything that is against the civil service code; and some provision has been made for civil servants to be able to make complaints. But these codes, like so much else, are not statutory; the government of the day can change them on the hoof.

Since Labour came to power there has been criticism of the big increase in public funds spent on advertising the government's policies (sometimes in documents purporting to be the objective work of civil servants) and sounding public opinion as to their popularity, both of which activities might more appropriately be paid for by the Labour party than the taxpayer. It is hard to believe that civil servants did not raise an eyebrow at this expenditure; it seems not to have been explicitly approved by Parliament.[60] There have been more press reports of ministers bullying civil servants.[61] And the government, in the name of efficiency, has pressed forward measures that threaten the traditional civil service values to the point where the Committee on Standards in Public Life in its *Sixth Report* felt it appropriate to consider 'whether, and if so why, the traditional core values should be sustained' and 'also the effect of the government's present programme of reform upon them'.[62] The committee addressed three issues.

Firstly, the conflict between the preservation of core values and the increasing use of outsiders. In March 1999 the Government in a White Paper on *Modernizing Government* piously said, 'we must not jeopardize the public service values of impartiality, objectivity and integrity,' but went on to say:

> We will bring in more people into the Civil Service from outside. We will hold more open recruitment competitions for people at various career stages. We will make greater use of short-term contracts. We will increase secondments to and from the public sector, the voluntary sector and the private sector.[63]

In a rather brief and seemingly despondent discussion of this policy, the Committee on Standards in Public Life said the government will have to consider carefully how the public service ethos is to be maintained if a substantial proportion of appointments is made from sectors where different values hold priority. (In the words of Sir Robin Butler, businessmen get used to worrying about the bottom line, whereas civil servants get used to worrying about equity of process.) The committee did not challenge government policy or suggest that outside appointments be restrained. They merely recommended that heads of departments should ensure that there are 'training and induction opportunities for short-term outside appointees...at which ethical issues within the public sector are examined; and they noted that there had been a disappointing response to a recommendation in their first report in May 1995 that surveys be made to see how much staff understood about ethical standards.[64]

Secondly, the committee has been concerned since its first report that performance-related pay arrangements for permanent secretaries may undermine the political impartiality of civil servants. In the *Sixth Report* it emphasized the need for 'independent validation' of arrangements under which permanent secretaries now have to agree to targets at the beginning of the year and accept pay according to their success in hitting them. Since, so far as I know, the objectives agreed with permanent secretaries are not made public, it is impossible know to what extent, if at all, they are made to chase short-run political targets to please their ministers, who are now obsessed with propaganda, rather than the long-term development of the public services for which their department is responsible.

Thirdly, the committee was concerned that the provision of impartial advice by the civil service might be marginalized by the importation of external advisers.

The main safeguard for the public service proposed by the committee is the introduction of a Civil Service Act, a measure first recommended by Northcote–Trevelyan 150 years ago. The committee said:

> Old as is the debate, we consider that it has acquired fresh importance because of the radical reform of the civil service that this government is pursuing. On any view, the civil service should be seen as not solely the property of the government of the day but as a national asset.[65]

The government in evidence said that it had such an act in mind but could not promise to include it in the next legislative programme. The process of consultation to determine the contents of an act had not been begun. In short, the government by its words and inaction indicated that it did not care much for such an act; it was dragging its feet. The committee, after expressing impatience, reacted by saying:

> A timetable for the implementation of the government's commitment to a Civil Service Act should be produced as soon as possible. In particular a target date should be set for the process of consultation on the scope of such an Act.[66]

That was in January 2000. Nearly two years later, Sir Richard Wilson, the Secretary to the Cabinet and Head of the Civil Service, told a House of Commons committee that he wanted to leave a draft Civil Service Bill when he retired in less than a year, and that he had cleared with the prime minister an early start on a wide-ranging consultation, with the hope of gaining as wide an amount of support as possible across party lines.[67] The unanswered question is when this government or any other will find it politically expedient to allocate parliamentary time for a Civil Service Bill, which in its very nature will limit the power of ministers *vis-à-vis* their civil servants, one of whose jobs is to stop them being corrupt.

3. The pursuit of private interests by civil servants

There is an obvious likelihood that civil servants are and will be more strongly tempted than before to be helpful to persons in the private sector who might offer them remunerative employment. Market testing and the putting out of work to private firms has been encouraged; movement in and out of the civil service has been strongly encouraged; performance-related pay and provision for early retirement have been introduced with the purpose of increasing mobility; civil servants have been encouraged to adopt friendly attitudes to business and, like others in society, to admire mobility and pursue private gain; their careers are less secure than they were; and as ministers have introduced more political advisers, their influence with ministers has declined.

There used to be the notion that top civil servants were granted good pensions, knighthoods and other Honours so that their advice and decisions would not be influenced by the prospect of jobs with business when they retired: good civil servants would confine themselves in retirement to work for public bodies and charities. That was never quite true. Of the 18 civil servants who have retired since 1919 from the three top posts in the home civil service – Secretary to the Cabinet, Head of the Home Civil Service and Head of the Treasury – fifteen have taken business directorships, usually several, after they retired; only three – Lord Bridges, Lord Trend and Sir Horace Wilson – appear not to have done so.[68] One suspects that top civil servants, with these three notable exceptions, have felt, like school prefects, that they were so greatly respected, so virtuous and so far above suspicion that they could do things that they would have frowned upon if they had been done by lesser persons.

Official policy, formulated in the inter-war years, has been that there is nothing intrinsically wrong in government employees, civil or military, accepting business appointments when they retire, but since there are cases 'which might lend themselves to misunderstanding', official assent should be asked for. (An instance of the use of the denial formula.) To provide advice to the prime minister, who heads the civil and military services, a vetting committee of public figures was set up in 1975. Since the first report of the Committee on Standards in Public Life, the rules have been made slightly more demanding, the procedure has been applied to ministers as well as to public servants and, in order to make the procedure more open, the committee now publishes an annual report.[69] But the system still relies wholly on the sense of honour of public servants and the private employers to whom they go. The maximum sanction is the recommendation of a waiting period. There are no penal sanctions and, so far as I know, no civil or military servant has been stripped of his or her pension or Honours for misbehaviour of this kind.

The outflow to business has grown greatly. In 1996–97 there were no less than 1,019 applications from senior officials (military and civil) for approval of business appointments; 86 per cent were approved unconditionally; 14 per cent subject to conditions, usually meaning delay. Of these applications, 360 were under the Departmental heading 'Defence'; 86 under 'Inland Revenue' and 82 under 'Customs and Excise'.[70] In the two tax departments, officials who know the tax system have increasingly been induced by the offer of large salaries to join firms that advise taxpayers how best to minimize their tax bills: a case of gamekeepers turning poachers.

So far, no scandals have broken over business appointments since policy towards movement became more lax, but that does not mean that nothing has been happening: as we have seen, scandals are erratic, sometimes climactic, revelations of reality. The most notable scandal over a civil servant improperly soliciting a business job occurred in the 1930s; and in the 1980s the conduct of two officials was criticized in the Scott Report on the arms to Iraq affair. These cases are interesting for what they reveal about the problem of relations with business and how circumspectly that problem has been handled. They are described in Appendix B.

A new cause for concern is that there has been a big increase in the number of private sector employees lent by business on secondment to the civil service. The number of staff seconded to the civil service is reported to have risen from about 600 before the 1997 election to 1,317. The arrangements under which these secondments are made appear to be rather informal, and there have been allegations that companies lending staff are getting favours in return. It has been reported that the chairman of the Committee on Standards in Public Life is in favour of a register that would spell out where the secondees come from and what they are doing.[71]

Recently there have been two cases, which may be a sign of the times, of extreme corruption by a civil servant. In 1994 Mr Foxley, a retired Ministry of Defence official who had been in charge of ammunition contracts receiving a salary of £20,000 was sentenced to 4 years in prison for having received more than £1.5 million in bribes.[72] In 1997 Mr Allcock, a tax inspector in charge of an elite team to track down City fraudsters, in particular those who had never registered for tax, was found to have engaged in fraud on a 'breath-taking scale' and was sent to prison for five years. He had accepted money to the value of £150,000, trips to Monte Carlo, a Caribbean cruise, Concorde tickets and the services of a prostitute from the wealthy Arab businessmen he was supposed to investigate. In addition, he is believed to have cost the taxpayer millions by not registering the taxable income of those who bribed him.

The latter case seems to be an example of how the civil service tradition of trusting the sense of honour of one's colleagues and subordinates and implicitly denying the possibility that anyone in the public service would misbehave has endured into an era when those social and moral assumptions have been failing. In a report on the case to Parliament the head of the National Audit Office stated that weak management controls and naive assumptions about the honesty of tax inspectors had created a culture where corruption could exist undetected.[73] Which, if you remove the pejorative tone, could be a description of how a system based on trust should work: a system where corruption could not exist undetected would be a system based on distrust, and that would be destructive of trust. What is reassuring is that the National Audit Office proceeded to review the case and express strong views to Parliament on the need for improvements: the system for auditing public expenditure and reporting to Parliament, which is the prime deterrent to the misappropriation of public funds, is intact.

4. Contracting out

Foster and Plowden, two distinguished proponents of the market approach to government who have advised British governments, acknowledge that the contracting out of the provision of public goods and services to private suppliers (for which they also use the terms 'separation' and 'contractorization') is likely to lead to more fraud. They quote an American analyst writing of the experience of the United States:

> The irony is rich – despite the enthusiasm for entrepreneurial government and privatization, the most egregious tales of waste, fraud and other abuse in government programmes have often involved criminal activity by the government's private partners and weak government management to detect and correct these problems. Why...? The answer in brief is that competitive prescription is not a magic bullet... Government's relationships require...aggressive management by a strong competent government. The competition prescription does not so much reduce government as fundamentally change its role.[74]

Another problem is that, in pursuit of efficiency, the traditional administrative culture in which prior approval was required for the purchase of, say, boots at an economical price, followed by precise check and audit that what was approved was done, has been replaced by a managerial culture. The emphasis is now on assessing alternative ways in which a budget can be used so as to achieve the objective for which it was provided, with the follow-up consisting of the evaluation of the results. The new system, which requires that responsibility for spending be delegated down the line and that checks are less narrow, provides greater opportunities for corruption than the old and must be harder to police and harder to audit after the event.

Foster and Plowden argue that as public employment becomes more like that in the private sector, more rigorous methods to prevent and detect fraud will have to be adopted, and conclude on a sobering note:

> But if the costs are not to be very high, the public sector must follow the private sector in accepting that some level of fraud is inevitable and not cost-effective to reduce. This will be unattractive to the House of Commons Public Accounts Committee, and to similar institutions in other countries, which have argued that only an absence of fraud is tolerable... But whatever measures are adopted, separation must be expected to result in more fraud. If it happens without the necessary safeguards, in some areas at least the costs of separation could outweigh the benefits.[75]

Loss of honesty is one thing, but there is another aspect to the policy of reducing the civil service in favour of contracting out: the civil service may cease to possess – or be prevented from building up – the management and technical skills, in which it was always weak, that are required if contracts with private suppliers are to be advantageous to the public sector in terms of cost, delivery on time and quality of the product. A series of major failures of government computer systems has led to a highly critical report from the Public Accounts Committee, which said that many contracts did not impose high-enough penalties for failure, that skilled computer managers should be brought in to ensure that systems were delivered on time and budget, and that there should be more scrutiny of external contracts to ensure that they are properly negotiated.[76] In its annual report on major defence projects the National Audit Office recently criticized worsening delays and cost overruns, some of them of astonishing proportions: two antitank weapons, one portable, one airborne, are expected to be completed approximately ten years late; of 25 projects just one was due to be delivered on schedule.[77] And it has been reported that the Ministry of Defence police is investigating allegations by a former employee of British Aerospace, our biggest defence contractor, that its subsidiary, Marconi, has cheated the taxpayer of millions of pounds by overcharging for minor jobs, a practice that he attributed to a combination of opportunism by Marconi and 'sloppily written' contracts.[78]

Since the policy of contracting out tasks and reducing the size of the civil service has been driven by dogma, one wonders how often the employment of consultants, recruiting agencies and other profit-making firms instead of civil servants has been extravagant rather than economical of taxpayers' money. I know of no case where work has been brought back into the civil service on grounds of economy.

Independently of the Committee on Standards in Public Life, the Public Accounts Committee of Parliament and the Audit Commission have for a considerable time being pressing for improvements in financial accounting and auditing of public agencies to which the spending of so much public money has been delegated. I do not know what the result has been.

Assessment

I shall apply the same rough method of assessment to these recent problems as I used in the previous chapter, asking (a) had behaviour sunk when enquiries were instituted – or were new higher standards being demanded; and (b) what action has been taken and what results are visible.

1. The bribing of MPs

There is little doubt that behaviour has deteriorated as the cult of greed, the growth of lobbying and social change caused MPs to be less inhibited in selling their influence. The remedial action, consisting of better monitoring by the new Parliamentary Commissioner, looks inadequate. The proposed anticorruption measures that are to be included in the new Criminal Justice Bill should help to deter some of the worst abuses – though the timing of that legislation is uncertain.

2. Party Funding

Party funding standards fell as both parties competed intensely for money from businessmen with which to finance media-dominated election campaigns. An Act has been passed which introduces limits on total national election expenditure by a party, forbids foreign contributions and requires disclosure of all substantial contributions; and an Electoral Commission has been established to monitor what happens. This should check the decline in standards and may raise them. But the limits on electoral expenses are so high that there is still a strong incentive to party leaders to ignore the increased transparency and accept contributions in exchange for the promise of favours. Moreover loopholes in the new law are already being discussed: as happened after the 1883 Act, new corruption may develop around the new higher standards.

3. Sale of Honours

This has recently been as scandalous as it was in Lloyd George's time, except that the money from the sales has not gone into the prime minister's pocket, but into the funds of his or her party. Leaders of both main parties have been involved. The amended vetting procedures introduced with the interim reform of the House of Lords, and those proposed for the final reform, continue to rely on shaming the leaders of the political parties who now dispense most peerages and, it is proposed, should continue to do so. The actual and proposed vetting bodies are denied the power to stop corrupt nominations. The compulsory disclosure of substantial contributions to party funds and the law against foreign donations should help.

4. The arms trade

The international arms trade, which has grown since the beginning of the Cold War, has been a burgeoning source of corruption in the Third World and amongst the politicians of the exporting countries, including Britain. The OECD Convention and the new English law against bribing foreigners are steps in the right direction, but its success will depend on how far the exporting countries, led by the United States, manage jointly and sincerely to enforce restraint and deal with such problems as the payment of bribes through foreign subsidiaries. Part of the arms trade is as elusive and rotten as the drugs trade.

5. Patronage in the public services

Standards have declined as appointments, notably those to the NHS, were politicized more overtly and aggressively than before. The new energetic Commissioner for Public Appointments achieved a victory when in March 2000 she upbraided the Ministry of Health for politicizing appointments to the Health Service and caused it to establish a new NHS Appointments Commission, in some degree detached from the ministry. This is a somewhat encouraging test case of the efficacy of the new monitoring bodies which, lacking a statutory basis, operate by reporting and shaming politicians who may be shameless. But it also indicates how much depends on the character of the monitor and, behind that, on whether ministers, who appoint the monitors, risk choosing persons who may criticize them.

6. The civil service and ministers

As the ability of civil servants to restrain ministers, which was regarded as an element in our unwritten constitution, was diminished, standards of ministerial conduct towards their civil servants fell. To protect officials from being bullied by ministers to act wrongly, or acting wrongly for their own benefit, non-statutory codes of conduct for ministers and civil servants have been introduced. The Committee on Standards in Public Life has recommended in strong terms that codes of this kind be enshrined in a Civil Service Act, which would also prevent the civil service being further knocked about without the approval of Parliament. But the Government has been dragging its feet.

7. The pursuit of private interests by public servants

This has been encouraged and the opportunities for corrupt behaviour have become wider as market behaviour, business models and mobility have been espoused; and it is proposed that the law should no longer treat corruption by civil servants with differential severity. Feeble action to prevent misbehaviour has consisted in the introduction of a civil service code (which sets out obvious rules) and greater publicity in the form of an annual report from the committee that vets movements from the public service to jobs in business. Misbehaviour of this kind is invisible to the public until a scandal occurs, usually as a result of an accidental revelation. That has not happened yet.

8. Contracting out

Contracting out, together with the policy of delegating responsibility for spending decisions down the line to 'managerial' civil servants, has increased the scope for corruption. This may take the form not just of the misappropriation of public funds but of collusive deals with consultants and contractors from whom the newly mobile civil servants may expect future employment or other rewards. Moreover the new system is harder to police and audit than the old.

Summary and Conclusion

In the light of this list, what summarized answer can one give to the question, had standards fallen before inquiries and action were considered? I would suggest that under the first six headings above – the bribing of MPs, party funding, the sale of Honours, the arms trade, patronage in the public services and the conduct of ministers towards civil servants – standards of behaviour, after sliding from the wartime peak, tumbled towards the end of the century. Under the last two headings – the pursuit of private interests by public servants and contracting out – opportunities for corruption have been greatly increased with consequences we cannot yet see. In short, the evidence against politicians is pretty damning; as yet there is little evidence against civil servants.

What then of remedial action? There is one case – the limitation of election expenses – where standards have been set, by statute, of a kind the country has not known before, and a new permanent electoral commission has been created to supervise the new regime; and there is the new law against making bribes to foreigners, though it looks leaky. In the other cases, it looks as if the decline in standards may have been checked or retarded, though it is too early to make more than a most tentative judgement. It cannot be said that there has been a return to the standards of the previous era when dedication to the public service rode high. The new mechanisms created to defend standards are of uncertain efficacy. They mostly consist of non-statutory monitoring bodies that can be abolished or doctored by the government of the day; and their means of operation is to report publicly (apart from the vetting committee for Honours which just leaks) to those they monitor: the Parliamentary Commissioner reports to MPs; the Commissioner for Public Appointments and other bodies report to ministers.

One might call this a system of gentle deterrence. What results it will produce will depend, as any such deterrence system must, on the sense of shame of those who are tempted to misbehave, and on the likelihood of their exposure and punishment if they do. The balance struck between reliance on honour, the counterpart of which is shame, and reliance on deterrence still leans towards reliance on honour.[79] That is understandable and probably laudable. To jump from a system based on honour to a system based on distrust and strongly punitive deterrence would be to provoke distrust. But one may still doubt whether it is prudent to rely so much on non-statutory bodies that, for their efficacy, depend on the honour of ministers, in particular prime ministers. They are the persons most directly and intensely engaged in the pursuit of power, most ready to kick aside anything they think obstructs their chances of electoral success.

I cannot think of another instance where a modern democracy has systematically undone the system by which uncorrupt public services were brought into being. One can see why it happened. The administrative elite with Victorian values produced by the Northcote–Trevelyan approach became, like other elites, self-perpetuating; in the 1960s it was criticized by the Fulton Committee for having failed to develop modern technocratic and managerial expertize; it has been perceived by the Thatcher government and its successors to be dedicated to obsolete values and incapable of producing the results that the government wants. Whether the new regime has increased the efficiency of the public services, or that of the economy, it is impossible to judge now. Nor will it ever be easy to judge. Too many things influence economic performance.

What explanations can one offer for what has happened in Britain? I have suggested two: firstly, that the weakening of positive pressures for uncorrupt government that used to come from military competition and from popular demands for more government have given freer rein to the natural tendency for competition for power and wealth to be pursued by corrupt means. Secondly, that the evolution of society, in particular the growth of a new and ever wider middle class, invited politicians to seek power by attacking high tax, big government and its elite structures, at the same time promising to demolish the constraints imposed on economic behaviour by the old order, without addressing the question whether that might risk more corruption. I am sure others can produce more refined and complex explanations.

That social pressures of these kinds have produced such radical change in Britain's institutions is partly the consequence of two constitutional factors. The first is that our eccentric electoral system has given Mrs Thatcher, Mr Major and Mr Blair majorities in the House of Commons even though none of them ever won more than 44 per cent of the votes cast at an election. Under the voting systems typical of other European countries, Britain would have been governed by coalitions; the policies of the strongest party would have been modified by its coalition partners.[80] The second, which I have emphasized, is that our system of government, based on unwritten conventions, has enabled the executive to make radical changes in how the country is governed without having to present legislation to Parliament and listen to the views and suggestions of its members. An unwritten constitution could be, and has been, gutted by inconspicuous means.

1 2

Recapitulation and Conclusion

My starting point was the suggestion, which I derived years ago from a conversation with Gunnar Myrdal, that instead of asking the conventional question, 'why is there so much corruption about and what can be done about it?' one should ask, 'why was corruption ever suppressed – as far as it was?' A change in question can be a useful step in the advance of understanding any subject. A new question, giving a different angle of vision, can make one see familiar things differently and start following new paths of enquiry.

I should like readers principally to judge what I have written by whether they are persuaded that the change in question I have proposed is likely to contribute to the understanding of corruption and the problems of suppressing it. I do not suggest that the conventional approach should be discarded, only that it be supplemented by the new question.

I have become convinced on pragmatic grounds that the proposed change in approach is useful. The institutions required for the suppression of public corruption are rather familiar – well paid military, police and civil services selected by merit; an independent judiciary; laws and economic regulations that inhibit corruption, or at least do not induce it; good audit systems; a press that is uninhibited in exposing corruption. Everyone who has studied the history of corruption, or the problems of corruption today in any part of the world, comes up with a list like that. The question to which no satisfactory answer has yet been found is, what has sometimes given rulers the will and the ability to introduce these institutions, which, in their very nature, constrain the degree to which they, the rulers, can pursue power and wealth?

The question leads one to look at history; and it led me to the conviction that one needs to adopt an evolutionary approach in order

(a) to observe the ups and downs of corruption and (b) to search for the forces that have generated those ups and downs.

The Observation of Corruption

The first step was to define public corruption in a manner that fitted the approach. The commonest prevailing definition of public corruption is 'the abuse of public office for private gain', or words to that effect. It has the merit of being short, comprehensible, translatable and indisputable. But it is static. It implies, unless you pause to think about it, that corruption is always and everywhere the same thing: it is misbehaviour. You are directed to a moral stance, not to better understanding.

The definition to which I have been led is:

> The breaking by public persons, for the sake of private financial or political gain, of the rules of conduct in public affairs prevailing in a society in the period under consideration.

This makes the meaning of corruption specific to time and place: it emphasizes that what is regarded as corrupt differs from one time to another and from one society to another. It helps one to see corruption as the product of the evolution of societies, each with its own history. It helps one to see that corruption is endemic: the essential aim of the rules that govern a society is to limit the ways in which people pursue power and wealth, for example, by forbidding them to poison their rivals, bribe voters, misappropriate funds or break contracts. People are always tempted to do such things. Some will yield to that temptation. Therefore there will always be corruption – so long as people pursue power and wealth. And there will be attempts to suppress corruption wherever people seek to have well-ordered societies in which to lead their lives and pursue their economic interests.

Changes in the level of corruption in a society are the outcome of the interplay between the evolution of rules and the evolution of their observance: corruption is the gap between the two. Each side of this relationship influences the other. For example, some new rules may reduce corruption, others, such as the prohibition of drink or drugs, may increase it and bring enforcement into disrepute.

In order to detect changes in the level and nature of corruption one is driven to look at scandals. They are a uniquely important source of evidence of what corruption is currently going on. In societies that are tolerably well ordered and open, they are episodes when evidence of public corruption is revealed that is firm and can be quoted without fear of prosecution for defamation. Years after the event one may also have evidence from memoirs and official papers.

It is not at all easy to infer from scandals in what direction the trend of corruption is going. The frequency of scandals is an uncertain indicator since they tend to occur infrequently and by accident. Moreover, the absence of scandals or a decline in their number may mean that the monitoring mechanisms that reveal corruption, notably the press, the police and the audit systems, are being obstructed or ignored; and vice versa. All the same, it would be foolish if, after examining a society in which there appeared to have been no marked change between two periods in the efficiency of the monitoring systems but a marked change in the frequency of scandals, we did not raise our eyebrows and look closely at the nature of the scandals past and present to see what was going on.

To do that it is useful again to distinguish rules and enforcement, so as to look separately at the rules that are being violated (allegedly or certainly) and the response by the relevant authorities, and see how each has evolved between the periods one is comparing. One needs to ask firstly: what is the behaviour in each scandal in a given field (e.g. election finances) that is regarded as corrupt? By comparing the answers for two periods one should get an impression whether the rules, formal or informal, in that field have been eroded, tightened or remained unchanged; and similarly one may also be able to see whether observance in that field has changed. Secondly did the government, extensively defined to embrace all the public authorities, including the police and judiciary, institute an uninhibited enquiry or did it shuffle? And if misconduct was found, was action taken, in the shape of punishment, improved monitoring or remedial legislation, to tighten the rules and/ or improve enforcement? Or, on the contrary, was it found politically preferable to let the rules become looser and/or let enforcement slip? Again one may be able, by comparing two periods, to judge if the government has become less or more favourably disposed to corruption.

In Chapters 10 and 11, I used this approach to analyse British scandals in the twentieth century. I believe the approach might be used more widely, for example, for comparing what is happening in different countries – though not of course in those countries where censorship or lawlessness means that there are no well-defined scandals. The EU comes to mind. In Brussels, countries with high standards of conduct are being merged with countries, including potential members, with rotten standards. In any democratic association of societies of this kind there is a risk that the good will be dragged down, rather than the bad pulled up. In the case of the EU, corruption seems particularly likely to be encouraged rather than discouraged by the institutions and policies that have been adopted so far, in particular the provision of vast subsidies paid out by national governments with little supranational supervision. What matters is not just the standard of conduct in Brussels, about which there have been major scandals, but standards in member countries. Will members with low standards take effective steps to check corruption? And will relatively clean members let it spread. One can think of many forms of corruption in EU countries that might usefully be analysed and currently monitored. A good starting point might be to analyse the various recent scandals over election funding in EU countries, comparing (1) what behaviour has been regarded as corrupt under the rules of each of the several countries where scandals of this kind have occurred; (2) how each scandal has been investigated; and (3) what remedial action has been taken.

Explanations

My exploration of the reasons why corruption was suppressed (as far as it was) in the eighteenth and nineteenth centuries in northwestern Europe, is tentative in the extreme. I am sure complex evolutionary processes were at work into which I have scarcely penetrated. Moreover, I have looked at only four countries. I hope others will tackle the question, look at more countries and do better.

My interest in the two explanatory forces I have concentrated on—military competition and the popular demands for better government generated by the Enlightenment and age of revolutions – was intensified by the thought that, having been important causes of reform in Europe in the past they have ceased now to be so. The reversal may be a clue to what has been happening recently.

As regards military competition, there is nothing new in the proposition that the pursuit of military strength was a motive for reforms in the efficiency of government and was an important element in the building of the modern nation state. Nor is it very novel to suggest that those countries that were most successful will have tended to expand, and that their success put pressure to reform on their neighbours with whom they had land frontiers. My aim has been to draw attention to this phenomenon in the study of why corruption was suppressed and, secondly, to point up that it was the product of military technology and social conditions of the time.

Those conditions have now been absent in Europe for a few decades, principally as a result of huge technological advances in the means of destruction achieved during the Cold War. The result is that Europe is now like the United States in its years of innocence. The military need for nation states with strong central government has faded, for the time being at least. (No one can predict the future.) The justification of government has come to lie principally, if not solely, in the provision of law and order (including the suppression of terrorism), education, health and other services, and in the regulation of economic activity so as to protect producers, consumers and their surroundings from the costs of unconstrained competition. All these except the first are functions with respect to which different sections of society have different interests and opinions. The unifying force of respect for the nation state has diminished, perhaps most extremely in Britain where pride in empire was once so strong.

Amongst the changing social forces that have recently influenced the tide of corruption, what seems most relevant is the spread since the end of the Cold War of market economics and criticism of big government, which carries with it an increase in respect for the pursuit of private gain as compared with public service. The demise of command economies of the Soviet type, in which the gains from breaking rigid, inefficient rules were so pervasive as to induce habitual corruption, must be counted a long-term gain, though in Russia there has so far been an increase in corruption as a result of trying rapidly to create a market economy without the legal framework and governmental institutions that are its prerequisites. The effect on the countries of western Europe is more ambiguous. There has been a wave of scandals in many countries but this may partly be because the ending of the Cold War has diminished the ability of governments to conceal what they are doing in the name of national security, and has increased the freedom of the judiciary and media to expose what is happening.

The most striking development is the apparent emasculation and displacement of two old British elites – the patrician politicians and the administrative class of the civil service. These two elites that helped to produce 'clean government' in Britain served each other. They shared an Oxbridge educational background; they shared, or at least respected, a notion of public service. And they shared power: the civil servants advised ministers what was possible and executed their instructions; ministers respected their civil servants for advising them – though they might bring in a few outside advisers when they wanted new policies – and they delegated the task of executing policy to them. Those ministers that did not come from Oxbridge had usually come up through the professions or trades unions; they had a more austere notion of what conduct was acceptable than the politicians of today.

It is understandable that Mrs Thatcher, bent on the reduction of government, on breaking up the bureaucracy and on introducing business practices, should have found these elites to be obstacles to her reforms. Indeed the reduction of the two elites can be seen as part of the ascent to power, under the leadership of Mrs Thatcher and her successors of both parties, of the new middle class, a process that has made Britain come to resemble the United States. But those are matters for historians and evolutionary sociologists.

Two developments to watch with respect to public corruption are going to be:

1. Whether the power of the civil service to restrain ministers from corrupt behaviour has been permanently diminished. It looks like it, since the old structure has been so radically dismembered. Yet permanent secretaries still report to Parliament that the money voted for their department has not been spent improperly. And it should not be forgotten that the civil service was pushed around severely by Lloyd George, only to bounce back.
2. Whether the new non-statutory codes and monitoring mechanisms put in place on the recommendation of the Committee on Standards in Public Life will be effective in restraining the behaviour of today's ministers and members of Parliament.

Implications for the Third World

I see no grounds for expecting standards of public conduct in Third World countries now to be anything like those that have evolved in northwestern Europe. The evolution of their societies has been quite different. Military competition, except perhaps in one or two temporary instances, has not helped to induce cleaner government. The main popular demand for reform that shaped these nations has been the demand for independent government, something quite different from the demands for better government that welled up in Europe.

The constitutions and legal codes with which the ex-colonies emerged at independence typically contained rules which, rather than having evolved locally, had been imposed by colonial rulers from Europe and were then adopted, with modifications, at the time of independence. These rules were not deeply rooted. The institutions required to keep corruption in check were young and frail. Typically, only a small minority of the population was Western-educated and versed in the adopted rules. In these conditions it would have been astonishing if the new rules had not come to be widely broken as people saw, and competed for, the power and wealth that were newly opened to them. Of course, what happened was not the same in all parts of the world. There are great differences between, for example, Africa, Latin America, China and the Islamic world. But severe corruption is common to them all.

I cannot identify domestic evolutionary forces in these countries that look as though they are now producing cleaner government. That may be because I have not studied the matter closely; but I doubt it. Periodically, corrupt regimes have been ousted, which is indicative of resistance to corruption at some level. But the new leaders often seem to fall into the bad old ways, a tendency that seems to be at least as pronounced in democracies as in autocracies. This is perhaps not surprising since, in either case, the new leaders will have taken over a system of power that has been fuelled by corruption and will have found themselves in command of persons versed in its practice; resistance to reform is likely to be pervasive. Revolutionary military leaders who have taken over power and brought with them a relatively uncorrupt military elite seem to have achieved greater results – one thinks of Atatürk, Nasser and Mao – but the effects of their reforms in checking corruption have been far from permanent.

The most outstanding success story has been that of Lee Kuan Yew, the benevolent autocrat of Singapore, a city-state that had been ruled by Britain. His success owes something to factors I have touched upon. Since Singapore had no natural resources, it was not vulnerable to corruption on that account by international corporations seeking concessions. The acquisition of sufficient military strength to maintain law and order and prevent outside interference after the break with Malaysia was an important early aim: in his memoirs Lee Kuan Yew tells how he sent for Israeli military advisers, persons well versed in stopping the disruption of a newly independent state. He and a significant number of his collaborators were educated in Western ways. But he rejected Western prescriptions for Third World countries, with their emphasis on individualism, democracy and a free press, and followed something closer to the Prussian model, with the important difference that his aim was economic growth not military expansion. He achieved so much only because he was a hardheaded pragmatist and an exceptional individual. In the words of Henry Kissinger:

> In the case of Lee Kuan Yew...the ancient argument whether circumstances or personality shapes events is settled in favor of the latter. Circumstances could not have been less favorable. Located on a sandbar with nary a natural resource... Singapore seemed destined to become a client state of more powerful neighbours, if indeed it could preserve its independence at all.
>
> Lee Kuan Yew thought otherwise. Every great achievement is a dream before it becomes a reality, and his vision was of a state that would not simply survive but prevail by excelling. Superior intelligence, discipline and ingenuity would substitute for resources. Lee Kuan Yew summoned his compatriots to a duty they had never previously perceived: first to clean up their city, then to dedicate it to overcome the initial hostility of their neighbours and their own ethnic divisions by superior performance. The Singapore of today is his testament.[1]

What has struck me when looking at trends in corruption in Britain and other rich countries is how unhelpful to the suppression of corruption in the Third World has been much of the behaviour of the rich countries and their international corporations.

We live in a world that is more open than before to international trade, investment and finance. At the centre of it are institutions – notably the World Bank and OECD – which, as part of their effort to aid economic development, try to help Third World countries suppress corruption. They advocate the introduction or improvement of the standard mechanisms for uncorrupt government: they run programmes for training public servants, for improving education and so on. These policies, which are commendable, can be fruitful in countries where the rulers have the will and the clout to reduce corruption. But often that is not so; the ruler's power rests on corruption and he or she has an incentive to keep it that way.

It is hard to see how the international economic agencies and their member governments can introduce incentives that would cause corrupt rulers to say to themselves 'if I do not attack corruption I may be punished so severely that I shall lose power, whereas if I attack it I shall be rewarded so generously that my hold on power will be maintained or enhanced.'

Not only are the rich countries and their agencies in this respect impotent, they commonly have been and are accomplices in corruption abroad, encouraging it by their actions rather than impeding it. I leave aside the unanswerable general question whether the current wave of laissez-faire is increasing or reducing corruption in the world compared with what it might be in some unknowable alternative world.[2] Consider four specific problems.

Firstly, there was the uninhibited use by both sides in the Cold War of corruption and covert operations, including 'destabilization' by arming dissidents, assassination, election rigging and the like, to topple regimes and obstruct the legitimate access to power of political parties perceived to belong to the other side.

Secondly, firms from the rich countries have been in the habit of paying bribes to rulers and officials in order to gain export contracts, notably for arms and construction projects. In doing so they have broken the rules that apply to bribery within their home country, pleading that since bribes are customary in many Third World countries they are driven to use them in those countries in order to compete with exporters from other rich countries. The new OECD pact is designed to stop this; and Transparency International is doing good work exposing this kind of corruption. But it remains to be seen how far it will be possible to enforce the pact and stop dodges such as the use of intermediaries.

Thirdly, there is the problem of the corruption-inducing effects of the purchase, by the rich countries and their international corporations, of concessions in Third World countries to exploit natural deposits of oil, copper, gold, diamonds and the like. Payments are made to rulers that often violate local rules (let alone Western rules) and also help to keep corrupt rulers in power and feed their personal bank accounts in safe havens. The huge wealth that comes from the possession of natural deposits is a major source of power for corrupt rulers in the Third World and is also the source of power of many of the barons of today's Russia who bought their mines and oil fields in corrupt deals at the time of privatization. It is hard to see any solution other than transparency and criticism. It would take an unprecedented degree of united dedication to the checking of corruption for the international community to agree that the oil and mining companies of the world should boycott corrupt regimes, somehow defined, let alone manage to enforce such an agreement.

Fourthly, the drug trade. The international law and national laws in the rich countries that prohibit drugs, produce a scarcity value irresistible to producers, smugglers and dealers. Crime and corruption is fostered across the world, most conspicuously in the drug-producing countries of Asia and Central America and on the smuggling routes from those areas to the rich markets in Europe and North America. Governments and civil society in these areas are undermined, indeed sometimes destroyed, by the violence and corruption that goes with the drug trade; and in our own societies the gangs who run the trade violently defy the police and undermine law and order. This is probably the most important way in which the policies of the rich countries foster corruption and violence. Yet the effect on the Third World seems scarcely to enter discussion of alternative drug policies in the rich countries. The legalization of drugs and the introduction of a regime of taxation and regulation, comparable to that applied to tobacco and alcohol (or, in the case of hard drugs, comparable to the regime for prescription medicines), might do more to reduce corruption in the world than any other measure the rich countries could take.

Public corruption may have beneficial effects by liberating enterprise from ill-judged government regulations and can certainly be consistent with rapid economic growth: the United States in the nineteenth century, Italy and a number of Asian countries in the second half of the twentieth century are examples.[3] But it also has economic costs; and if it goes too far it can cause economic collapse: the former Soviet Union, many parts of Africa and the drug lands are examples. Short of that extreme, public and private corruption has social costs, for example, damage to the environment, to health and to personal and public safety as a result of rules being flouted; and when it becomes severe, the sight of rule-breaking, unfairness and, in extreme cases, violence, can undermine the quality of life.

Since we appear now to be facing an epidemic of public and private corruption across much of the world, there is every reason to confront the problem, but it does not attract the kind of informed discussion and research effort that is given, say, to global warming. People seem to avoid looking closely and comparatively at corruption, perhaps for fear of pointing fingers at individuals, institutions, nations, races or religions. But reluctance to name or investigate an identifiable problem is as irrational and counter-productive in the case of public corruption as it is in the case of a threatening endemic disease: it does not serve the interests of the peoples afflicted by the problem.[4] An evolutionary approach may help dispel the taboo by shifting emphasis away from moralizing towards understanding.

Appendix A

The Differences Between Private and Public Corruption and the Constraints on Them

The Definition of Corruption

I have defined public corruption as: 'The breaking by public persons, for the sake of private financial or political gain, of the rules of conduct in public affairs prevailing in a society in the period under consideration.'

The definition distinguishes both the category of person who breaks rules and the kind of rule they break: the persons are public officials and politicians; the rules are those relating to the conduct of public affairs. If a public official or politician breaks a rule unrelated to the conduct of public affairs, for example, by stealing property from his neighbour or speeding, we do not count that offence as public corruption, though we may think that by committing the offence a public person casts doubt on his or her suitability for public office.

When we talk of private corruption we mean dishonesty between private persons in economic transactions. We do not mean speeding, murder or a wide range of other offences. The rules, written and unwritten, governing economic transactions, and hence the meaning of private corruption, have evolved to different standards in different societies. In modern Western society the main actions that we regard as corrupt are:

1. The giving or taking in cash or kind of bribes, meaning payments made to induce a person to do something that is wrong and known to be wrong.
2. The granting or taking of favours, i.e. the pursuit of private advantage where scarce assets (jobs or tickets to the opera) are allocated, instead of being sold for what the market will bear or allocated by an open procedure. The most persistent practices in this category are patronage and nepotism in the allocation of jobs.

3. The over-charging of customers with respect to the quantity or quality of goods or services.
4. The under-paying of suppliers.

It may not be customary to apply the term corruption to items 3 and 4 above, but I think it is best. The paying of a bribe is a way of indirectly over-charging the ultimate customer (or under-paying the ultimate supplier) by corrupting his or her agent. For example, a bribe paid to the representative of a firm (or government) in order to win a contract is a means of getting that contract at a higher price than would have been accepted in an unbiased competition. A dishonest contractor may use bribery in order to get a building contract or he may fail to produce work of the required quality, or both. In every case he is a corrupt contractor, i.e. a contractor lacking in integrity who swindles his customer.

Private persons, besides being corrupt in transactions with other private persons (including firms), may be corrupt in transactions with the state, for example, evading tax, making false claims for benefits and subsidies, and paying bribes to get government contracts. We can call these categories 'private-to-public corruption' and 'private-to-private corruption'.

Thus we have four categories of corruption:

1. Public persons breaking the rules governing their public conduct.
2. Public persons acting corruptly in their private transactions.
3. Private persons acting corruptly in dealings with the government.
4. Private persons acting corruptly in transactions with other private persons or agencies.

Constraints on Corruption

Two factors constrain corruption. One is moral virtue: the belief that to be corrupt is wrong and shameful. The other is deterrence, meaning fear of being found out and suffering punishment or market damage.

As regards moral virtue, each society will at any time have evolved a set of standards. Those standards will apply broadly to all the four categories listed above. Deterrence, on the other hand, does not operate in the same way in all categories.

As regards category 1, the chances of a public person being found out if he or she acts corruptly is dependent on the integrity and efficiency of the government institutions for auditing government transactions and on the mechanisms for monitoring the conduct of public persons. Once found out, a culprit's chances of being punished depend how severe public persons are to one another when there is evidence of corruption: they may cover up misconduct out of a desire to protect the reputation of the system or, where public corruption is common, a desire to prevent exposure of misconduct by public persons other than the accused, including perhaps themselves; and for similar reasons they may apply only token punishment or none when guilt has been established. All of this depends on the standards prevailing in the public system at the time. In England, we have a recent law designed to protect 'whistle-blowers'; whistle-blowing is a dangerous occupation that is in the public interest.

As regards category 3 (private persons behaving corruptly in transactions with the government), deterrence again depends on the efficiency and integrity with which the public system detects and punishes infringements. In detecting corruption, the government is unlikely to be aided by private persons reporting one another. There is an economic reason for this: if one private person knows or suspects another of cheating the government, he has a negligible incentive to stick his neck out and report the matter. Suppose, for example, that there are a million taxpayers, each with the same tax liability, and one evades paying his tax; if tax rates are raised to compensate the consequent loss of revenue, the burden on others is an increase in the tax rate by one millionth; and the consequences are similar if a person obtains cash benefits or other public funds to which he is not entitled. There are also social reasons why public corruption is unlikely to be reported by private persons: in most countries the tax liabilities and social benefits of individuals are confidential; added to which some people retain from their schooldays a feeling that sneaking is bad.

In categories 4 and 2, which represent what happens when people are engaged with one another in private economic activity, matters are different. If one private person cheats in economic transactions with another, his or her victim (another private person or a public person acting in his private capacity) is likely to find out what has happened; if and when they find out, their incentive to react is direct and undiluted: what the corrupt dealer gains his or her victim loses; it is a zero-sum game. The victim is also likely to be as uninhibited as the law permits in warning others against the corrupt dealer. There is thus an element of market deterrence; and by the same token there is some incentive for sellers to be seen to be honest and thereby achieve trust.

These mechanisms are far from perfect. The information available to buyers about the quality of products is commonly less than that in the possession of sellers; and information about products will inevitably tend to be uncertain where those products are highly variegated or subject to rapid innovation. Moreover in modern economies sellers will often be large organizations with far greater economic power than consumers. This has been compensated to some extent by the growth of consumer groups and laws for consumer protection. Thus, because the hassle and costs of going to court are great, consumer groups have been given the right to go to court to stop bad practices. Since imperfect or calculatedly misleading information is the basis of swindling, the purpose of many consumer protection measures is to improve information, starting with rules setting standards for weights and measures and labelling. But the essential point is that in private transactions there is a kind of in-built deterrence against cheating that is absent from cheating in public transactions. It may be a weak force but it can be reinforced.

Appendix B

Three Cases of Apparent Conflict of Interest in the Conduct of Officials

Sir Christopher Bullock

The most serious conflict of interest case occurred in the mid-1930s when Sir Christopher Bullock, the permanent secretary of the Air Ministry, while negotiating a government contract with Imperial Airways, which was partly owned by the government, solicited a job with the airline and discussed the award of an honour to Sir Eric Geddes, its chairman with whom he was negotiating.[1] Geddes requested Bullock to desist but Bullock persisted in his overtures until Imperial Airways complained to the authorities. Sir Warren Fisher, permanent secretary of the Treasury, responded by setting up a board of inquiry of senior civil servants over which he presided. Bullock claimed that his aim had been to strengthen the management of Imperial Airways. The inquiry learnt that Bullock had also arranged a directorship for himself with an insurance company with which the Air Ministry had dealings and had tried to get a peerage for its managing director. The report of the inquiry made no mention of the latter case but found Bullock's conduct 'completely at variance with the tenor and spirit' of the code established in 1928; it exonerated him to some extent by saying it was their 'opinion that he at no time appreciated the gravity or fully realized the consequences of what he was doing...' He was dismissed from the service but not otherwise penalized. He was apparently an ambitious and pugnacious man who was nicknamed 'Napoleon' because of his size and temperament. For years afterwards he persisted in claiming that he had been wrongly treated. After the war he managed to get his case reviewed by Lord Jowitt, the Lord Chancellor, who, having read the papers, concluded that the matter had been properly handled but thought that Bullock ought to have been allowed to resign. Sir Edward Bridges, the head of the civil service, like a solicitous and sensitive headmaster, felt so uneasy about the dismissal that in the early 1950s he saw Bullock several times and, when Bullock asked to be fixed up with a job at one of the Big Five Banks, Bridges went so far as to speak to the Governor of the Bank of England about the propriety of passing on that request. A detailed account of the case by Richard Chapman gives one an unusual glimpse into the patronage that Bridges possessed, or was perceived to possess, at this time. For example,

> Bullock...said that the Treasury had thousands of directorships at its disposal, yet had never offered him one and he thought this very odd, bearing in mind the injury which had been done to him. Bridges found this difficult to handle because the reason why Bullock had never been offered a Government directorships was that he was not a very easy person to deal with and was not the kind of person officials would want to recommend as a Government representative. Bridges therefore pointed out that there were not as many opportunities as Bullock thought and in any case the final decision on appointments did not rest with officials. Bridges said he recognized that Bullock was entitled to make the point and he would take note that he had made it. This only produced a statement from Bullock that he was not asking for a job but was quite capable of asking for one when he did want one. Nevertheless he thought "the machine" had behaved very badly to him in never offering him one.[2]

The two other cases are to be found in the Scott report of 1996 on the arms to Iraq scandal. They concern the Ministry of Defence (MOD), a department where the interests of private firms and the government were by 1996 tightly intertwined.

Air Vice Marshal Howard

In the 1980s Air Vice Marshal Howard, the most senior RAF expert on aviation medicine, provided advice on about a dozen occasions to Tripod Engineering, a British private firm that was bidding for an Iraqi air force contract to supply an a 'aeromedical system' (including a human centrifuge and ejector seat training rig). Scott judged that there was nothing wrong with that, given the Air Vice Marshal's remit.[3] What followed was another matter. When official relations between Britain and Iraq became distant and ambivalent, the Air Vice Marshal went along out of uniform to a meeting in London between Tripod Engineering and three Iraqi officers. In a note to the MOD a year later he said that, 'he was present as a consultant to Tripod and did not represent the Royal Air Force or HM Government.' Scott commented that, 'The presence of a senior RAF officer at a meeting of this kind was ill judged.'[4]

When the Air Vice Marshal subsequently offered advice on whether an export license should be granted for the project he 'was enthusiastic in his advocacy of the export opportunities afforded by the project'. There was nothing improper in that. The licence was granted, after which Lord Trefgarne, the minister in charge, 'was content for Air Vice Marshal Howard to continue to provide advice to Tripod, provided that the Air Vice Marshal had no more contact with the Iraqis.'[5] A few months later, however, Air Vice Marshal Howard retired; and in the next month he, without seeking permission, entered a consultancy agreement with Tripod to provide advice in connection with the Iraqi contract. For this advice he received remuneration of an undisclosed amount. He admitted to the Scott Inquiry that he had not sought permission to work for Tripod. Yet he had on his retirement signed a document in which he certified that he was aware of an RAF circular setting out the rules concerning the acceptance of business appointments after leaving the service. Having had the rules drawn to his attention, he agreed that he should have sought permission but said that 'the failure to seek permission was certainly not deliberate.' It was argued that he would have received permission if he had asked for it.[6]

Scott concluded:

> The rules were, however, expressly designed to counter suspicion, whether or not justified, that the advice and decisions of a Crown servant might have been influenced by the hope or expectation of future employment with a particular firm or organisation... AVM Howard's actions, however unintentionally, were apt to give rise to precisely the suspicion which the rules were designed to avoid.[7]

Mr Hastie

The case of Mr Hastie is so bizarre that one might well think it came from a television farce about Whitehall. It concerns the granting of an export licence to British Aerospace (BAe), the leading British arms manufacturer, to sell Hawk trainer aircraft to Iraq.

The Head of Defence Sales at the MOD, Sir Colin Chandler (as he later became), had been recruited into that job from BAe where he had been responsible for supervising the marketing efforts of BAe's operating divisions, including the division responsible for the Hawk. While still at BAe Sir Colin had recruited Mr Hastie to the marketing side of BAe, from which position Mr Hastie had been 'in regular correspondence' with the MOD regarding the Hawk project.[8]

In March 1988, Sir Colin arranged for Mr Hastie to be seconded to the MOD for a year (later extended to 18 months) during which BAe continued to pay him. Sir Colin explained that he had arranged this move after talking to Mr Hastie's boss at BAe and agreeing with him that, 'it made sense to use [Mr Hastie's] talents' at the MOD, 'for a short period whilst BAe took a long term view as to his future'. (One notes that BAe's interests take first place in this explanation of the secondment.) Sir Colin created the position of Business Development Adviser (BDA) for him at the MOD and gave him the task of setting up a system to help small firms promote their arms exports. But Mr Hastie, though on the BAe payroll, also provided advice about the Hawk project; he was in touch with BAe; and he helped in the preparation of an MOD paper supporting the project when the government was considering whether to grant an export license.[9]

The multi-hatted nature of Mr Hastie's position became absurd in April 1989 when there was an exhibition of military equipment in Iraq. British firms wanted to exhibit their weapons but since the Foreign Office did not want the British Government to be too visible in Iraq it was decided that no representatives of the MOD should go to the exhibition and there should be no MOD stand. But it was agreed that BAe might exhibit a Hawk aircraft.

At the last minute the team leader from BAe was refused a visa because he had previously been a military attaché in Baghdad. (Presumably he was an ex-officer who had been taken on by BAe – one of the many movements in that direction.) BAe at short notice asked for Mr Hastie to be allowed to go to the exhibition in place of the ex-military attaché. Sir Colin Chandler personally took the decision that Hastie should be allowed to go and told him to say that he was there on behalf of BAe. The Foreign Office, when they learnt of the decision after Hastie had already left, sent to the Embassy in Baghdad a telegram which ended with a charming touch:

> The MOD believe that the Iraqis were keen for Hastie to be included because they continue to believe him to be a member of BAe. They may equally well know that he is not. Either way, we are anxious to ensure that Hastie and his team are scrupulous in presenting Hastie only as a member of BAe... In particular, he should not give out MOD visiting cards.[10]

Scott's opinion was that Mr Hastie, through no fault of his own, had been placed in a position of potential conflict between interest and duty. Mr Hastie and Sir Colin Chandler argued in their different ways that there had been no conflict of interests. They perceived their two hats to be one. That seems bound to happen if, as in the case of military aerospace, any industry, with government encouragement, becomes a national, but not a global, monopoly, and the government is both its sole domestic customer at home and acts as a promoter of its sales abroad. Where the hats should not be perceived to be one (because there is a true difference of interest between the government and the industry) is over decisions whether to develop new weapons which cost huge sums of public money in implicit subsidies and bring profits to the industry regardless of whether they work or are needed, or whether they can be exported.[11] (The alternatives are to buy from abroad or do without.) This conflict of interest can become lost to sight when the government, by uniting with the industry to promote its exports, causes the employees of the two sides to see themselves as working together for a common cause.

Notes

Chapter 1. Introduction (pp. 1–3)

1. The conversation took place in Stockholm in the 1970s. I remember that we talked at length about the reasons for corruption in India, a country in which we had both lived, and ended up agreeing that it would be interesting to try turning the question on its head. I cannot remember who proposed the idea. I expect it was Gunnar Myrdal. His conversation used to be carelessly scattered with new ideas. I was taken by the idea. I suggested it unsuccessfully to others and, at about the end of 1995, I decided to try tackling it myself.

Chapter 2. General (pp. 5–19)

1. Papers and books on corruption almost invariably include discussions of the definition of corruption. See, for example, Vito Tanzi, *Corruption Around the World*, IMF Staff Papers, vol. 45, no. 4, Washington, December 1998; or Robin Theobald, *Corruption, Development and Underdevelopment*, Duke University Press, Durham, N Carolina, 1990, Chapter 1. For my approach to the distinction between public and private corruption see Appendix A.
2. The amount of corruption might be measured, in theory at least, absolutely or relatively. That is to say, one might, if data existed, measure the total number of decisions that is made corruptly; or one might measure what percentage of decisions is made corruptly. The percentage measure seems the more useful concept. It indicates the average honesty of public persons, independent of the size of the society and the extent of its rules and government activity. I shall not attempt to make quantitative estimates of these concepts, the measurement of which is highly problematical.
3. See G R Searle, *Corruption in British Politics 1895–1930*, Oxford, 1987; and Anthony Trollope, 'The Civil Service as a Profession', *The Cornhill Magazine*, vol. iii, 1861.
4. W G Runciman, *A Treatise on Social Theory*, Cambridge, 1989, vol. II.
5. For the importance of military competition in the evolution of machinery for mobilizing resources see John Brewer, *The Sinews of Power—War, Money and the English State, 1688–1783*, London, 1989; Philip Harking and Peter Mandler, 'From "Fiscal-Military" State to Laissez-faire State, 1760–1850', *Journal of British Studies*, vol. 32–1, January 1993; Michael Mann, *States, War and Capitalism*, Oxford,

1988; Charles Tilly, *Coercion, Capital and European States, 990–1990*, Oxford, 1990; and Charles Tilly, 'War Making and State Making as Organized Crime', *Bringing the State Back In*, ed. P B Evans, D Rueschmeyer, and T Skocpol, Cambridge, 1985, pp. 169–191.

6. A seminal work on the relation between military competition and the building of nation states is a lecture by Otto Hintze, delivered in 1906, 'Military Organization and the Organization of the State', *The Historical Essays of Otto Hintze*, ed. Felix Gilbert, Oxford, 1975, pp. 178–215. See also Volker R Berghahn, *Militarism: the History of an International Debate, 1861–1979*, Leamington Spa, 1981, pp. 14–15.

7. Martin van Creveld, *The Rise and Decline of the State*, Cambridge, 1999. See also the observations on the rise and decline of the sovereign state in Michael Howard, *The Invention of Peace: Reflections on War and International Order*, London, 2000.

8. Adam Smith, *The Wealth of Nations*, Book V, Chapter 1, Everyman, London, 1910, vol. 2, pp. 180–1.

9. D Herlihy, *The History of Feudalism*, London, 1970; and, as regards the origins of the feudal system, Chris Wickham, *Land and Power, Studies in Italian and European Social History, 400–1200*, London, 1994, Chapter 1.

10. Geoffrey Parker, 'The Military Revolution 1560–1660—a Myth?' *Journal of Modern History*, vol. 48, no. 2, June 1976, pp. 193–214.

11. An efficient system for government borrowing, such as England created when it followed the Dutch model by introducing Parliamentary guarantee of loans and creating the Bank of England in 1694, could be a help. The benefit in the English case was not simply that the government could borrow on better terms through a better capital market but also that financiers were put in a position where they were able to restrain the government from excessive borrowing and insist on linking it to taxation; at the same time they had an interest in the survival of the government in war and in its solvency. The relationship between the political world and the new financial world that emerged in London at the end of the seventeenth century is brilliantly analysed in Bruce G Carruthers, *Politics and Markets in the English Financial Revolution*, Princeton, 1996.

12. A Hourani, *A History of the Arab Peoples*, London, 1991, p. 218; and Peter Robb, *Midnight in Sicily*, London, 1998, p. 230.

13. C B A Behrens, *Society, Government and the Enlightenment*, London, 1985, *passim*.

14. William H McNeill, *The Pursuit of Power: Technology, Armed Force and Society Since AD 1000*, Oxford, 1983, suggests that after the feudal age market behaviour (in which people sought profit through specialization, trade and accumulation) displaced command behaviour (in which people obeyed tradition and orders from above) in both the civil economy and the military economy. Starting in the Italian cities and the Low Countries, specialization and trade over long distances grew and so did the need for new weapons and professional armies: as the civil and military systems were commercialized they stimulated each other economically; both escaped the dead hand of traditional behaviour and static technology. In expounding his thesis McNeill offers a great many details about weapons and methods of war.

Chapter 3. Prussia/Germany (pp.21–32)

1. A J P Taylor, *The Course of German History—A Survey of the Development of Germany since 1815*, pp. 28–9.
2. James J Sheehan, *German History, 1770–1886*, Oxford, 1989, p. 60; and C B A Behrens, *Society, Government and the Enlightenment: the experiences of Eighteenth Century France and Prussia*, London, 1985, p. 79.
3. Sheehan, *op. cit.*, p. 64.
4. C B A Behrens, *op. cit.*, London, 1985, p. 79.
5. *Ibid.*, p. 70.
6. *Ibid.*, p. 64.
7. Hans-Eberhard Mueller, *Bureaucracy, Education and Monopoly: Civil Service Reforms in Prussia and England*, California, 1984, pp. 76–8.
8. Behrens, *op. cit.*, p. 67.
9. C B A Behrens, 'Government and Society', *Cambridge Economic History of Europe*, vol. V, ed. E E Rich and C H Wilson, Cambridge, 1977, p. 576.
10. Count Mirabeau, *The Secret History of the Court of Berlin—a Series of Letters written between July 1786 and January 1787*, Eng. trans., London, 1789, pp. 245 and 343–4.
11. Behrens, *Society, Government and the Enlightenment: The Experiences of Eighteenth Century France and Prussia*, p. 81.
12. Sheehan, *op. cit.*, p. 88.
13. France's poor performance seems have shaped the opinions of eighteenth-century English luminaries about the level of military expenditure a nation can bear. In *The Wealth of Nations* (1778) Adam Smith wrote that 'Among the civilized nations of modern Europe, it is commonly computed that not more than one-hundredth part of the inhabitants of any country can be employed as soldiers without ruin to the country which pays the expense of their service'; and Gibbon wrote that, 'It has been calculated by the ablest politicians, that no state, without being soon exhausted, can maintain above one-hundredth part of its members in arms and idleness.' Gibbon may have derived his view from Smith. Adam Smith, *The Wealth of Nations*, Book V, Chapter 1, London, 1910, vol. 2, p. 186; E Gibbon, *The Decline and Fall of the Roman Empire*, Chapter 5, 1st para.
14. H A L Fisher, *A History of Europe*, London, 1936, p. 746.
15. Alistair Horne, *How far from Austerlitz?*, London, 1996, p. 329.
16. Behrens, *op. cit.*, p. 186.
17. Horne, *op. cit.*, p. 198.
18. Sheehan, *op. cit.*, p. 305.
19. Behrens, *op. cit.*, pp. 192–3.
20. Sheehan, *op. cit.*, pp. 298–9.
21. John R Gillis, *The Prussian Bureaucracy in Crisis, 1840–1860: Origins of an Administrative Ethos*, California, 1971, p. 25.
22. Behrens, *op. cit.*, p. 193.
23. Sheehan, *op. cit.*, pp. 433–4.
24. *Ibid.*, p. 432.
25. Max Weber cited in Sheehan, *op. cit.*, p. 430.
26. Sheehan, *op. cit.*, p. 691.
27. Gillis, *op. cit.*, p. 132.
28. Sheehan, *op. cit.*, p. 718.
29. Gillis, *op. cit.*, pp. 120–42.
30. *Ibid.*, p. 179.

31. Edward Crankshaw, *Bismarck*, London, 1981, pp. 153–5, 165–6, 196–7, 277, 293, 335–6, 357–360. Some of these allegations are disputed. For example, Lothar Gall in his *Bismarck – the White Revolutionary* (trans. by J A Underwood, London, 1993, vol. 2, p. 5.) attributes Bismarck's financial success to the fact that he found in Meyer Carl von Rothschild and, later, Gerson Bleichröder, 'bankers who administered his revenues and property with the utmost skill'. He tells us that 'The fact that a heavily indebted country squire owning two relatively small estates became in the space of a few decades a man of means who left his children assets running into many millions of marks already provoked speculation among Bismarck's contemporaries. Such speculation has never entirely ceased to this day. However, a meticulous, expert and wholly unprejudiced examination of Bismarck's fortune has meanwhile come up with definitive proof that there can be no question of any irregularities here, not even in the indirect sense of taking advantage of official information.' For this vindication he refers to Fritz Stern's *Gold and Iron—Bismarck, Bleichröder and the Building of the German Empire* (London, 1977). But Stern's work lends support to a less flattering view. For example, his description of how Bleichröder (with some Rothschild financial support) and Bismarck bought shares in railways, the nationalization of which Bismarck was pushing through, would surely be regarded as corrupt today. Stern tells us that 'A very large part of Bismarck's personal fortune was invested in railroad shares precisely during these years of anticipated nationalization.' and that 'In his frequent letters to Bismarck, Bleichröder never alluded to their common financial interest in the matter, but Bleichröder could count on Bismarck's intense concern, and a direct mention of their financial stake would have been gratuitous.' (Stern, *op. cit.*, p. 212).

Chapter 4. France (pp.33–44)

1. C B A Behrens, 'Nobles, Privileges and Taxes in France at the end of the Ancien Regime', *Economic History Review*, 1962–63, pp. 458–9.
2. C B A Behrens, *Society, Government and the Enlightenment*, London, 1985, pp. 73–4.
3. William Doyle, *Venality—the Sale of Offices in Eighteenth-Century France*. Oxford, 1996, pp. 3–7.
4. Julian Dent, *Crisis in Finance: Crown, Financiers, and Society in Seventeenth Century France*, Newton Abbott, 1973.
5. *Ibid.*, p. 48. England solved the problem by the Petition of Right, whereby those who lent to the king could claim repayment. It left untouched the proposition that 'the king can do no wrong', which was abolished by the Crown Proceedings Act in 1947.
6. *Ibid.*, p. 65.
7. *Ibid.*, pp. 188–9.
8. A Cobban, *A History of Modern France*, London, 1962, vol. 1: 1715–1799, p. 14.
9. A J Sargent, *The Economic Policy of Colbert*, London, 1899, pp. 17–18.
10. Dent, *op. cit.*, pp. 106–107
11. Sargent, *op. cit.*, p. 25.
12. C B A Behrens, 'Government and Society', *The Cambridge Economic History of Europe*, vol. V, Cambridge, 1977, p. 577.
13. Robin Briggs, *Communities of Belief—Cultural and Social Tensions in Early Modern France*, Oxford, 1995, p. 175.
14. Neither Francis I (1515–47) nor Henry II (1547–49) summoned the Estates General.
15. Cobban, *op. cit.*, p. 12.
16. Behrens, *op. cit.*, p. 553.

17. See Bernard Pujo, *Vauban*, Albin Michel, Paris, 1991, p. 239 and pp. 292–300; and Vauban, *Projet d'une Dixme Royale*, présentation de Jean-François Pernot, Association des amis de la Maison Vauban, 89830 Saint-Léger-Vauban, 1988. Saint Simon in his memoirs gives a dramatic account of Vauban's decline and death following the harsh treatment of his book, claiming that *'De ce moment, ses services, sa capacité militaire, unique en son genre, ses vertus, l'affection que le Roi y avait mise, jusqu'à croire se couronner de lauriers en l'élevant, tout disparut à l'instant à ses yeux...le malheureux maréchal...mourut peu de mois après, ne voyant plus personne, consommé de douleur...'* But Saint-Simon's account is contradicted by Pujo *op. cit.* and is denied by Vauban's descendants in the notes on display at the château of Bazoches, south of Vézelay, which was his home and is, by the way, the place where Richard Coeur de Lion spent the first night of the Third Crusade, having set out together with Philip Augustus, King of France, from Vézelay on 4 July 1190. See Steven Runciman, *A History of the Crusades*, Cambridge, 1954, vol. 3, p. 36.
18. For a most readable account of the life of John Law and his antics in France, see Janet Gleeson, *The Moneymaker*, London, 1999.
19. For the revisionist view that Necker was falsely accused of misleading accounting by opponents who would suffer from his reforms, see Robert D Harris, *Necker, Reform Statesman of the Ancien Régime*, California Press, 1979, and his *Necker and the Revolution*, University Press of America, 1986.
20. Marcel Marion, *Histoire Financière de la France depuis 1715*, Tome II, 1789–92, Paris, 1927, pp. 176–178.
21. *Ibid.*, Tome IV, p. vi.
22. Clive Church, *Revolution and Red Tape: the French Ministerial Bureaucracy, 1770–1850*, Oxford, 1981, pp. 179–80.
23. Louis Bergeron, *France under Napoleon*, trans. R R Palmer, Princeton, 1981, pp. 38–9 and 50.
24. Michael Roberts, *Gustavus Adolphus and the Rise of Sweden*, London, 1973, pp. 125–7 and 189–192.
25. J E C Bodley, *France*, London, 1898, vol. II, Chapter VI, 'Corruption under the Third Republic', pp. 272–317.
26. See Chapter 8, pp. 98–9.

Chapter 5. The United States (pp.45–58)

1. These infectious diseases, such as smallpox, measles and flu, against which the Europeans had evolved substantial resistance, came from domesticated animals such as cows and sheep that were indigenous only in Eurasia. See Jared Diamond, *Guns, Germs and Steel—the Fates of Human Societies*, London, 1997, pp. 210–214; and as regards the history and causes of genocide in America and elsewhere, see his *The Rise of the Third Chimpanzee*, London, 1992, pp. 250–78.
2. See Julian Perry Robinson, *The Problem of Chemical and Biological Warfare: a study of the historical, technical, military, legal and political aspects of CBW and possible disarmament measures*, Volume I *The Rise of CB Weapons*, Stockholm International Peace Research Institute (SIPRI), Stockholm, 1971, p. 215.
3. Terrence J. McDonald, introduction to William J Riordon, *Plunkitt of Tammany Hall*, New York, 1994, p. 5.
4. S E Morison and H S Commager, *The Growth of the American Republic*, vol. 1, Oxford, 1937, p. 368.

5. *Ibid.*, p. 369.
6. Daniel Ball, 'Crime and Mobility among Italian-Americans' in A J Heidenheimer (ed.) *Political Corruption—Readings in Comparative Analysis*, New Jersey, 1970, p. 160. fn.
7. Morison and Commager, *op. cit.*, vol. 2, 1942, p. 222.
8. *Ibid.*, pp. 68 and 222–3.
9. *Ibid.*, p. 233.
10. *Ibid.*, p. 224.
11. John A Gardiner, 'The Politics of Corruption in an American City', in A J Heidenheimer (ed.), *op. cit.*, p. 185.
12. James Bryce, *The American Commonwealth*, London, 1895, vol. 2, p. 579.
13. D W Brogan, *An Introduction to American Politics*, London, 1954, p. 124.
14. Bryce, *op. cit.*, vol. 2, p. 51.
15. *Ibid.*, p. 387
16. *Ibid.*, p. 388.
17. Samuel P Orth, *The Boss and the Machine*, Yale, 1919, p. 73.
18. William L Riordon, *op. cit.*, p. 28.
19. *Ibid.*, pp. 49–51.
20. *Ibid.*, pp. 54–7.
21. Bryce, *op. cit.* and Orth *op. cit.*
22. Brogan, *op. cit.*, p. 125.
23. C F Adams Jnr 'A Chapter of Erie' and 'An Erie Raid' in F C Hicks (ed.), *High Finance in the Sixties*, Yale, 1929; and Orth, *op. cit.*, pp. 72–3.
24. C E Merriam, *Chicago: A More Intimate View of Urban Politics*, 1929, cited in Brogan, *op. cit.*, p. 130.
25. James Q Wilson, 'Corruption: the Shame of the States', in Heidenheimer, *op. cit.*, p. 300.
26. Lincoln Steffens, *The Struggle for Self-Government*, New York, 1906. p. 40.
27. Morison and Commager, *op. cit.*, vol. 2, p. 367.
28. Steffens, *op. cit.*
29. Heidenheimer, *op. cit.*

Chapter 6. Britain in the Eighteenth and Nineteenth Centuries (pp.59–73)

1. G R Elton, *The Tudor Revolution in Government: Administrative Changes in the Reign of Henry VIII*, Cambridge, 1953, *passim*.
2. John Brewer, *The Sinews of War—War, Money and the English State, 1688–1783*, London, 1989, p. 40 & 42.
3. Mark Kishlansky, *Monarchy Transformed, Britain 1603–1714*, London, 1996, p. 224.
4. Brewer, *op. cit.*, pp. 88–114.
5. L B Namier, *England in the Age of the American Revolution*, London, 1930, and *Crossroads of Power—Essays on 18th Century England*, London, 1962.
6. I was surprised to find that this sort of thing went on in a small way in my own college until the second half of the nineteenth century. According to the evidence given on 4 July 1867 by J L Hammond, Bursar of Trinity College, Cambridge, to the Committee of the House of Commons on the Oxford and Cambridge Universities Bill of 1867, it was customary for each tutor to invest for his own benefit the caution money his pupils deposited with him on admission. See

D A Winstanley, *Later Victorian Cambridge*, Cambridge, 1947, p. 243, and pp. 1867, XIII, pp. 248–9.

7. J H Plumb, *Sir Robert Walpole: the King's Minister*, London, 1960, p. 206.

8. Stanley Ayling, *Edmund Burke: his Life and Opinions*, London, 1988, pp. 120–21.

9. John Torrence, 'Social Class and Bureaucratic Innovation: the Commissioners for Examining the Public Accounts, 1780–1787', *Past and Present*, no. 78, pp. 56–81. See also J E D Binney, *British Public Finance and Administration 1774–1792*, Oxford, 1958.

10. Torrence, *op. cit.*, pp. 56 and 80.

11. *The Gentleman's Magazine and Historical Chronicle*, 1786, p. 83.

12. *The Edinburgh Review*, April 1810, p. 203. The article is anonymous, but F W Fetter in 'The Authorship of Economic Articles in the Edinburgh Review, 1802–47', *Journal of Political Economy*, vol. LXI, June 1953, p. 247, says 'probably Brougham'.

13. John Ehrman, *The Younger Pitt*, London, vol. 1, pp. 174–8, 239–56 and 318; and vol. 3, pp. 102–9, 258–76, 472–4 and 676–83.

14. A Farnsworth, *Addington, Author of the Modern Income Tax*, London, 1951.

15. *Ibid.*, pp. 67–8.

16. Arthur Hope-Jones, *Income Tax and the Napoleonic Wars*, Cambridge, 1939, p. 33.

17. B R Mitchell, *British Historical Statistics*, Cambridge, 1988, Chapter 11, tables 4 and 12.

18. Philip Harling, *The Waning of 'Old Corruption': The Politics of Economical Reform in Britain, 1779–1846*, Oxford, 1996, p. 4.

19. Alan Ryan, 'Utilitarianism and Bureaucracy', in Gillian Sutherland (Ed.) *Studies in the Growth of Nineteenth Century Government*, London, 1972, p. 40; and Percival Spear, *India, A Modern History*, Michigan, 1961, p. 209.

20. The Northcote–Trevelyan report on the home civil service and the Macaulay report on the Indian civil service. Both are reproduced in full in *The Civil Service: Report of the Committee 1966–68*, vol. 1, Cmnd 3638, Appendix B.

21. H C G Matthew, *Gladstone, 1809–1874*, Oxford, 1986, p. 84.

22. *The Civil Service: Report of the Committee 1966-68*, *op. cit.*, pp. 108–09.

23. Andrew Roberts, *Salisbury—Victorian Titan*, London, 1999, p. 74; Anthony Trollope (the novelist, who spent most of his life working as a civil servant in the Post Office in which he rose to a high position), describes his own entry to the civil service and criticizes competitive examination in *An Autobiography*, London, 1946, pp. 44–52, and tells us on p. 111 that, 'Sir Gregory Hardlines was intended for Sir Charles Trevelyan—as any one at the time would know who had taken an interest in the Civil Service'; see also two articles by him, 'The Civil Service as a Profession', *The Cornhill Magazine*, vol. III, 1861, pp. 214–228; and 'Competitive Examinations', *ibid.*, vol. IV, pp. 692–712. J M Bourne, *Patronage and Society in Nineteenth Century England*, London, 1986, p. 166.

24. *Dictionary of National Biography*.

25. David Cannadine, *G M Trevelyan, a Life in History*, London, 1992, p. 5.

26. See *Life Letters and Diaries of Sir Stafford Northcote, First Earl of Iddlesleigh*, ed. Andrew Lang, London, 1890, *passim*.

27. Hew Strachan, 'The early Victorian army and the nineteenth century revolution in government', *English Historical Review*, 1980, pp. 782–809; and Sutherland, *op. cit.*; and G E Aylmer, 'From Office-holding to Civil Service: the Genesis of Modern Bureaucracy', *Transactions of the Royal Historical Society*, Fifth Series, Volume 30, 1980, pp. 91–108.

28. Richard Johnson, 'Administrators in Education Before 1870: Patronage, Social Position and Role', in Sutherland, *op. cit.*

29. Jennifer Hart, 'The Genesis of the Northcote–Trevelyan report' in Sutherland, *op. cit.*
30. Sir Charles Edward Trevelyan, 'The Purchase System in the British Army', *Tracts on National Defence.*
31. A L Lowell, *The Government of England*, New York, 1919, p. 463.
32. H C G Matthew, *The Gladstone Diaries*, Oxford, 1982, vol. VII, p. 193.
33. Gladstone M M S 44347, cited in E Hughes, 'Postscript to the Civil Service Reforms of 1855', *Public Administration*, XXXIII, (1955), pp. 305–6.
34. H C G Matthew, *Gladstone 1809–1874*, Oxford, 1986, pp. 173–4.
35. D W Brogan, *An Introduction to American Politics*, London, 1954, p. 296.
36. E J Hobsbawm, *The Age of Revolution: Europe 1789–1848*, London, 1962, p. 191. See also Elie Halévy, *The Triumph of Reform, 1830–1841*, London, 1927.

Chapter 7. Britain's Indian Connection (pp. 75–95)

1. P J Marshall, 'The British in India: Trade to Dominion' in *The Oxford History of the British Empire*, Roger Louis, (ed.) Oxford, 1998, p. 493.
2. Lucy S Sutherland, *The East India Company in Eighteenth-Century Politics*, 1952, pp. 51–3.
3. *Ibid.*, p. 81. For a description of how one of the worst of the Company's servants, Mr William Bolts, abused his position to make a fortune by swindling the local people, see Philip Woodruff, (the pen name used by Philip Mason for this book, not for his other works) *The Men who Ruled India*, London, 1965, vol. 1, pp. 104–13.
4. J S Furnivall, *Colonial Policy and Practice: a Comparative Study of Burma and Netherlands India*, Cambridge, 1948, p. 27.
5. Eric Stokes, *The English Utilitarians and India*, Oxford, 1959, p. xiv. Of interest too is 'Bureaucracy and Ideology: Britain and India in the Nineteenth Century', by the same author in *Transactions of the Royal Historical Society*, fifth series, vol. 30, London, 1980, pp. 131–56.
6. For an account of the difficulties encountered with the zamindari system see R E Frykenberg, *Guntur District*, Oxford, 1965.
7. Sir Edward Blunt, *The I.C.S.*, London, 1937, p. 34.
8. *Memoirs of William Hickey*, vol. 1, 1749–1775, ed. Alfred Spencer, London, 1914, p. 115.
9. *Ibid.*, pp. 117–8.
10. *Ibid.*, p. 124.
11. J W Kaye—*Life of Sir John Malcolm*, London, 1854, pp. 5–8.
12. An entertaining picture of the life of a civil servant in India, based on his experiences on a visit to India in 1863, was written by Macaulay's nephew. See G O Trevelyan, *The Competition Wallah*, London, 1907.
13. Percival Spear, *India: a Modern History*, Michigan, 1961, p. 208.
14. C H Philips, *The East India Company, 1784–1834*, Manchester, 1961, p. 1.
15. Percival Spear, *op. cit.*, pp. 208–9; and C H Philips, *op. cit.*, pp. 124–32.
16. Eric Stokes, *The Peasant and the Raj*, Cambridge, 1978, p. 94.
17. J M Bourne, *Patronage and Society in Nineteenth-Century England*, London, 1986, pp. 100–101.
18. House of Lords, April 9, 1813, Col. 723–7.
19. 53. Geo. III, C. 155.
20. William Cobbett, *Charter Papers* 14, cited in C.H. Philips, *The East India Company, 1784–1834*, Manchester, 1961, p. 290.
21. House of Commons, July 10, 1833, Col. 525.

22. *Ibid.*, Cols. 525–6.
23. *Ibid.*, Col. 746.
24. 3 and 4 William IV C. 85, CIII–CIX.
25. *Ibid.*, CIX.
26. Woodruff, *op. cit.*, vol. 1, p. 283.
27. House of Commons, July 8, 1853, Col. 1436.
28. The Macaulay report of November 1854 on The Indian Civil Service, reproduced in Appendix B of the Fulton report on *The Civil Service*, June 1968, Cmnd 3638, pp. 120–1.
29. *Ibid.* p. 125.
30. House of Lords, June 13, 1853, Col. 5–6.
31. House of Commons, June 23, 1853, Col. 618.
32. *Ibid*, June 24, 1853, Col. 747.
33. *Ibid.*, July 22, 1853, Col. 671–4.
34. *The Times*, 28 July 1953; see also 7 and 8 April, 29 July and 2 August 1853.
35. C H Philips, *op. cit.*, p. 15.
36. Trevelyan, *op. cit.*, pp. 120–4.
37. Woodruff, *op. cit.*, vol. 1, pp. 179–80.
38. J M Compton, 'Open Competition and the Indian Civil Service, 1854–1876' *English Historical Review*, 83, April 1968, p. 281; PP 1876, LV, pp. 311–12; the figures are for the 15 years 1860–74.
39. The figures refer to the proportion of consuls under the Roman Principate who were the sons, grandsons or great-grandsons of consuls and the proportion of successful candidates for the Chinese civil service of the twelfth and thirteenth centuries AD who were the sons, grandsons or great-grandsons of civil servants. See W G Runciman, *The Social Animal*, London, 1998, p. 167.
40. *The Civil Service, Evidence submitted to the Committee under the Chairmanship of Lord Fulton*, vol. 3(1), p. 21.
41. 'Observations on Cramming' appended to a 'Letter from the Civil Service Commissioners to the Under Secretary of State for India' dated 16 March 1875, PP 1876, LV, pp. 316–8; 'Letter from J A Godley, Under Secretary of State for India to the Secretary of the Civil Service Commission' dated 24 July 1889, PP 1890 LIV, pp. 403–7; and minute of dissent by Sir A Arbuthnot, *ibid.*, pp. 3–7; and Oscar Browning, Comment on the Report of the Indian Civil Service Syndicate addressed to Members of the Senate of Cambridge University, dated 1 March, 1883.
42. Bradford Spangenberg, 'The Problem of Recruitment for the Indian Civil Service During the Late Nineteenth Century', *Journal of Asian Studies*, XXX 2 (1971) pp. 341–60.
43. For a discussion of the differences between the Spanish imperial bureaucracy and the ICS, see John Leddy Phelan, *The Kingdom of Quito in the Seventeenth Century—Bureaucratic Politics in the Spanish Empire*, University of Wisconsin, 1967, pp. 153–5.
44. PP 1889 LVIII, 127–460. and PP 1890 LIV, pp. 125–226.
45. Woodruff, *op. cit.*, vol. 2, p. 249.
46. See M McMullan's remarks on the functions of corruption in 'Corruption in the Public Services of British Colonies and Ex-Colonies in West Africa' in Arnold J Heidenheimer, *Political Corruption—Readings in Comparative Analysis*, Transaction Books, New Jersey, 1978; and John A C Greppin 'The Uses of Bribery' *The Times Literary Supplement*, October, 1998, p. 31. Also relevant is the discussion of the relative merits of direct and indirect rule in J S Furnivall, *op. cit.*
47. For an eloquent late statement of this vision of the civil service, see Sir Edward Bridges, *Portrait of a Profession: the Civil Service Tradition*, Cambridge, 1950.

Chapter 8. The Evolution of Independent Judiciaries (pp.97–124)

1. B A C Behrens, *Society, Government and the Enlightenment: the experiences of Eighteenth-Century France and Prussia*, London, 1985, p. 89.
2. Louis XIV *Mémoires*, II, 399, cited in M. Marion, *Dictionaire des Institutions de la France aux XVII et XVIII Siècles*, Paris, 1923, p. 314.
3. H A de Colyar, K C, 'Colbert', in *Great Jurists of the World*, Sir John Macdonell and E Mason (eds), London, 1913, p. 275.
4. Behrens, *op. cit.*, p. 95.
5. *Ibid.*, p. 94.
6. *Ibid.*, p. 97.
7. Louis Bergeron, *France under Napoleon*, trans. R R Palmer, Princeton, 1981, p. 32.
8. F Grivart de Kerstrat, 'France' in Shimon Shetreet and Jules Deschênes (eds), *Judicial Independence: the Contemporary Debate*, Dordrecht, 1985, pp. 66–67.
9. *Le Monde*, 14 January 2000, pp. 1, 8 and 16;, *The Times*, 14 January 2000, and *The Economist*, 22 January 2000, pp. 44–5.
10. See leading article, *The Times*, 9 July 2001; *The Economist*, 2 June 2001, p. 4; *Le Monde* 1 June and 10 July 2001 and much detailed reporting on previous dates; David Ignatius, 'In France, a Chance for Politics to Break With a Dirty Past', *International Herald Tribune*, 4 June 2001; and Helen Trouille, *L'Affaire URBA,: Opening a Can of Worms*, unpublished paper, University of Bradford, Yorkshire.
11. Behrens, *op. cit.*, p. 100.
12. *Ibid.*, p. 101.
13. James J Sheehan, *German History, 1700–1886*, Oxford, 1989, p. 70
14. Behrens, *op. cit.*, p. 115.
15. John R Gillis, *The Prussian Bureaucracy in Crisis, 1840–1860: Origins of an Administrative Ethos*, California, 1971, pp. 120–42
16. Shimon Shetreet, 'Judicial Independence: New Conceptual Dimensions and Contemporary Challenges', Shetreet and Deschênes, *op. cit.*, p. 605.
17. Peter Schlosser and Walther Habscheid, 'The Federal Republic of Germany', *ibid.* pp. 84–5.
18. Shetreet, *op. cit.*, p. 605.
19. J S Furnivall, *Colonial Policy and Practice, A Comparative Study of Burma and Netherlands India*, Cambridge, 1948.
20. F W Maitland, *The Constitutional History of England*, Cambridge, 1908, p. 7.
21. W S Holdsworth, *A History of English Law*, vol. VI, London, 1924, p. 234.
22. W S Holdsworth, *A History of English Law*, vol. I, London, 1956, p. 646.
23. *Ibid.*, p. 425.
24. *Ibid.*, p. 438.
25. *Dictionary of National Biography*, London, 1895.
26. *V and A Magazine*, September–December 1998, p. 17. I am indebted to Mary Stirling for bringing this to my attention.
27. John Lord Campbell, *The Lives of the Lord Chancellors and the Keepers of the Great Seal of England*, London, 1846, p. 517.
28. *The Parliamentary History of England from the Earliest Period to 1803*, London, 1811, vol. VIII, p. 414.
29. See Chapter 6.
30. *The Tryal of Thomas Earl of Macclesfield*, 1725.

31. *Report of the Select Committee on Sinecure Offices*, July 1834, pp. 7–9 and *Minutes of Evidence taken before the Select Committee on Sinecure Offices*, 28 April 1834.
32. Holdsworth, *op. cit.*, 1956, vol. 1, p. 445.
33. Sir Thomas Skyrme, *History of the Justices of the Peace*, Chichester, 1994, pp. 35–6.
34. *Ibid.*, p. 35.
35. Lords Lieutenant were first established in reign of Henry VII with the task of putting down local unrest, using the local military forces and assisted by the magistrates. Apart from advising on appointments, their functions nowadays are mostly ceremonial.
36. Skyrme, *op. cit.*, p. 671.
37. The Royal Commission, chaired by Lord James of Hereford, reported in July 1910.
38. Elié Halévy, *A History of the English People in the 19th Century, vol. I, England in 1815*, (published in French in 1913), trans. by E I Watkin and D A Barker, London, 1949, pp. 22–3.
39. The Right Hon. Lord Lane, 'Judicial Independence and the Increasing Executive Role in Judicial Administration', in Shetreet and Deschênes, *op. cit.*, pp. 525–6.
40. *Ibid.*, p. 528.
41. In the other two colonies, Connecticut and Rhode Island, the judges were appointed by the legislature.
42. Skyrme, *op. cit.*, pp. 1045–1087.
43. James Bryce, *The American Commonwealth*, London, 1893, vol. 1, pp. 19–20 and 505–6.
44. *Ibid.*, p. 229.
45. *Ibid.*, p. 230.
46. *Ibid.*, p. 265 and 271. Bryce's observation requires little or no qualification today.
47. Robert B McKay and James M Parkinson, 'The United States', in Shetreet and Deschênes (eds), *op. cit.*, p. 358.
48. Bryce, *op. cit.*, vol. II, pp. 118–9.
49. McKay and Parkinson, *op. cit.*, pp. 368–9.
50. *The Washington Post*, 4 August 1996, p. A14.

Chapter 9. The Twentieth Century (pp. 125–152)

1. The figures for 1880 to 1960 are from Angus Maddison, 'Origins and Impact of the Welfare State', 1883–1983, *Banca Nazionale del Lavoro Quarterly Review*, XXXVII, (1984), p. 57; for later years *OECD Economic Outlook*.
2. In Germany the figures for 1929 will have been increased by the expenditures to relieve the extremely high levels of unemployment and the low level of GDP; and the same will have been true to some degree of Britain.
3. W G Runciman, *A Treatise on Social Theory*, vol. III, Cambridge, 1997.
4. *SIPRI Yearbook*, 1976, pp. 152 and 1998, pp. 228–33. Note that in 1954 German military expenditure consisted largely if not wholly of payments to the occupying powers of 'occupation costs'.
5. Alan T Peacock and Jack Wiseman, *The Growth of Public Expenditure in the United Kingdom*, Oxford, 1961.
6. Anthony Quinton 'Thought' in *Edwardian England 1901–1914*, Simon Nowell-Smith (ed.) , Oxford, 1964, p. 291.
7. Mark Harrison, (ed.), *The Economics of World War II*, Cambridge, 1998, *passim*.
8. Estimates supplied by Mary Acland-Hood, formerly of SIPRI. For analyses of

military research and development expenditures in the Cold War see *SIPRI Yearbook of World Armaments and Disarmament*, 1972, pp. 149–239; 1973, pp. 252–95; 1984, pp. 165–74; and 1987, pp. 153–8.

9. Mark Malloch Brown, administrator of the UN Development Program, and Jayantha Dhanapla, UN under secretary-general for disarmament affairs, *International Herald Tribune*, 26 January 2000.

10. BBC News 2 January 2000.

11. Mary Kaldor, *New and Old Wars: Organised Violence in a Global Era*, Polity Press, Cambridge, 1999, Chap. 5.

12. For a fascinating account of how mercenaries were hired by the government of Papua New Guinea to recover from local rebels the copper mine on the island of Bougainville and how the operation was exposed and ended in farce, see Michael Bilton, 'Death and Dollars' *The Sunday Times Magazine*, 2 July 2000, pp. 32–47.

13. For an excellent account of the descent into corruption, tyranny and strife of the former Belgian Congo see Michela Wrong, *In the Footsteps of Mr Kurtz—Living on the Brink of Disaster in the Congo*, London, 2000.

14. Christopher Andrew, *For the President's Eyes Only: Secret Intelligence and the American Presidency from Washington to Bush*, London, 1996, *passim*.

15. *Ibid.*, pp. 172–3.

16. *Ibid.*, p. 371.

17. Jon Lee Anderson writing on the Pinochet affair in the *Sunday Telegraph*, 25 October 1998, Review Section p. 2.

18. The *Sunday Telegraph Magazine*, 31 January 1999, p. 14.

19. Daniel Patrick Moynihan, *Secrecy, the American Experience*, Yale, 1998, p. 214.

20. For example, information is coming out about how Belgian forces, after several attempts by themselves and the CIA, murdered Patrice Lumumba, the post-independence leader of the Congo, a country with deposits of uranium and other minerals of importance to the West. See *The Times*, 8 June 2001.

21. *Le Monde*, 24–25 October 1999, p. 17.

22. Steve Weinberg, *Armand Hammer: the Untold Story*, London, 1989; and Tom Bower, *Tiny Rowland: a Rebel Tycoon*, London, 1993.

23. *The New York Times*, 20 August 1995, p. E3.

24. *The Memorial and Claim of Eugenie Caron de Beaumarchais by her agent John Augustus Chevallie for a balance due to his estate for sending sundry Arms, Ammunition, etc.*, Letouzey et Ané, Paris, 1951, vol. 5, p. 1217.

25. Anthony Sampson, *The Arms Bazaar*, London, 1988.

26. *Ibid.*, pp. 221–2.

27. *Ibid.*, pp. 234–5.

28. See Chapter 8.

29. *Financial Times*, 20–21 December 1997; and *Private Eye*, 9 January 1997, p. 26.

30. *The Guardian*, 5 March 1999, p. 2.

31. *The Economist*, 16 January 1999, p. 28.

32. See, for example, Mark Phythion, *The Politics of British Arms Sales Since 1964*, Manchester, 2000.

33. *Construction and Arms Industries Seen as Leading Internal Bribe-Payers, New Transparency International Survey*, Transparency International, Berlin, 20 January 2000.

34. D Held, 'Farewell Nation State', *Marxism Today*, December 1988, p. 15.

35. The bribing of the Olympic Committee over where the games should be held is a poignant example of international corruption invading an organization founded on the highest ideals. See Andrew Jennings, *The Great Olympic Swindle*, New York, 2000.

36. Anatole Kaletsky, 'Let the whistle blow', *The Times*, 11 February 1999; and for details of the mass resignation and its causes, *The Times*, 17 March 1999.
37. See, for example, 'EU aid to Albania: Stinking Fish', *The Economist*, 27 October 2001.
38. S E Morison and H S Commager, *The Growth of the American Republic*, Oxford, 1937, vol. 2, p. 367.
39. James Q Wilson, 'Corruption: the Shame of the States', in A J Heidenheimer (ed.) *Political Corruption—Readings in Comparative Analysis*, New Jersey, 1970, p. 301.
40. Theodor Eschenburg, 'The Decline of the Bureaucratic Ethos in the Federal Republic' in A J Heidenberg (ed.) *op. cit.*, p. 259 *et seq.*
41. *Time* magazine, that barometer of orthodox public concerns, ran a cover story in its issue of 22 June 1998 headed 'The Cancer of Corruption', in which it listed some of the biggest scandals that have hit the world; for evidence on our four countries see the special issue on 'Sleaze: Politics, Private Interests and Public Reaction', *Parliamentary Affairs*, Oxford, vol. 48, no. 4, October 1995.
42. *International Herald Tribune*, 24 January 2000.
43. For a useful review of the problem and current approaches to it as seen by a senior international official, see 'Corruption Around the World—Causes, Consequences, Scope and Cures' IMF *Staff Papers*, vol. 45, no. 4, December 1998.

Chapter 10. Britain in the First Half of the Twentieth Century (pp.153–163)

1. In the case of the judiciary, patronage continued but was increasingly constrained. The Lord Chancellor, advised in different ways as regards magistrates and judges, made appointments. See Chapter 8.
2. For an appraisal of the evidence see Roy Jenkins, *Sir Charles Dilke—a Victorian Tragedy*, London, 1958, chap. xvi.
3. G R Searle, *Corruption in British Politics, 1895–1930*, Oxford, 1987, pp. 21 and 23–4, and *passim*.
4. Philip Magnus, *King Edward the Seventh*, London, 1964, p. 389.
5. Alan Doig, *Corruption and Misconduct in Contemporary British Politics*, London 1984, p. 74.
6. Searle, *op. cit.*, p. 11.
7. *Dictionary of Business Biography*, London, 1984, vol. 1, pp. 391–95.
8. Searle, *op. cit.*, p. 44.
9. Robert Blake, *The Conservative Party from Peel to Churchill*, London, 1970, p. 244.
10. M Pinto-Duschinsky, *British Political Finance, 1830–1980*, American Enterprise Institute for Public Research, Washington, DC, 1981, p. 34. Also Searle, *op. cit.*, pp. 85–6; and Blake, *op. cit.*, pp. 143–4.
11. W Ivor Jennings, *Cabinet Government*, Cambridge, 1936, pp. 341–2. For Disraeli's approach to patronage see Robert Blake, *Disraeli*, London, 1966, pp. 386–92 and 680–96.
12. *Ibid.* p. 35.
13. Searle, *op. cit.*, p. 90 and 153. For a fuller account of Salisbury's attitude to Honours see Andrew Roberts, *Salisbury—Victorian Titan*, London, 1999, pp. 668–76.
14. Pinto-Duschinsky, *op. cit.*, 1981, p. 45.
15. A J P Taylor, *English History 1914–1945*, Oxford, 1965, p. 74.
16. John Grigg, *Lloyd George, from Peace to War, 1912–1916*, London, 1985, pp. 48–66.

17. Searle, *op. cit.*, p. 309.
18. Robert Blake, *The Decline of Power 1915–1964*, London, 1985, p. 96.
19. Pinto-Duschinsky, *op. cit.*, 1981, p. 44.
20. Searle, *op. cit.*, pp. 355–76.
21. The Honours (Prevention of Abuses) Act, 1925.
22. Pinto-Duschinsky, *op. cit.*, pp. 105–110; Searle, *op. cit.*, pp. 406–7; and J. Walker, *The Queen has been Pleased*, London, 1986, pp. 94–115.
23. See the list in Walker, *op. cit.*, pp. 100–101.
24. Pinto-Duschinsky, *op. cit.*, p. 112.
25. Searle, *op. cit.*, p. 409.
26. For a full account of the affair by an author who came to the view that Boothby had been treated too harshly, see Robert Rhodes James, *Bob Boothby—a Portrait*, London, 1991, pp. 192–228 and 270–98.
27. Searle, *op. cit.*, pp. 412–3.
28. *Halsbury's Laws of England*, London, 1990, vol. 11(1), paras. 281–4.
29. R S Sayers, *History of the Second World War: Financial Policy 1939–45*, London, 1956, pp. 28–9.
30. For an excellent analysis of the case and of the procedure used to enquire into it, see Madeline R Robinson, 'The British Method of Dealing with Political Corruption' in *Political Corruption: Readings in Comparative Analysis*, ed. A.J. Heidenheimer, New Jersey, 1978, pp. 249–58.
31. *Parliamentary Papers, Commons*, vol. 530, 20 July, 1954, Cols. 1178–1184.

Chapter 11. Britain in the Second Half of the Twentieth Century (pp.165–199)

1. Brian Brivati, *Lord Goodman*, London, 1999, pp. 45–63; and Ian Gilmour, *Dancing with Dogma*, London, 1992, p. 197. Brivati, p. 50 writes that 'We know that at least two of his [Goodman's] clients were being "economical with the truth" about what happened on the trip.'
2. Francis Noel-Baker, 'The Grey Zone', *Parliamentary Affairs*, 1961–62, vol. 15, pp. 91–2.
3. Richard Crossman, *The Diaries of a Cabinet Minister*, London, 1977, vol. 3, pp. 210 and 406.
4. Alan Doig, *Corruption and Misconduct in Contemporary British Politics*, Penguin, 1984, p. 217.
5. Doig, *ibid.*, Chap. 5, *passim*.
6. Doig, *ibid.*, pp. 204 and 216–8.
7. The Committee on Local Government Rules of Conduct which was appointed by Mr Heath in October 1973 and reported in May 1977.
8. Doig, *ibid.*, p. 346 and House of Commons, 15 June 1979, Col. 343.
9. Doig, *ibid.*, pp. 230–1 and House of Commons 17 June 1976, Cols. 731–2.
10. Ben Pimlott, *Harold Wilson*, London, 1992, pp. 725–7.
11. *The Times*, Wednesday, 5 May, 1999, p. 22.
12. Brivati, *op. cit.*, p. 277.
13. Brivati, *op. cit.*, p. 278.
14. For a concise summary of the 'cash for questions' case, see Law Report, Court of Appeal, *The Times*, 30 March, 1999, p. 40.
15. Alexis de Tocqueville, *De la démocratie en Amerique*, Gallimard, Paris, 1986, vol. 1, p. 331; the author's translation.

16. *Transcripts of Oral Evidence to the Committee on Standards in Public Life*, 15 February 1995, p. 368. On the new career politicians see also Peter Riddell, *Honest Opportunists*, Hamish Hamilton, London, 1994.
17. *First Report of the Committee on Standards in Public Life*, Cm 2580, May 1995, p. 3 and 15.
18. *Sixth Report of the Committee on Standards in Public Life, Reinforcing Standards, Review of the First Report on Standards in Public Life*, Cm 4557, January 2000.
20. See the first and sixth reports of the committee.
21. *Raising Standards and Upholding Integrity: the Prevention of Corruption*, Cm 4759.
22. See p. 161 above.
23. *Financial Times*, Weekend 10/11 November 2001, p. 4.
24. Anti-terrorism, Crime and Security Act 2001, Part 12, Clauses 108–110.
25. *The Guardian*, Leader, 19 November 2001.
26. Peter Bottomley, 'A shadowy group in the House—Elizabeth Filkin deserves an apology and an invitation to continue as parliamentary commissioner', *The Guardian*, 16 November 2001; and Chris Blackhurst, 'A woman scorned—Elizabeth Filkin is a tireless guardian of parliamentary probity. So naturally she had to go', *The Independent*, Friday Review, 9 November 2001.
27. Diana Woodhouse, 'The Parliamentary Commissioner for Standards: Lessons from the 'Cash for Questions' Inquiry' *Parliamentary Affairs*, vol. 51, no. 1, January 1998, p. 59.
28. Andrew Roberts, 'Now we know the price of a policy (it's £1m)' *Sunday Telegraph*, 18 July 1999. And for a longer list of donors to the Labour Party, derived from a leaked party document, see *Sunday Telegraph*, 6 September 1999.
29. *Financial Times*, 1–2 April 2000; and *The Independent*, 9 April 2000.
30. See, for example, *The Times*, 25 November 1999, pp. 1, 4 and 5.
31. Michael Pinto-Duschinsky, 'Farewell the lesser spotted donator', *The Times*, 29 July 1999.
32. See, for example, *The Times*, 8 November 2001, pages 1, 8, 9 and 21; Patrick Wintour, 'Wakeham says ministers wrong on Lords reform', *The Guardian*, 12 November 2001; and Anthony Howard 'If MPs fail to strangle the Lords Bill they should find they have clinched their claim to being considered wimps', *The Times*, 13 November 2001.
33. First leader in *The Times*, 8 November 2001.
34. *The House of Lords—Completing the Reform*, white paper issued by the Lord Chancellor's Department, Cmd 5291, 7 November 2001.
35. Numbers of life peers per prime minister from *The Times*, 8 November 2001, p. 8. For Harold Macmillan the period in office is counted from the 30 April 1958 when the Act creating life peers received the Royal Assent and came into force.
36. Website of the House of Lords Appointments Commission.
37. Stewart Chaplin, 'The Stained-Glass Political Platform', *Century Magazine*, June 1900, quoted in *Brewster's Dictionary of Phrase and Fable*, London, 1977, p. 1144.
38. *The House of Lords—Completing the Reform, op. cit.*, para. 66.
39. Guy Peters, 'Morale in the public service: a comparative inquiry' *International Review of Administrative Sciences*, vol. 57, no. 3, September 1991, p. 422.
40. Opening statement by Sir Michael Bett, First Civil Service Commissioner, *Sixth Report of the Committee on Standards in Public Life*, Cm 4557—II, p. 192.
41. See for example 'Blair set to purge Whitehall elite' *The Times*, 8 June 2000.
42. *Report of the Committee on the Civil Service*, June 1968, Cmnd 3638, vol. 1. For the precursor of the committee see *The Administrators—the Reform of the Civil Service*, a report by a Fabian Group, June 1964.
43. See for example, William Plowden, *Ministers and Mandarins*, IPPR, 1994; and *The*

Civil Service in an Era of Change, Peter Barberis (ed), Dartmouth, 1997; Simon Jenkins, *Against the Grain—Writings of a Sceptical Optimist*, London, 1994, pp. 31–8; Ian Gilmour, *op. cit.*, pp. 184–6; the evidence of Professor Peter Hennessy to the Committee on Standards in Public Life; and the evidence of Lord Kennet to the House of Lords Select Committee on the Public Services in November 1996.

44. Parliamentary Report, House of Lords, 6 June 1994, Col. 970.
45. *The Spectator*, London, 27 November 1993, p. 5.
46. Richard A Chapman, *Ethics in the British Civil Service*, London, 1988, p. 56.
47. *Parliamentary Affairs*, vol. 48 (1995), p. 188.
48. *The Commissioner for Public Appointments, First Report 1995–1996 and Second Report 1996–1997.*
49. *The Commissioner for Public Appointments, summary of his first report, 1995–1996.*
50. *The Times*, 30 December, 1999.
51. *Public Appointments to NHS Trusts and Health Authorities, A Report by the Commissioner for Public Appointments*, March 2000, p. 23 and 33.
52. See NHS Executive's announcement of the creation of the Appointments Commission, NHS Website update of 3 January 2001, and the Commissioner for Public Appointments, Sixth Report, 2000–2001.
53. *The Committee on Standards in Public Life-Transcripts of Oral Evidence*, Cm—4557-II, pp. 8–9.
54. Christopher D Foster and Francis J Plowden, *The State under Stress: Can the Hollow State be Good Government?* Open University Press, 1996, p. 77.
55. A brief but influential statement of the case against handing executive tasks to independent boards was made in the Haldane report in 1918. *Ministry of Reconstruction: Report of the Machinery of Government Committee*, Cd 9230, 1918, paras. 31–33.
56. Evidence of Dr. Peter Hennessy, *The Committee on Standards in Public Life—transcripts of Oral Evidence*, 15 February 1995, p. 364.
57. *Sixth Report of the Committee on Standards in Public Life*, Cm 4557-1, January 2000, paras 4.65–4.67.
58. Foster and Plowden, *op. cit.*, pp. 231–2.
59. Memorandum by Sir Christopher Foster and Mr Francis Plowden, *Evidence taken before the House of Lords Select Committee on the Public Services*, 19 November 1996, p. 18.
60. See 'Labour spends £22 million on focus group fascism', *The Sunday Times*, 28 February 1999, p. 3; and 'Vacuous drivel is a disgrace to Civil Service', Peter Riddell, *The Times*, 14 July 2000.
61. See, for example, 'Bullying ministers sicken mandarins' *The Sunday Times*, 31 May 1998, p. 12
62. *Sixth Report of the Committee on Standards in Public Life*, Cm 4557-1, January 2000, paras 5.6.
63. *Modernising Government*, Cm 4310, March 1999. para 5.19.
64. *Sixth Report of the Committee on Standards in Public Life*, *op. cit.*, paras 5.25–5.27, 5.49.
65. *Ibid.*
66. *Ibid.*, para 5.53.
67. Peter Riddell, 'Rules must be changed to protect Civil Service integrity', *The Times*, 2 November 2001.
68. The 15 are Lord Hankey, Sir Warren Fisher, Sir Richard Hopkins, Lord Normanbrook, Lord Sherfield, Sir Frank Lee, Lord Helsby, Lord (William) Armstrong, Lord Croham, Lord Hunt, Lord Bancroft, Lord (Robert) Armstrong, Sir Douglas Wass, Sir Peter Middelton, and Lord Butler. Statistics based on entries

in *Who's Who* and the DNB. The number of persons mentioned is small since the three jobs were often combined in the hands of one or two civil servants.

69. For debates of policy in this area see in particular *Eighth Report of the Treasury and Civil Service Committee of the House of Commons*, and the related evidence.

70. *The Advisory Committee on Business Appointments, First Report, 1996–98*, Cabinet Office, July 1998, p. 45. Since some officials apply for approval of several appointments when they retire or resign, the number of applicants is less than the number of applications.

71. *The Times*, 24 April 2000, p. 6.

72. *The Times*, 26 and 27 May 1994.

73. *The Independent*, 25 June 1999.

74. D F Kettle cited in Christopher J Foster and Francis J Plowden, *The State Under Stress—op. cit.*, p. 109.

75. Foster and Plowden, *op. cit.*, p. 124.

76. *The Times*, 5 January 2000, p. 12.

77. *The Independent*, 6 July 2000, p. 12.

78. 'Defence company accused of cheating ministry of millions', *The Sunday Times*, 2 July 2000.

79. See Alan Doig, 'People or Positions? Ensuring standards in the reformed public sector', in Peter Barberis, *op. cit.*, pp. 95–103.

80. Mrs Thatcher at her greatest victory won 44 per cent of the votes cast (33 per cent of the electorate including those who did not vote); Mr Major in 1992 won 42 per cent of the votes; and Mr Blair since 1997 has had a majority in the House of Commons greater than Mrs Thatcher ever won, having in 1997 gained only 43 per cent of the votes cast (31 per cent of the electorate) and in 2001, when the turnout slumped, 41 per cent of the votes (24 per cent of the electorate).

Chapter 12. Recapitulation and Conclusion (201–211)

1. Foreward by Henry A Kissinger to Lee Kuan Yew, *From Third World to First, The Singapore Story: 1965–2000*, New York, 2000. pp. ix–x.

2. One may note an anarchistic element in US economics that can be partly explained by the history of that country. Where, as in the US romantic ideal, settlers cleared land and set up their individual homesteads, there was initially little or no government, and attention was focused on local problems. It was natural to debate whether to join together to build a schoolhouse or subscribe to a fire engine. The absence of government was the starting point and the problem was how much government was desirable, how much should be created. In Europe, government was taken for granted. Government had been there for many generations and provided the framework within which society had evolved. The question of concern was how to change government so as to make society more satisfactory. The difference in approach can be seen in books on what used to be called public finance. European books typically used to explain historically why governments did what they did and debated the economic justification for those functions and for changes in them. Then US books came along which asked whether there was any justification for each and every kind of government activity, thereby imparting rigour but also an ahistorical tinge of anarchy.

3. For a useful review of the arguments about the effects of corruption see Robin Theobald, *Corruption, Development and Underdevelopment*, Durham N Carolina, 1990.

4. Gunnar Myrdal discussed at some length, but did not himself breach what he called the taboo on research into corruption. See *Asian Drama: an Inquiry into the Poverty of Nations*, New York, 1968, vol. ii, pp. 937–58.

Appendix B   (pp.217–221)

1. Eunan O'Halpin, *Head of the Civil Service: a Study of Warren Fisher*, Routledge, London, 1989, Richard A Chapman, *Ethics in the British Civil Service*, London, 1988, and the report of the board of inquiry, PP 1935–36, vii, 474–6, *passim*.
2. Richard A Chapman, *op. cit.*, pp. 173–4.
3. Sir Richard Scott, *Report of the Inquiry into the Export of Defence Equipment and Dual-Use Goods to Iraq and Related Prosecutions*, HMSO, London, 15 February 1996, para D2.366.
4. *Ibid*. D2.373.
5. *Ibid*. D2.391.
6. *Ibid*. D2.394–5.
7. *Ibid*. D2.396.
8. *Ibid*. D6.29.
9. *Ibid*. D6.31–3.
10. *Ibid*. D6.39.
11. Sam Brittan, 'No defence for arms subsidies', *Financial Times*, 5 July 2001.

Index

Italicized page numbers indicate quotes